DADS DON'T BABYSIT

Towards Equal Parenting

David Freed and James Millar

First published in 2018 by
Ortus Press, an imprint of Free Association Books

A CIP Catalogue of this book is available from
the British Library

ISBN: 978-1-91138-316-1

Typeset by
Typo•glyphix
www.typoglyphix.co.uk

Printed and bound in Great Britain

David:

For Charlotte and Little Bear

James:

For Ros, my equal partner in everything

CONTENTS

INTRODUCTION

When Serena Williams returned to tennis in 2017 for the first time since giving birth the event was accompanied by a tell-tale headline that goes to the heart of the issue. A number of news outlets described her partner Alexis Ohanian as babysitting their child. "Serena Williams' multimillionaire husband babysits as wife returns to court[1]" was typical.

There are three big issues here.

Firstly, and most importantly given the title of this book, *the idea that a man can babysit his own child*. Babysitting by its very nature is temporary and being done as a favour to someone else. Being a father is not. Just googling the word babysit brings up a definition that babysitting means looking after a child while its parents are away. It is looking after a child on behalf of the responsible parent. Alexis Ohanian is the child's parent. Unless he's Dr Who, a father cannot be away and there at the same time.

Most men that have taken the opportunity to spend some quality time with their children out and about without a woman around will have had someone suggest they are 'babysitting'. No, they are parenting. Yet the sight and the concept of a man just looking after his own children remains the exception and is consequently worthy of comment.

Just the other day I was in a card shop on the local high street. I go there for all my card-buying needs at least in part because the folk running the shop are friendly, helpful, considerate people. Ahead in the queue was a man with his toddler son. "Where's Mum today?" enquires the ostensibly considerate shopkeeper. Not a great question to ask, and here's why.

For Mum may have been up a mountain, or battling a supervillain. The parents could be separated, or worse she could have passed away. More likely on a Saturday morning, she could have just been in bed. Yet in an effort to make unthinking small talk the man at the counter points to something unusual – a man looking after his small child on his own. He expects to see the mum there. The mum just before them in the queue with her pushchair was unsurprisingly not greeted with "Where's Dad today?", because it's a daft question to ask.

Before we start worrying about guys being 'oversensitive' when they don't like being told they're babysitting / on daddy duty / doing daddy daycare / being lazy for not working / asked where mum is all the time, or any similar rap, the problem with these terms when applied to dad is *not* necessarily any offence it might cause. It is unlikely that the guy will shed tears over it (and not just because he's had a lifetime of being told that big boys don't cry).

The problem is what it represents and reinforces in our culture: men cannot fundamentally be responsible for kids, they always have to do the childcare on behalf of someone else. There is a deep and underlying expectation that the only truly responsible parent is Mum, and she *must* be that responsible parent. She cannot share that ultimate responsibility with another, and especially not with a man. There's an expectation that Dad is 'doing Mum a favour' by looking after his own child, because he can't be the fully responsible parent.

This remarkably stubborn perception throws up all sorts of barriers for both parents being able to make a full and free choice about how to organise their parental lives: not the statement about a babysitting dad itself, but all the assumptions and expectations that are going on behind it.

It is in practice a modern day equivalent of a man seeing a woman he doesn't recognise in a boardroom and asking if she could grab him some coffee before the new boss arrives. What a prat when it turns out she is in fact his new boss.

WHAT IS NORMAL?

This matters because to describe a man looking after his children as babysitting makes him feel that he's doing something odd and it needs an explanation. It implies that him parenting on his own is unnatural and temporary until the real parent gets back. This could challenge him in a good way that might up his determination to push back against these norms. More likely, given the weight and volume of those norms, he will follow the path of least resistance. It will make him withdraw from a role that makes him feel different.

Most of us don't want to stand out, to be pointed at, discussed, looked at with a quizzical gaze. We may want to stand out for doing something good, not for doing something odd.

His children will pick this up if folk make these comments. Don't underestimate the ability of kids to take their cues from the world around them – the things they see and hear from all sorts of sources. We don't need to take away gender completely, but we surely all want our children to be able to make up their own minds about the roles they can and want to pursue in life rather than having limits placed on their horizons.

For now a man taking primary responsibility for his children remains odd, and *most* people don't want to be odd. We want to change that expectation on dads; not to force everyone to share responsibility, but to make it a real choice with fewer pressures and social stigmas pushing them into a traditional arrangement that may not work for them, and in practice, as we'll see, they may not really want. The aim is to make equally shared parenting and even the possibility of dads being the 'main' carer of their kids more acceptable and a free choice for *both* parents.

DIFFERENT SEX, DIFFERENT EXPECTATIONS

Which brings us to the second issue in that Serena Williams headline. Serena is the greatest tennis player in all human history. Consider that a moment. Some might make the case for Roger Federer, but he's never won a grand slam title while pregnant like Serena did in 2017 at the Australian Open. And he never will.

Yet somehow being the best in the world ever at something is not enough. The tone of the coverage of her return to action was not a celebration of her comeback after maternity leave, instead it was marked by the implication that somehow she's not a good enough mother because she's leaving her baby with the child's father to 'babysit'. Now she's a mother that is her primary role, not tanning the opposition and winning every tennis title imaginable. Serena Williams is currently as close as humankind is going to get to a superwoman. And yet it isn't enough.

The only comparable sporting achievement we can think of in the same league as Williams winning while pregnant is when Tiger Woods won the US Open golf with a broken leg in 2008. Undoubtedly impressive. When he came back to the sport following that injury did anyone ask who was looking after his children? His second child was born just a couple of months before the first major championship of 2009. There was no mention of his partner babysitting while he spent four days on the course.

Because it's different for women and men. The two sexes are judged by different standards. Women have known this for long enough, and suffered under that system. For women, good enough invariably isn't enough according to the rules of almost every society through history. Looking good enough isn't enough, hence the multi-million pound cosmetics industry aimed squarely at females. Behaving good enough isn't enough, hence girls are brought up to be demure and obedient while the phrase 'boys will be boys' excuses all manner of male misdemeanours. And being a good enough parent isn't enough, hence the constant pressure on women to be superwomen or tiger mothers while men can drop in and out of family life as they see fit as long as they contribute some or most of the cash.

The flip side of that has perhaps powered the women's rights movement. Just getting the vote wasn't good enough, reproductive rights weren't good enough, taking down demeaning lads mags wasn't good enough. They have not broken the stigmas and limitations attached to being a women. It's why the feminist fight goes on.

Yet men are victims of those societal strictures too. And by taking steps to allow men to remodel the rules that apply to them, just as women have been doing with increasing success in the last century, we can make life freer and better for everyone.

There's the third problem with the Serena Williams headline. Her husband is described as a multimillionaire. The tennis star is worth about $150 million compared to Ohanian's net worth of $9 million. And yet the headline focusses on his value and her implied neglect as a mother.

Above we noted that men can drop in and out of family life as long as they front up some money. And that is how a father's role has often been portrayed; men have choice over the extent of their involvement. The problem is what sort of a choice has that been and what sort of a choice is it today.

The traditional view has been that family life is something men ought to avoid; striding through industry racking up cash and status is what to strive for. Men don't want that any more. A slew of studies and surveys has found that men want to spend more time with the people they love the most. They want more time with their newborn babies, their kids as they grow up, their partners for mutual love and support through the tides of life.

But there's a weight of research showing that doesn't happen. Men tend to remain in full-time employment following fatherhood while a much higher proportion of women reduce their hours and often their ambitions. We've called this chasm between what people want and what happens in reality the 'paternity gap', in line with its close relative, the gender pay gap.

And that's in a best case scenario; too many women are simply eased out of the workplace when they become mothers because their requests for flexible working, the possibility they'll have to drop everything to care for a sick child – things that are not expected to afflict male workers – are more trouble than their worth to a boss in pursuit of that perfect combination of healthy profit and an easy life.

In the home men spend less time with their children. That's not because they are busy keeping house. No matter the family set-up, even if the female partner is in full-time employment and the man is not, the likelihood is that it's the woman doing the lion's share of domestic work. There is not a country in the world where men do more domestic work than women.

Recently the job of organising and keeping track of those chores – from making sure the household runs smoothly, to cooking, to ironing, to knowing which kids have after school club, detention or a play date in the park – has been dubbed the 'mental load'. The fact that it has its own trendy moniker is progress. And it's an intriguing title too. For men portrayed as physically and mentally stronger are surely better suited to shoulder a load.

The term 'mental load' has also been born out of an increasing focus on mental health. And here the traditional view of men as stoic and strong is breaking down. It's part of the answer as to why men are saying they want more family time. Because it's nice. (Most of the time.)

Men who are around their families more have better relationships with their wives and with their children. In turn that nourishes their mental health. Stronger support networks and deeper relationships are undoubtedly a good thing. Yet men are invariably given the message that these things are best avoided in favour of talking about football.

ARE MEN REALLY VICTIMS?

The statistic that suicide is the biggest killer of men under forty-five has been highlighted routinely by various admirable campaign groups in recent years to the extent that it's fairly well embedded in policy makers' minds. It's clearly an important, pressing and ultimately tragic issue. Is it a particularly male crisis? It's also widely reported that more women than men attempt suicide, it's just that men, for a number of potential reasons, are actually killing themselves. It may well be that the genders have more in common than what separates them in terms of the reasons they reach the most desperate state.

Not according to the 'meninists', a fairly odd group of anti-feminists who decry the repression of men by a mean and castrating 'matriarchy', because equal rights are painful for those on the top. We really need to distance ourselves from these guys at the outset. Meninists, who sometimes also style themselves men's rights activists (MRAs), seize on the male suicide statistics and paint them as proof that men, invariably white men such as themselves, are under attack from a society that has historically grown increasingly sympathetic to women.

Meninists think men are victims because their world view is that if women gain rights then men must be losing something. The main thing meninists long for is the right to fight, and to look down on women; too many combine the two. They are much less keen on the statistic that every week two women die at the hands of domestic abusers.

Rights are not a zero-sum game. We can all gain – emotionally, financially, even physically –because more involved dads tend to live longer if men get more involved in family life. More rights for men to take a bigger role as fathers goes hand in hand with more rights for women. They are in fact mutually reinforcing.

So when we describe men as victims it is meant in a very different way to the definition provided by meninists. The meninists think men are victims of feminism. We believe it's feminism that will set men free and that men are victims of the strictures that they themselves have been complicit in creating and supporting down the decades.

Describing men as victims is not to deny they have huge privileges. That would be foolish because it's plain to see. Being a man means you get to have tons of advantages in life just because of the contents of your pants. That's unfair and we'd like to change it. But let's not pretend that it's not brilliant being able to swagger around the place largely ignorant of the threat of sexual violence, never having to face being ignored, talked over or talked down to just because of your sex.

Being a man comes with huge benefits. So much so that many don't even notice it. As Grayson Perry puts in his book, *The Descent of Man*: "talking to men about masculinity is like talking to fish about water". The downside is you have to be a 'man'. If you want to access the privilege you have to sign up to some sort of masculinity. In fact even if you don't want the privilege you still get it, and you are still impacted by its straitjacket. You're expected to live up to a macho definition of 'manliness' that can often be at odds with what you want to do with your life, as we'll see.

WORKING DADS AND MUMS

So let's look at what masculinity means in this context. It still suggests men should be the provider for their wives and families. In more and more households the woman makes the most money, but that's still not the norm by a long way. According to a 2015 study, in 78% of two-parent families the man is still the main breadwinner[2].

Indeed somebody actually bothered to survey women about how they would feel about earning more than their male partners and found among some it is an issue. Has anyone ever asked a man how he feels about being the breadwinner? There's your problem right there. You can even find articles asking if a wife earning more than her husband will 'wreck' the marriage[3]. Again, there are no articles asking the reverse question.

And at work attitudes remain out of time. Presenteeism, the idea that workers should be present even if they aren't actually achieving anything, is rife and it disproportionately infects men. Great strides have been made in opening up flexible working to workers, but whether it actually represents progress is brought into question by the way the right to request flexible working is used. It's mainly women taking it, it's mainly women expected to take it, the latter backed up by research that shows men are far more likely than women to have their flexible working request turned down.

Similarly first Labour in 2010 and then the Conservative–Liberal Democrat Coalition government introduced a proper policy of shared parental leave that came into force in 2015. This allowed parents to split time off to care for their baby. It would be a bit much to expect shared parental leave to become the norm within just a few years but it's not even close.

Most intelligent estimates put uptake at around 5% of eligible dads, with up to 40% of new dads not being eligible in the first place. That's within the government's expected range, so on that count it's not been a failure. By any other standard it isn't working. When we look at other countries in Europe that have had similar policies for longer, they also have equally dismal uptakes by dads.

Work is of course the biggest draw on any adult's time and consequently the thing that keeps them away from their children. Everyone needs to earn a living so we need to look at ways to alter the world of work to fit with modern priorities.

Policy will be a big driver here. Just introducing shared parental leave and broadening the right to flexible working has not been enough. Both are significant achievements. Family life has a foot in the door of the workplace. And firms, particularly big companies with cash to spare who are desperate for any advantage in attracting the best employees, are piloting expanded and enhanced policies that build on the statutory minimum. They would not have been doing that if the policies had not been put in place by government.

But there's clearly huge scope for improvement. Government can speed up and embed the normalisation of different working and leave practices – if it wants to. We'll set out how that could be achieved in a way that gives men a genuine choice to define their own role within the family and, crucially, gives women the same freedom. And we'll explain why government ought to press ahead because such policies are not just good for its citizens but will also boost the economy.

CULTURAL INFLUENCES

The problem goes much deeper than parental leave and the workplace. The most recognised fictional father in popular culture is Homer Simpson. And he's a buffoon. *The Simpsons* may be funny but the humour comes from recognition. He's an act that means something to many viewers, and reinforces the idea that men and parenting only go together with hilarious consequences.

In a home with pre-schoolers Homer Simpson is replaced by Daddy Pig of the ubiquitous Peppa Pig cartoon. Again he's incompetent and a figure of fun. Where are the men doing domestic tasks and childcare well, taking a backseat while Mummy goes on an adventure?

It's easy to reject this stuff as unimportant. Suggesting *The Simpsons* is taken off air isn't going to make you popular (we're not suggesting *The Simpsons* is taken off air, it's too funny). *Peppa Pig* is just a five minute frippery right? Well no, actually. Adults, and even more so kids, take their cues from the culture that surrounds them whether that be on TV, the adverts on the side of a bus or simply the division of labour in the kitchen at home.

If kids especially are told by telly that it's normal for men to behave in a certain way they'll believe it, particularly when they are at the pre-school *Peppa Pig* watching age because that's when they are trying to figure out who they are and how they fit into the world. *Peppa Pig* is political.

Adults consume culture too. The news in particular tends to seize on every half-baked experiment or trendy popular science book that points to some sort of genetic fundamentalism when it comes to the difference between the genders. *Men are from Mars, Women are from Venus* has sold fifty million copies. In more recent years the focus has switched to human brains. Increasingly journalists talk with conviction about different bits of the brain lighting up in experiments that prove one thing or another. All they prove is that people like certainty.

The brain is a very complicated thing and it doesn't light up to order. What we do know is that male and female brains have much more in common than they do differences; that when a man looks after a baby the same chemical processes take place in his brain as in a woman's. Luckily in recent years there's been a growing push back against those that choose to focus on any tiny difference, with actual science and bald statistics volleyed back at them. The latest research is telling us two things that we're now understanding about parental biology: caring is natural, for women *and* men; and there is no relevant or substantial difference in parenting abilities between the sexes.

We need to challenge the bad science and explain that men looking after babies is the most natural thing in the world. Because it is. Society, from grandparents to lazy advertising execs, reinforces the idea that maternity is somehow a natural experience. Of course for most women it is a vital and normal part of their life cycle. But the real experience of labour doesn't immediately lend itself to sounding natural. We make it sound natural by the way we talk about it.

Fatherhood, and more specifically, involved and responsible fatherhood, is normal too. Most men will go through it. So we need to convince men who say they want to do more parenting that it's okay to do so and they will most likely be really good at it. Culture and science have a role to play there.

MAKING CHANGE HAPPEN

For things to change, men need to act. For while men may be victims of the societal strictures that push them away from or even out of family life they have one huge advantage – agency, the ability to make change happen.

Feminists have to fight to get heard. Movie mogul Harvey Weinstein's unpleasant and possibly illegal behaviour didn't only come to light last year. Women had spoken about it for years but they hadn't been listened to. The vital change that the #MeToo movement has brought is that it showed that even today a woman's voice is invariably worth less than a man's. That's unacceptable and hopefully we're moving on to a stage where that will no longer be the case. Unfortunately, with every sector tainted by sexual harassment scandals the scale of the problem and the distance we still have to travel become clearer.

But men have influence, power. It's men that could have stopped Weinstein in his tracks if they'd chosen to. Men who can speak up for the voiceless and get an audience. Of course that's not the world we want but it's the world we have and we can use it to everyone's advantage if men are willing to act on their convictions. It may be largely down to the simple twist of fate that put a penis in their pants, but men can speak out and be listened to and that power can be harnessed to achieve political and societal change.

In terms of power the 'worst' it's going to get for men in human history is equality. Hopefully equality will open up a new definition of power that is measured not so strictly in terms of money and politics but in terms of the power to choose your path in life, to be free to make quality choices about the directions you take in life, regardless of your genitalia. Women can put their careers first, and men can choose their families over their jobs. That's freedom.

It's important to be clear what we mean when we talk about freedom for both sexes here. We're talking about men, women and indeed couples together having a quality choice about how they share the benefits and burdens of parenting. A choice where all the options apart from one have very high costs – economic and social – is not a decent choice. It's like the freedom to scrape a living in poverty or starve. It's not a quality choice and it's not real freedom.

The more stigmas and costs attached to each option, the worse the quality of the choice. Sure, not every step we take in life needs a high quality choice, but adding a sprog to the brood is a life changing milestone that will have rippling effects on all other aspects of both parents' lives. It is a choice worthy of our effort to make better.

It is not about forcing couples to share parenting in a way that doesn't work for them. That would be wrong. It is about improving the real quality of the choice that they make. As we see from the paternity gap, this is simply not the case today.

Talking is the first and easiest step to take. How often does a group of men get together and discuss family issues? When does that discussion take in the joy of family life rather than jokey comments about 'er indoors, nagging, sex, and the demands of children?

Let men speak up. If men can tell a pollster they want to spend more time with their children let them say the same thing to their friends in the pub or more importantly to their partners. It could be something she's longing to hear.

Men can challenge those who lazily reinforce gender norms but how many do? Not enough; including the authors of this book. One of the triggers for the title was a visit with my children to the nation's favourite shop that sells the necessities for children: school clothes and Percy Pig sweets. A stout middle-aged member of staff asked: "Babysitting for the afternoon are you?".

As mentioned, using the b word in front of the children normalises, reinforces in fact, the idea that a father looking after his children is somehow unusual. But I did not challenge the shop lady and one of the asks of this book is not just that men, and women, speak up for equality but to create a society in which a man caring for his offspring (and that plainly includes adopted or step children or any of the other family arrangements we have these days) is not regarded as unusual.

The steps we propose to make things better are not big asks. They are clear, simple, and affordable steps that can be taken to achieve the goals we want to see and which could affect huge change in a short space of time. And there is a growing momentum to look at these issues and tackle them. Westminster's Women and Equalities Committee took the time to look into the issue of fathers in the workplace at the end of 2017. They would not have done so if there wasn't pressure to do it.

But it's not only about taking down barriers through public policy and the boardroom. Just as pertinent was something the MP Jess Phillips, who sits on the committee and who is routinely described as 'gobby' for having the temerity to be a woman who speaks up, told us about the hearings.

She said "What struck me about listening to the men talking was it would have been exactly the same if it had been a bunch of mothers talking. I had to keep being 'well yeah that's the same for women'. The one difference was that we expected them to do something about it."

Men can make change happen. Dads need to stand up (or stay at home) for their rights, and for the rights of their partners. We're not calling for a revolution. All the asks in this book are simply extensions of what is already happening. But a revolution could result. A world in which boys and girls have more options ahead of them in terms of the role they play in the society they inhabit, a world in which men and women enjoy better, more equal relationships benefitting their health, their happiness and their wallet.

We're asking for men to take responsibility and make the world a better place.

THE STRUCTURE OF THIS BOOK

The first part of this book makes the case for why sharing parenting more equally can be good for the whole family. We'll explain why men should get on board and get involved more in family life. And the role women can take in making that happen. There is clear evidence that more engaged fathers are a good thing on any number of metrics – essentially, good dads are good for everyone.

Part II explains more about the paternity gap, and raises questions about why it's there, and why the numbers on dad's involvement aren't meeting up to what parents want. Part III busts some of the myths about the biological differences between mums and dads, and explains why instincts to care for kids are in fact parental, not just maternal.

Part IV goes through how these arguments and so many others have seeped into our everyday lives, and built up limiting expectations on dads: expectations and stigmas that amount to a 'babysitting handicap' confronted by dads thinking about taking their turn in childcare. Part V talks about the flip-side of these pressures, of forcing all the real responsibility of childcare squarely on women.

Part VI looks at how these expectations don't just start in the workplace and can't only be challenged in parliamentary committees. They are part of the way we bring up our kids. To help our kids grow up freer and more well-rounded, we need to be willing to challenge that, and teach our boys that they can be 'good little dads' if they want to be. Finally, we'll offer a simple list of solutions: a manifesto for a better fatherhood and more equal parenting.

First, let's look at the evidence for the benefits a bit more closely before pondering why, if those gains are so clear-cut, men aren't already clamouring to be let into the kitchen. Then we'll consider what's needed to make change happen so that in the future, when it comes to their own offspring, men care for, parent, nurture, raise, look after, love them – anything but babysit them.

Part I

THE FAMILY HAT-TRICK

Why sharing parenting should be a real option for parents

1

SHARING PARENTING

The idea that the nuclear family includes '2.4 children' still lingers, even when the average child count has dropped to 1.7. That's because – and this in no way delegitimises any alternatives – most children are still raised in such a set-up. But families are about more than just numbers. The image of the nuclear family still includes Mum raising the kids and Dad offering a protective and supportive gaze when he returns from a hard day's work. The man goes out of the home to work, the woman takes care of the childcare. The 'natural' way of the world.

We've been treated to different reasons for this set-up being the best way of doing things, from an efficient division of labour, to playing, to the biological strengths of the sexes. These arguments have made it difficult if not impossible for parents to have any real choice about how they split parenting. They have shaped how the world of childcare works, and what is expected in the workplace. They curtail the choice of most parents to choose to share parenting equally, or to even consider letting the dad become the main responsible parent instead of the mum.

If you're told that one of two options is going to be not just impossible, but also damaging to your family, and if every attempt you make to go down that path is treated as weird or is blocked by others, you're not really able to make a free choice about what's best. You're left with the only choice available, which means in the end it's not a real choice: you're just stuck with one way of doing things.

Of course sharing parenting more equally between both parents is not an option for some families either because it is simply better for one parent, mum *or* dad, to take the lead as primary carer for most of the time or because one parent is not around by dint of choice or tragedy. However for the vast majority of families sharing parenting can be a good choice. And we'll make the case why for many couples it may be a better choice than the alternative, and why sharing parenting deserves to be treated on a fair footing with the idea that Mum takes the lead on childcare alone, and Dad is kept at arm's length.

Some try to make this out to be a zero-sum game. *If dads get more time with the kids, they'll love Mum less; dads can only suffer from being expected to know how to clean up baby-poop; the economy will go under if we support dads in paternity the same way we support mums in motherhood.* Some think that men's rights are 'abused' by maternity rights, others that maternity rights would be jeopardised by giving dads better rights. All of these arguments are nonsense, and we can look to the latest research to prove it.

Shared parenting should be taken more seriously as something that gives Dad, Mum, and the kids a win, not to mention the real benefits it can bring to the economy.

2

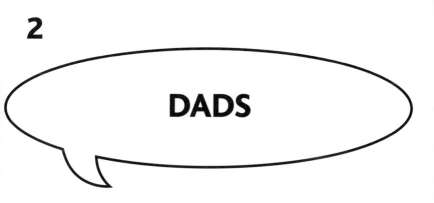

IT MIGHT NOT BE EASY, BUT IT SURE AS HELL IS WORTH IT

Now my baby and I have really got that bond, that he developed before with his mum. More so now, I feel like he's my little buddy and we're a little team and just spend our days together and do stuff together. It's kind of like you're best mates. But I didn't have that beforehand.

Jason (9 months leave), Fathers On Leave Alone[4]

Formerly the Cabinet Minister with responsibility for families, Michael Gove wrote a piece in *The Times* in 2008 arguing why it was awesome to be a hands-off dad[5]. "When tiredness sets in, in the hour before bedtime when tears come more easily, there's many a dad I know who finds that urgent work demands his absence, colleagues need to be called, papers submitted." Clearly referring to the task left to his wife, Gove explains that the pyjama-clad kid will "grab the book you've been reading for the past three years, which they've now outgrown, and which everyone else in their class now regards as babyish, insist that you read it".

He goes on to moan that the bedtime routine is a terrible travail that dads should avoid at all cost. Instead they should sneak in when the mum has done all the hard work, and get the cuddles during the 'sweet-spot' just before they settle down for sleep at the end of the day. So, in sum, that dad gets to miss most of the upbringing of his kids, but manages to squeeze in a few happy minutes just before bed-time.

We can only feel sorry for the men who buy into this. The moment your baby arrives, your whole world is going to change. You can either sit on the edge of the pool, dip your toes in and comment on how nice it is to get wet, like Gove, or you can say "screw this, I'm diving in". The invigorating feeling of being immersed in refreshing water as you start the swim, and moving in a way you never could on dry land is something that the toe-dipping-only people will never get the chance to know. When it comes to being an involved dad, people like Gove may just not understand quite what they're missing.

Contrast this to stay-at-home dad and author of *Dad Blog UK*, John Adams, who sums up the contrast he's noticed between dads who buy into the Gove way of thinking, and those who dive in to parenting: "When talking to both types of guys at the pub, the difference is really clear. The involved dads will talk about their kids' school lives, want to talk about how they're coming along and the funny things they get up to. They're just happy talking about their kids. They have a much better knowledge of their kids' school lives, happiness and their worlds than the other dads." We want to talk about things we enjoy, and when you're involved with bringing up your kids, that's your kids.

Of course, there's a whole range of dad types. At one end of the scale there's the absent dad who spends little time around his kids at all; there's the toe-dipping-type or the 'stand-back' dad; or the mum's assistant who occasionally picks up a bottle to give to his partner or 'does her a favour' by picking his own kids up from school one day a week. At the other end of the scale is the fully responsible dad, who doesn't see his partner as being more at the helm of looking after the kids, because he is just as much a parent as she is. The dads who embrace every part of being a dad fully.

It's these fully active and responsible dads who are breaking the norm, and who often come across their own version of the 'glass ceiling' when getting into fatherhood. Though it's more a glass floor, childcare being associated with women, and therefore any man seeking to trade in full-time work to take on more hands-on parenting is seen as stepping down. What it has in common with the glass ceiling is that it is mainly patrolled by men.

Dads who get involved like this, who fully dive into being a proper, responsible, and equal parent for their kids, often struggle to understand why every guy that has a kid doesn't do this, because it really is awesome.

Satisfaction

The feeling of your little person falling asleep on your shoulder as you're carrying them because they trust you like no-one else in the world, is a feeling you can't put into words. When they get scared or upset, they run to you for a hug. Every involved parent knows this feeling is golden, even if it's slightly tarnished when they do it in the hours of darkness when you're trying to sleep or enjoy some 'special' time with your partner. That golden feeling doesn't happen by not being around for your kids, and it happens more the more time you spend looking after them.

Listening to the toddler getting bathed from downstairs (as Michael Gove would if he accidently gets home to his own children too early, ironically having spent his day with giant man-baby Boris Johnson) isn't a happy experience – you only hear the crying when the shampoo comes out. But when you're involved, you also see the smiles, have the chats, try out the new toys. You have the conversation about the lion-shaped toothbrush and why red and pink aren't the same colour. It's worth it in a way that you can't see when you're not in the bathroom.

Ryan recently became a father to his first kid, little Orán. There's no shortage of time that Ryan has to talk about his new son. "I'm normally really motivated to get up and spend my time getting ready, but I'm now finding it really difficult to get out of bed in the morning because he's awake. I just get that time to spend watching him making his little noises. Him and me time. It's just great."

Ryan joins countless other dads who can benefit from spending more time with their kids and get more involved with their upbringing. While these benefits for dads have been largely ignored in the past, there is now an increasing amount of research pointing to the benefits that active parenting can bring to men. First off, the closer dads are to their babies and kids, the more satisfied the dads feel with their lives[6].

The huge United Nations-backed, State of the World's Fathers report sifted evidence from around the globe and concluded: "Men who are involved in meaningful ways with their children report this relationship to be one of their most important sources of well-being and happiness. Studies find that fathers who report close, non-violent connections with their children live longer, have fewer mental or physical health problems, are less likely to abuse drugs, are more productive at work, and report being happier than fathers who do not report this connection with their children."[7]

Being involved in parenting is a virtuous circle. The more involved you are as a dad, the more rewarding parenting becomes. You may not realise it when you're explaining to a three-year-old that they can't have ice-cream for dinner and managing their meltdown after you've announced this injustice. But being the involved parent for those moments means that you're going to bond with your kids more and enjoy the upside of parenting like you've never enjoyed something before.

Let's be honest, a toddler having a meltdown over nothing can be tough. But even the best jobs have plenty of drudgery, arguments with colleagues, and moments where we question our career choice. We just hope, like with parenting, that they'll be outweighed by the good times. It takes time and effort but for parents who put in the hard graft of the sleepless nights and arguing with unreasonable tiny versions of themselves, the rewards are magnified.

Research has also shown that the more time dads spend as sole carers for their kids in two-parent households, the stronger their bonds and interactions with their kids become. This isn't rocket science, yet the paternity gap is still gaping, and it took until 2008 for researchers to start to make this claim and back it up with data[8].

Living in an apartment in South London, Justin and Chloe had their first child, Josh, just over two years ago. Justin explains that his work meant that he couldn't spend the time he wanted to around his new toddler. This meant that whilst Josh got very close to Chloe, he saw Justin much the same as he saw other people in the family. "You're told that you're all of a sudden going to have this really close bond with your baby, like they'll suddenly have this strong attachment. But it was really tough in the beginning and it takes time to form the bonds."

> "Josh was really clingy to Chloe for the first year. He wouldn't let me or anyone else take him and do stuff for him, which was really difficult on Chloe, but also really upsetting for me. I was helping out but Josh wasn't really connecting with me. But he did spend nearly all his time around Chloe, so it makes sense."

Justin noticed however that "he's started to come to me a little more freely recently, which feels great. I've spent several weeks with a lot more time around him, holiday and coming home early, and it's really paying off. I've had a lot more time to play with him and look after him. But I know that if I spend just a few weeks needing to work later or travel more I'll have to start from scratch and he'll get really clingy to just Chloe again."

He says what every dad in his situation feels: "I know it sounds bad but it's nice to feel wanted and loved by your kids. You really need that sometimes. It's just so great when they turn round and run over to you or give you a spontaneous hug! It's deflating when they don't."

One extensive study covering detailed interviews from dads across eleven developed countries, including the UK, demonstrated something that just a bit of on-your-own parenting experience can show is fairly obvious. These bonds and the sense of satisfaction are more pronounced when dads have a good chunk of time on their own with their babies[9]. Taking charge and owning the task at hand makes parenting even more satisfying.

Purpose like you've never felt it before

Men that are more engaged with their children and family life, who take on more of the mental load – that's the term for keeping on top of when sports day is, which kid needs a packed lunch tomorrow and whether everyone in the house has enough clean pants – live longer and enjoy better mental health.

They have purpose. They are more social, are less prone to depression, more self-aware, more self-confident, and more mature. The list goes on, and the evidence is mounting that dads benefit from being closely involved in parenting in ways they don't always see before being an involved dad. Arguably the clearest reason for all these perks that dads get for being more involved stems from a new purpose when they fully commit to the their role as dad.

Ali, with two kids, works in the public sector and, ignoring pressure from his boss, took shared parental leave for his second daughter. "There's no doubt in my mind that I've bonded more with Julia, my second, than my first. She's still tiny, but there's a really close connection. Since my wife had an emergency C-section, I also took on a much bigger role in feeding and caring for Julia right from the beginning. I did all the night feeds myself and was just really ready for it all. I was tired and exhausted, but was loving every second of it. I felt really needed. I just didn't get that with our first as my wife was able to do everything."

Ali goes on to explain that while taking shared parental leave, he bonded much better with his second daughter than he was able to with his first, "summarised in the proud moment when her first word was 'dadda'! I loved it. I was talking about my clever little girl's first word for weeks. Julia did laugh at my wife first, but I got her first smile, not just the ones trying to push out a fart. The real first smile. It feels silly but that means so much when you're a dad. You just feel you get more purpose in life."

David Shaul, the primary carer for his kids, talks about the first time he got to take his son out to the cinema in his blog, *Dad vs. World*: "When I was a kid I'd dream about being a professional footballer, having a big house and a flashy car, yet in this moment, sat just me and my lad watching a superhero film hand in hand I couldn't feel any luckier if I had any of those things. I'm living my dream, I just didn't know this was what I wanted until I had it."[10]

Sure, we have a sense of purpose in our careers. We want our jobs to go well, to be trusted and respected in what we do from the building site, to the beat or the boardroom. Historically, dads have stepped aside, though when it comes to having a big purpose in the home, all they have needed to do in the past is bring home the bread, and occasionally read a good-night story. That's no longer seen as a life purpose.

Mental health

Olivia Spencer's book, *Sad Dad*, explores the mental health issues that men can face when becoming fathers. We often assume that men can't get post-natal depression because that's for mums coping with the cocktail of post-pregnancy hormones, overwhelming responsibility and loss of control. But dads do report getting it, or something like it. And even if a father's problems don't manifest themselves in a full-blown depression, the causes can still have a significant strain on his mental health.

However, in most cases, unlike for women with PND, one of the main drivers behind mental health problems for fathers is a sense that they are being excluded from the relationship they knew, with their partner, and from the one they expected, with their baby. As Spencer explains, "men can get envious of their partners, and they can feel pushed out of their relationship by their own child."

Spencer goes on to explain that in many cases "the connection between the baby and the mother can become a problem for the father... Often, these feelings of exclusion will surface after the birth... Before the baby arrived, the father had a connection with his partner, but after the birth [if he's not fully involved] he has no immediate connection with either his partner or his child. Instead, she has the direct connection with the child and the father is the outsider."

This feeling of being outside the close core unit of mother and baby can be crippling for some, and drive them into depression. It's a beautiful thing to watch how close a mum and her baby can be together. But it's sad when you thought you'd be part of that too, and find out that you're left outside in the cold. For many, it doesn't need to get that far or be that extreme to still have a negative effect on a dad's happiness and wellbeing.

In many of these cases (albeit not all), if the dad was enabled and expected to take a bigger role in the family, and more real responsibility for bringing up the baby, it's not unlikely that they would feel more included. There are some big gains to be had for many fathers if they are able to get more involved and be a central part of the family unit.

Lasting relationships

It is, like so much of this subject, obvious when you think about it. Of course men who actually talk to their children and spend time with them, who make parenting a shared endeavour with their partner, enjoy better relationships.

And perhaps the most obvious reward of all for fully involved dads is that it's going to set you up with a lifetime-long strong bond with your kids. This is a two-way street between Dad and kid. Research shows that when dads are involved more with looking after their kids as babies, they'll be closer and more invested in them as they get older. Like a gateway drug, once dads get a little taste of being involved with their little ones early on, they can't get enough, and continue to have a close and satisfying bond with them as they grow up [11].

Our own experiences speak to this. James has two kids. He downgraded his paid employment to part-time second time around and it's noticeable that it's his younger child, the one he spent much more time looking after, that almost always turns to him for help and comfort. For his older child it's not one-sided, but the cry of "Mummy!" is heard much more.

For Dave, who split shared parental leave down the middle with his partner, there's a reassuring feeling that for a little over half the time when he and his wife are both around, his toddler's calls for comfort are aimed at Daddy. Sure his little guy's insistence that Daddy has to be the one to feed him breakfast at six o'clock on a Saturday morning can leave him bleary-eyed, but for some reason it's just obviously worth it. When your kids hurt themselves and need comfort and help, your instinct is to reach out to them. If your kid picks you over everyone else in the room to give that comfort, you can't help but feel it's great.

Being a more involved dad doesn't just mean better relationships in the home. There is an issue around men lacking support networks. Men rarely have as many friends as women. That's a crude generalisation but it speaks to a truth that while most women are brought up to talk to each other, men are not.

That lack of social support feeds into mental health. Of course women have mental health issues too, and we'll come to them in a bit, but they are often triggered for different reasons.

Just as kids with a loving and settled home life are more likely to find life easier, so the same goes for adults. It's easier to be confident and relaxed in social situations when you've got a firm grounding at home to build on. And other people want to be friends with the confident and relaxed guy. So his social circle grows, his confidence grows, his support network expands.

Confidence is another key aspect of mental health. But many men lack it around babies. A man may be able to walk into the boardroom and slap his metaphorical cock on the table to take charge of the meeting, but faced with the product of his loins, imposter syndrome can often kick in. It's a big step for a man to front up and take on childcare. Of course it shouldn't be but it is challenging a gender norm and it is something men are not expected to do.

Again, getting involved in parenting and being an active dad is going to fix this. If you do it from the beginning and go through the struggles and victories from when they're new-borns, you're going to be a more capable and confident father. That confidence and competence has all its own rewards, because we like being good at what we're doing.

So that decision about how both parents are going to share parenting should have a 'dad factor' for the sake of dads. For most of history, whilst men have been firmly in the driving seat, they've been cut off, or more likely cut themselves off, from what could be the route to a much more fulfilling life.

They've been kept away – not by women but by the society they created – from playing the role of a full and responsible dad with all the satisfaction and perks that brings with it. Men who are more engaged in fatherhood and family life are fitter, happier, and more productive. They have more purpose and a better relationship with their kids with all the rewards that that brings. And best of all it's not a zero-sum game – it applies to mums as well.

3

MUMS

SHARING THE LOAD

Mums, like dads, are also faced with the question of what sort of mum they want to be. But the pressures on Mum are the polar opposite from those on Dad. For mums who want to continue with their career and share parental responsibilities with their partner, life will become more difficult. But if they follow the direction that society pushes them towards, sacrificing their career and juggling more work inside and outside the home, then there's a good chance that the burden of responsibility will be very heavy indeed.

In the past, women have had very little control over their lives, handed as they were from father to husband. Each wave of feminism has won more in the way of control but one of the reasons we still have feminism is that there's still a way to go yet. And one of the remaining steps is to see mothers and fathers as equal parents giving the former a genuinely free choice in whether to stay at home and how long for.

Stress of parenting – wanting to share the load

We've heard people say that mums should not want to miss out on a second of their kids' lives, making out that it's 'fundamental' to being a woman to be the main parent, often to the exclusion of the dad. But being a parent – Mum or Dad – isn't just cuddles, giggles, and bike rides. It's also really tough.

Sarah, working in finance with two small kids at home, argues that it's "too much to have responsibility for on your own. It doesn't really work. If all of the burden is on one parent to work hard and do everything at home, it will push them to derail their careers to cope. Something will have to give with that much pressure. If you can split the pressure, share the burden, it's going to be much more manageable, and as a mum you're likely to be able to do more of what you want to do. And do it better as well."

Sarah's point is at the heart of why sharing parenting can offer big benefits for mums compared to the status quo for most families. Few involved parents will claim that parenting is easy. It's often not. We're not parents because it's easy, we're parents because, despite the times when it's hard, the rewards of getting that spontaneous hug are immense enough to make up for it. But that doesn't mean that only women should have to shoulder the hard stuff. Dads taking a bigger role in childcare and domestic work, with real responsibility for it, is going to cut the pressure on mums because there is simply less stuff for each parent to do.

Sarah's husband, Max, plays a bigger role in childcare than many dads, and he was able to play a bigger role for their second child than for their first. Sarah argues that the more of the burden Max took, the easier it became for her. It was easier for her to pick up and push her career forward and she'd managed to progress as a result, just as she'd wanted. She wouldn't have been able to do this if the pressure of parenting during the week was all on her shoulders.

Reduce the sole-burden or parental responsibility on mums, and more women could be happier, more productive, and fitter too. Many, if not most, women are holding down two full-time jobs. Paid employment, which may be a five day job condensed into fewer hours too, and running the household – the so-called mental load.

Mental load became a thing in 2017 after a comic strip by French artist Emma went viral. The illustration, entitled "You should've asked" explains how women do most of the household tasks, while men need to be asked to get involved. Perhaps the most pernicious example is the woman who asked her partner to get the baby's bottle out of the dishwasher before he came to bed, in anticipation of a night feed. When she stumbles bleary-eyed into the kitchen in the night to retrieve the bottle she finds he's done as he was asked, but everything else – the plates, dishes, cutlery etc – remain in the machine. The comic was met with the inevitable 'not all men' indignation from some. But it was celebrated by many more women who recognised the scenarios but particularly the concept of mental load.

The artist Emma explains that mental load means always having to remember which chores need doing, what the kids need for school next day, what bills need to be paid. The mental load is "permanent and exhausting work. And it's invisible," she says[12]. And it's being taken increasingly seriously.

According to the latest Office of National Statistics figures, women still do nearly twice as much housework as men in the UK. A huge Canadian study published in 2017 that tracked people at different stages of their lives found that, no matter their age, women did more chores. Which is why the latest State of the World's Fathers report released in 2017 made tackling the disparity in the amount of domestic work carried out by each gender its main priority. It opened with the blunt assessment: "Caregiving and unpaid care work are at the heart of any discussion of the state of the world's fathers, and at the heart of gender inequality. For all the attention paid to unpaid care work, however, in no country in the world do men's contributions to unpaid care work equal women's."[13]

The link to equal parenting is strong. First, if women bear the mental load alone they get fed up. Marianne, thirty-four and married to Rob, had her baby boy in 2015. After a year of maternity leave, she went back to work for three days a week. On becoming a toddler, their little angel made the predictable shift to becoming more prone to tantrums as he started to try out his will on the world.

Marianne explains that "this is really awful, and it makes me feel bad for saying it, but sometimes I just can't cope with him. I just don't know what to do. You just feel exhausted, like you've got no energy to deal with all the other things you need to do. It's a lot of pressure.

> "There are days when I really look forward to Rob getting home just because more people there might help. But when Rob gets back late, because of work or if he goes out to drinks with his work, it doesn't get any easier. I still have to get the food ready and handle the baby. It doesn't really stop until I get him to bed. It just feels like a lot."

There was more than a small hint of resentment from Marianne towards Rob for him not helping out more at home. But each time that resentment started to show, she made it clear that he also had to focus on his job, and that even the after work drinks were 'important for his career'.

After giving her interview with us, Marianne gave up her job. She argued that she liked 'getting out', but there was just too much going on with needing to look after a small child, and that 'something had to give'. Contrast to Sarah and Max where the burden was more shared, and Sarah was happier and more able to pursue the career she wanted, with no sign of resentment. Which makes the second link to shared parenting – sharing the mental load will make for a better relationship. Split the household chores rather than split up.

Thirdly, if men are more engaged and involved from the early days of parenting they're just going to have more understanding of what's needed. Any decent man seeing his partner buckling under the weight of the mental load would surely intervene. But if he's not at home he's not going to see it.

If men are given more opportunity to spend time looking after their kids from the off they are more likely to see themselves as something more than just a breadwinner. If parents share the mental load then the pressure is relieved a little and women can give more of their energy and focus to work and give the same but more willingly to their family whilst allowing dads to take on their fair share.

To sum up, a kid's tantrum shared is a kid's tantrum halved. Sharing this burden more with dads must be a win for mums and can pull everyone away from breaking point.

Mums' mental health

A study from 2007 showed that mothers whose partners were more involved with childcare were also less likely to experience depression[14]. Post-natal depression, depression in general, is complicated and its exact causes are likely to be as unique as the person with the condition. However there are broader causes that can be considered. When people don't feel in control mental health problems can begin and the isolation that accompanies a birth is not helpful. There's a reason it's called confinement.

Bridget Hargreave has battled PND and written a book on the topic, *Fine (Not Fine)*[15]. She told us: "The common thread is isolation. So these are women that are feeling isolated, they may still be going out and hanging out with NCT friends or whatever but you can still be lonely in that context."

Control is regularly mentioned too. Telling girls that in the twenty-first century they can achieve anything, then handing them a baby-shaped barrier and telling them they've got to surmount that while the boys don't, is bound to have an effect.

At least one in four new mums suffer post-natal depression, and the figure is likely higher because both admitting the problem and getting diagnosed are barriers many find too imposing.

In many of these cases a dad is still in the picture, just not able to take time out of work to share the responsibility for baby and childcare. Dad's having to work a full week, knowing his baby-mum is suffering and needing support, can be really tough when he wants to be there more for his family. But it's worse for the person going through depression. Having a partner cheerleading for them and able to understand could make a huge difference.

Bridget Hargreave spoke to a number of people, including dads, who had been through PND. She said: "I wouldn't want to simplify it to say the ones whose husbands did nothing suffered longer but it is interesting that the ones who have a more positive story, and then things got better, usually they list medication, getting therapy and they got help and the help almost always came from their partner. Not just helping in the practical sense but also the showing up, being present, being there, acknowledging you're ill. PND wasn't a journey or a path their partner could completely understand, but if they were there they could understand it more."

In the vast majority of cases having a partner who is around more and doing more to help in those early weeks of parenthood, and consequently more likely to be more involved beyond that phase, would be a good thing.

Bridget adds: "With PND there are three or four recognised causes. Usually it'll be a combination of those factors. So it's not as clear as simply improving one thing and the instance of PND will go down." But she agrees that even if it doesn't reduce the amount of people hit with PND it may be "milder or not last as long".

And she can even see a preventative effect. "Some women start to become depressed and anxious when they are pregnant. If you were pregnant but you knew that when the baby comes I'm not on my own because my husband's taking time off or I only have to get to three months and then I'm going back to work. [That might help.] It's knowing you have options. Having choices is key."

Giving men and women proper choice in how they handle childcare and the domestic duties that go with it could cut the pressure on mums and reduce the incidence of mental health problems among parents. Sharing the tough moments and the burdens of responsibility with the dad doesn't make the mum any less of a mum, it just makes it easier to be a mum.

Careers and minding the pay gap

Taking time out of work to look after your kids is going to have an impact on your career. And the longer you take the bigger that impact is likely to be. Maternity discrimination means over 50,000 women are fired every year just for becoming a mum. If you do get to return to work after your maternity leave, then you're likely to find your work colleagues treating you differently. You're now seen as a 'working mum' who isn't so serious about progressing in her career.

Taking a long stretch out of the workplace makes it all the more difficult to go back afterwards, skills get rusty and confidence ebbs away. In nearly all cases today, if one person in a couple is going to bow out of the workplace to bring up the kids for a while, it will be the mum.

Long maternity leave hurts careers. When MPs on the House of Commons Women and Equalities committee looked into the issue in 2016 a range of experts told them that leaving the workplace for more than nine months was a bad idea if you want to forge a career. US campaigner for better maternity rights Sylvia Ann Hewlett found that two years out of the workplace reduces a woman's earning power by 18%, permanently. Wait till the kids have started school to go back to work and earning power is cut by 38% for life[16].

On the other hand maternity leave of around six months has no significant impact over the course of an earning lifetime. Research also shows that when fathers work flexibly and share childcare responsibilities with their baby-mums, mothers are almost twice as likely to progress in their career[17].

Then there's the pay gap that largely emerges as a result of men and women's different roles in childcare. From 2017, companies in the UK were forced to publish data on their gender pay gap. In early 2018 when High St knick-knack emporium Oliver Bonas owned up to a 10% pay gap they squealed that the figures were unfair because they didn't take into account the number of women on the shop floor. But that's the point – that all the men in the company work in head office doing more senior jobs. And while the gender pay figures were poor for the firm the bonus pay gap was worse: the male employees are hoovering up bonuses at a higher rate than the females. It's worth pointing out that Oliver Bonas were far from the worst offenders – Easyjet, Virgin Money and the Co-operative Bank all had pay gaps of over 30%[18].

The BBC may have thought they'd weathered the storm in 2017 after admitting to a 10% gender pay gap compared to ITN and Channel 4, at around 20% and 30% respectively, only for the BBC's China editor Carrie Gracie to kick off a row about equal pay when she quit in protest at the start of 2018 because she was being paid less than other, male, editors.

Equal pay is covered by legislation – it's illegal to pay different sexes a different amount for the same work. But the pay gap persists. To explain and tackle it you have to look at maternity. In the workplace, if employers are expecting women to take a year off a few times in their 30s or 40s, or even needing to stop working after having kids, then they're going to feel unfairly biased against them. They don't currently expect men to do the same, however big their families get.

These things go a long way towards explaining why the pay gap between men and women for the same type of work starts after women have kids[19]. So the current expectations on mums and dads can actively harm Mum's career, which can't be good for her happiness, the family's finances, or the wellbeing of the whole family.

The problem with most chat about whether a mum should go back 'early' or not is that it's always framed as her having to decide between her career or her babies. Dads meanwhile are never challenged by others with this sort of dilemma. This doesn't need to be the case for mums if Dad is able to take his turn, if the couple opt for sharing parenting.

After the parental leave period there's the question of childcare. Which parent will go part-time? Which parent will pick up the mental load and attend the school Christmas concert, parents' evening, and ferry the kids to their afterschool clubs? The one that's earning less, obviously. The one that earns even less, because they've gone part-time and taken the full year out on maternity leave, because that's the natural order of things, because they are just 'better' at childcare.

That may breed resentment in a lot of couples. Not among all women who freely and willingly choose to throw themselves into it, but among a significant proportion who want a career and a family together. They may be depicted as wanting 'it all' but realistically that's like saying someone wants everything on the menu when in fact they are asking for just bread and water.

There are two ways of looking at it: if men take shared parental leave women can get back to the workplace sooner. Forgive us for stating the obvious but a year of maternity leave is twice the length of six months' shared parental leave for each parent. The sooner women get back to their desk, or factory or whatever workplace they occupy, the smaller the maternity penalty. Alternatively if men start taking an equal amount of parental leave compared to their partners, then employers have no reason to discriminate when hiring, firing, promoting, or just in their everyday dealings with employees of a different gender.

Either way if the parental leave playing field were evened up and if flexibility after that period was genuinely offered to both parents then employers would have to start rethinking their treatment of women. Parenting would become a smaller and more evenly spread issue between men and women. Dads taking their turn to look after the kids can help their baby-mum, both emotionally and professionally.

4

KIDS

MORE DAD MAKES FOR HAPPIER KIDS

For parents, however, the benefits to themselves of doing something are going to be worth very little if it's going to harm their kids. From babies to toddlers to kids and on to adolescence, Dad taking his turn benefits his little ones. The evidence on this front is really quite remarkable.

And yet we've seen dads taking over being sold as bad for the babies. Even when referring to two-parent households, it's not uncommon to see a tabloid headline announcing that children are obviously crippled when their mums 'abandon' them going back to work 'too early'. Mums are branded as 'selfish' for leaving their important maternal post to lesser adults[20].

First, it is clear now that mums going back to work is not bad for their kids[21], and that it can also be good for them, but also we're talking about dads taking on the role of the parent, so the kids are a long way from being abandoned.

One study tracking kids from birth into adulthood found that in two-parent households, when mums went back to work full-time earlier than normal, fathers became significantly more involved in childcare. The more equal split of parenting in these families led to better – not worse – outcomes for the kids[22].

It turns out that children whose fathers are engaged in family life from the off are just more likely to be better off. This is especially the case for kids where both parents share full responsibility. The more dads that share sole care of their kids with their partners, the better their offspring's mental wellbeing, happiness, job security, and educational attainment is likely to be[23].

Of course that's not possible for everyone – and there's plenty of evidence that conflict and disharmony between parents can have negative impacts on children sharing a household with adults that don't get on. But in the many families where it is the case, we should think about the positive impact of more engaged dads.

For a start the child benefits from double the love. Of course all parents love their kids. But just as babies aren't born with an understanding of how not to poo in the bath, they can't be expected to just understand that their parents love them, they need physical evidence of that. They need to be shown. And that just means being hands-on – talking to them, holding them, rocking them to sleep and, as they get older, playing with and teaching them.

First and foremost for dads is that their kids will be closer to them, and that bond will be stronger and last for longer. Love is a difficult thing to pin down, but it's fair to say that a father's love and a mother's love are essentially the same. Similar chemical reactions are being triggered in everyone's brain.

But the baby's brain is particularly flexible, everything it sees and hears in those very early days, months, and years contributes to its neurological architecture. Just the way a parent looks into their eyes affects the configuration of neurons within. And so the loving gaze of two parents multiplies the effect.

Dads being involved in baby-care for the first year doesn't just mean that babies are closer to their dads, but are also more sociable and confident with other babies and adults. The 2015 State of the

World's Fathers report pulled together reams of research and surmised: "Playful and affectionate interaction with fathers can predict children's positive social-emotional involvement with others, particularly with peers."[24]

Role models

And dads bring different things to the parenting table. Inevitably they have different interests, outlooks and perspectives that can only broaden a child's horizons. And while we'd like gender to be less important than it is today, we're not there yet. So men and women are different courtesy of the environment they grow up in, not because of any innate genetic gubbins. That means dads bring dad stuff to parenting. For example, given the strictures of masculinity, fathers tend to partake more in rough-and-tumble play but that helps kids learn the limits of aggression and violence.

The division of household labour does raise questions about what sort of role models fathers actually play – i.e. are they just perpetuating gender stereotypes? Or is it good to have a man in the house because children, and perhaps boys in particular, need a male role model? Much is made of adolescent boys going off the rails for lack of a decent male role model. But the evidence is that those teenagers are more likely to be victims of the toxic masculinity culture than to find themselves in bother for want of a man showing them how it's done.

"Fathers are important because more caregivers in a household are often better than one, not because they are male." Michael Lamb, author of *The Role of the Father in Child Development*, explains that when it comes to role models one role is much more important than another: "The characteristics of the father as a parent rather than the characteristics of the father as a male adult appear to be most significant."[25] And this applies to parents no matter their sexuality or even their exact relationship to the child. So, for instance, stepfathers can fulfil the same role.

Better prepared for the future

Over the longer-term, the more involved both parents are, the more confident, smarter and emotionally balanced the kids will be as they grow up.

Having a guess at what aspect of someone's childhood will have the biggest single impact on their educational success, and so their opportunities in life, we might list a few possibilities, including class, genes or poverty. But we'd be wrong. The single biggest indicator of a child's educational success is none of the above, it's paternal involvement[26].

This is all evidenced once the children of engaged parents get to school. Dads make kids smarter. It is remarkable that fathers can have that impact. Of course there's all sorts of stuff to unpack around that statistic about why it is the case but it seems to apply across class, gender, and even geography so for now let's just lap up the fact that it is the case.

Part of the reasoning is that kids who have dads around who are, crucially, fully engaged and taking an active part in the household, are better behaved, they are healthier, they are happier, they are less likely to get in trouble with the authorities and best of all they have a more positive view of gender equality. The boys don't look down on girls quite so much, the girls are go-getters. Dads are basically magic.

Just as parents want clever, well-behaved kids, so should society. Which is why mums' and dads' demands for a more equitable settlement when it comes to parenting and childcare should get a sympathetic hearing in the corridors of power. Sometimes though, the only way to get people on board is to point to the bottom line.

5

THE ECONOMY

WHERE THE MONEY IS

The shake-up caused by shifting domestic and childcare responsibilities to both parents is a big change. Arguably the biggest change for gender equality in half a century. If sharing parenting is made more feasible and families start to take it up, there will be huge social benefits for everyone involved. It would be simple to say that this is worth the costs. Most people would trade quite a bit of their income if it would make their family happier, healthier, and closer[27].

So when traditionalists start to cry that taking dads out of the workplace will suddenly wreak havoc in the economy and will cost too much, we should already start asking them why they think a little cash is more important than the happiness and life chances of our kids. Even if it did cost us, it would be worth it.

But – and here's what every economist, business owner, and politician wants to hear from a public policy – widespread shared parenting is good for the economy. A win for families is also a win for companies, wealth, and jobs if it's done right.

Retaining half the working population

Once we clarify the weird situation, that we've taken half the population out of the labour market indefinitely and held the other half back from doing something they could desperately need and benefit from, it starts to become clear that there are big gains to be had by shaking things up. Half a trillion quids' worth of gains.

According to OECD analysis[28], if there were as many women as men in the workforce the economy would swell by up to half a trillion pounds and get a 10% boost in GDP by 2030. That's hard to argue with. Of course it's up to women, and hopefully the same applies increasingly to men too, to decide whether they want to go back to work, and to what extent, once parenthood begins. But the more cautious estimate of reducing the gap between men and women leaving the workforce by half still adds to GDP by a huge 5%.

That's 5% to 10% of GDP we're missing out on right now because of unequal opportunities and expectations on parents: well over the tiny 0.8% the fully funded and widely used parental leave and day-care system in Sweden costs. These benefits are shared across both the families and companies they're employed by. That's better for business, and better for creating sustainable jobs.

And beyond the bald numbers there's the human factor: talented women lost to the workplace because they can't get the hours they want or because bigoted bosses simply force them out after childbirth because they don't fancy the hassle of having a mum on the team. Remember the latter affects over 50,000 women every year.

And men too who are either similarly forced to choose between work and family or, more likely, trapped by expectation and economics in long hours, full-time jobs they may increasingly come to resent.

Around nine months of leave from a workplace is the maximum time before an employee begins to fall out of touch with their old job. Longer than eight months out of the workplace, employees and employers start losing skills that damage their earning potential. So when for nearly all families mums are expected to use up all twelve months of their maternity leave without getting Dad to take his turn, it's hardly surprising that companies are going to take a hit to the value of their workforce when kids arrive.

Dr Ben Kerrane who runs a research project into parental leave, *Making Room For Dads*, experienced pushback against the policy. One business owner argued that if men were able to 'just disappear' from her workforce for 'months on end', it would bring unacceptable costs and uncertainty to many companies. Ben wasn't sure that she, and others arguing the same, had really thought their arguments through. They never showed similar concerns about maternity leave.

Imagine the real impact of more shared parenting on a business. If parents choose to take up shared parental leave as it stands and divide the time available down the middle, women would be able to return to work in half the time they did before, practically wiping out gender differences in earning power over a lifetime. Rather than half of your workforce receiving a huge career-limiting break in their careers, you have the parents in your workforce taking a much smaller skip before they step back in with the added skills that parenting brings.

A more equal uptake of parental leave would mean that businesses would either have to treat their workforces more equally, or discriminate against all parents or potential parents. This would presumably either leave these companies with a niche workforce of really square teenagers and old people, which is unlikely to work out for most industries, or change their mindsets to something altogether fairer.

Once the leave period was over, if women and men shared family responsibilities and didn't face the risk of leaving completely because their job couldn't fit with their childcare commitments, it'd be a more contented and productive workforce.

Business on the whole copes when a woman takes her full entitlement of twelve months away. If it has a problem with men taking half of that or even the same, then there's some fundamental sexism going on there, especially when it increases the chance that women will take shorter periods out. Retaining a huge chunk of your workforce and its talents can't be bad.

In countries that do have a more equal split between parenting roles, we have seen a steady growth in the number of women in the workforce. Nordic economies are doing pretty well. They weathered the financial crisis better, have more skilled workforces, and tend to house more innovative industries per capita[29]. Not all of this will have been due to their higher levels of gender equality, but clearly a more balanced workforce can play its role.

Diversity

Diversity improves the bottom line. The more diverse companies are, especially at senior levels, the more perspectives and healthy challenges they'll get. This leads to healthier companies.

There are a range of studies that try to explain this phenomenon, some arguing that a few extra women on boards don't make much of an impact, whilst others arguing that they do. But the more recent studies have shown that for companies facing the same challenges, higher numbers of women at all levels of management allow companies to outperform their competitors with male dominated workplaces[30]. This is hardly surprising since they are benefiting from being able to hire from the whole workforce, and not excluding half of it and ending up with the leftovers.

A frequent (not always valid) concern about increasing gender diversity in companies is that women can leave the workplace for maternity reasons and have less time to develop their skills compared to their male counterparts. By allowing dads to take half of the parental leave and half of the burden of taking care of the kids, we're not just having a neutral impact on the workplace, we're allowing both parents to preserve their talents and stay closer to the labour market and avoid the risk of becoming under-employed.

Businesses don't like uncertainty, even if change will benefit them in the long-run. More worrying though is their logic. Traditionalists claim that if you allow dads to take half the parental leave the mum would have taken, you're introducing uncertainty. Wait, here's an opportunity to allow the women in your workforce to not leave the company completely when their baby comes. Surely that's reducing rather than increasing uncertainty.

It seems to be that it breaks down another certainty that they had used to hire their workforce: that you can hire, promote, and raise the salaries of men without an eye on how old they are or how big their families are. In fact, if they have kids, then you can expect more from them as they'll need to earn more for their families. Women on the other hand, especially when they're of the age when they're likely to make babies, are reliably untrustworthy in such respects because they might announce maternity leave at any moment.

Jason, forty-two with two teenaged kids, works as a manager in a company that employs around 200 people. He admits that when looking for who to promote, they have to think about what he calls 'commitment' to the company. "If a woman's of childbearing age, that wouldn't stop me from hiring her. But when I put someone into a business-critical role, I want to know that they'll stay there for a good long time… If she then decides to take a year out to look after a baby, I'm in a mess. I have to get someone to do her job well, for a whole year, then make them leave at the end of it so she can come back. I reckon that costs companies a lot, so I have to be cautious."

Before we get too angry with Jason, let's remember he is trying to run a business that, if it doesn't do well, will go bust, losing the jobs of everyone in the company. This set-up puts women at a big disadvantage in the workplace, but it also pushes the idea that sharing parental leave and responsibilities could be bad for companies. Jason goes on to talk about how "risky it would be for dads to also be able to take the time out. I would then have to cope with twice as many people demanding to disappear for a year whilst I keep their job open."

So a boss builds a company on the assumption that, by-and-large, the senior and higher paying work is done by the reliable men, and the danger of maternity is limited by only giving a few high-profile jobs to women. The gender pay gap figures that firms were forced to publish in 2017 showed this to be common practice. When someone then comes along and says men are also dads, and that they can now also take parental leave, ask for flexi-time to look after their kids, or leave work early to do the school-run, and women might start sticking around the office more, the hiring practices in his business are going to look stupid. His competitors who had a better gender mix are going to be at an advantage, and it's all his fault for being sexist.

But, and it's worth repeating, if today a mum takes twelve months off work to look after a baby, if dad takes half of the time, she will only need to take six months. Alternatively, and preferably, if parental leave pay entitlements were expanded to allow both parents to take nine months off, nothing has changed in terms of how long the woman is out of the office.

Change might be worrying for people like Jason, but that doesn't mean it's not right anyway, and even in their company's best interest.

Motivating dads

What's more, men who have better mental health, who are more confident in their family and friend relationships, and who are given the freedom to choose their working hours and conditions, will be better employees.

I went back to work for three days a week after my parental leave was up so I could look after my toddler for the remainder of the week. It's far from two days 'off' but it's brought ample rewards. The three days that I'm in the office, I now feel more focused and a lot more productive than before, because not only do I now know I've only got three days to do everything, but my experiences as a parent have made me trim the fat in my working behaviours. More time and responsibility for my child has made me happier and more engaged at work.

As well as loyalty, there are gains in productivity. It may be a self-selecting group but we've yet to hear from a dad that took shared parental leave or flexible working and regretted it or, more pertinently here, felt it made him a worse employee.

As explained in the *Dad's Turn* blog: "parenting makes us better, not worse, workers. Whether our little trolls train us to have lightning fast reflexes because of their magnetic attraction to danger; or become adept at feigning interest in monotonous tasks; or they just force us to do and think about half a dozen things at once on almost no sleep; these little people are forging us into more efficient and more resilient employees."[31]

Back in 2015, then deputy Prime Minister Nick Clegg trumpeted shared parental leave as good for the economy with a vague promise of increased productivity. But the evidence backs him up. A survey of some of the world's biggest companies found folk content with their work–life balance put in 21% more effort, while those unhappy with their work–life split didn't work as hard, were prone to poorer health and therefore absenteeism, and were ultimately more likely to leave the firm[32].

Two in five dads report often having significantly disrupted concentration at work because of not being able to fulfil family responsibilities. Companies don't want employees who work long hours for five or more days a week if they're not able to concentrate. Another phenomenon that companies should be increasingly worrying about is 'father churn', where fathers or expectant fathers are changing employers because they cannot reconcile their family and work lives.

On the flip side, and explaining where the wider economic benefits from more equally shared parenting can come from, dads with access to flexible working to accommodate their childcare responsibilities are more satisfied with their employer and are less likely to consider changing employer than fathers with more rigid working conditions. Companies benefit from more loyal and happier workforces.

To top this off, as mums returning to work after maternity leave have been saying for a while, the more a dad is the sole carer for their kid, the more skills he develops that he can then bring back to the workplace[33]. This isn't just learning to change nappies, it's also becoming better at multi-tasking and developing patience, both of which most workplaces can benefit from[34].

Companies aren't just doing this as a favour to families; if the workforce as a whole takes on more shared parenting, companies benefit too. This leads to happier workers, more wealth and so more jobs and better jobs. It's hard to understand why any government or political party would not enthusiastically embrace a policy that can be shown to be good for men, women, and children as well as improving the economy. Especially one that is becoming more and more supported by parents.

Getting fathers more involved in family life, in bringing up their own children, can do all that. Why it's not more widely successful we'll come to later. But the evidence is mounting that the old-fashioned way of looking at things is certainly not the only way.

The traditional split of household responsibilities may be built into our expectations of parenthood, but it's not what's best for everyone. Given the huge benefits for all involved that can come from more shared parenting, it's worth making a more equitable split in childcare easier for parents to choose. However, despite being faced with strong evidence in favour of this relatively novel way of running the family, we are still a very long way away from making it a real feasible choice for most couples in the UK.

Part II

THE PATERNITY GAP

Where are all the dads?

6

DADS NOT GETTING INVOLVED

So, the benefits of shared parenting are many and various and hopefully clear now. If we lived in a world where those benefits were acted on you could expect around half the parents looking after babies and small children during the week to be dads; nurseries and schools to ring dads as much as mums when a child is ill; kids to look to both parents equally for comfort. Maybe men feel confident in asking for flexible arrangements at work and parental leave because it's widely accepted by employers that dads are meant to be as responsible for their offspring as mums. Men are happier with their lives due to closer and more satisfying relationships with their kids. Perhaps women who have kids keep the careers they want and represent around half of senior management. The old *Mumsnet*, *Mothercare* and *MadeForMums* have all realised that the word 'parent' includes mums *and* dads, and have updated their brands accordingly. Maybe dads spend about the same amount of time with their kids as mums do, and people generally accept the 'old husbands' tales' that dads know best when it comes to how to carry, calm, and potty train the little ones.

But we don't live in that world. In fact, just how far we are away from this situation is sobering.

During parental leave, I took my son to baby cinema every Wednesday. There, parents can catch a film for grown-ups but everyone accepts that babies are going to cry, giggle at inappropriate times, and crawl around causing mayhem. On one count, I saw around 100 other parents watching the film. Two were dads. This was pretty unusual, as there are normally none at all.

This is no mother-and-toddler group reluctantly rebranded as a 'parent'-and-baby activity. It's a lame excuse but it's true that social norms make it unusual for men to sing in public: they might be put off by the prospect of singing *Sleeping Bunnies* for the hundredth time. This is going to the cinema, an activity not known for excluding either sex, or for generally including singing. And yet hardly any dads in sight.

Now, the men may all have had bad experiences like the one time I took my daughter to baby cinema ten years ago when she was just a tot and the film being screened involved Ryan Gosling falling in love with a blow-up sex doll and it just felt a bit weird really. But it seems unlikely nearly all new dads would have been similarly put off.

This picture is a little less one-sided during the weekends. Taking my son to rhyme-time at the local library every Saturday and Monday (I get that twice a week may seem excessive) allows for a useful comparison. On Mondays there are few or no other dads, but the weekends tell a different story.

One Saturday session there seemed to be some dads around. It could be that dads prefer listening to an old lady reading *We're Going on a Bear Hunt* to watching the latest *Star Wars* film with a babe in arms. More likely it's because dads are at work during the week, and the mums are taking the babies out. But this just feeds into the idea that dads 'do their bit' on a Saturday morning rather then 24/7. It doesn't need to be that way.

But before we get the impression that the puzzle of equal parenting gets solved the moment dads clock off work, even when there are dads present we tend to notice them more than the mums. With a surprised comment from one of the other dads that there were so many fathers around, I counted six dads out of twenty-three adults (fifteen mums and two grandmas), and this was on a Saturday. What's more, twelve of the mums were on their own with their little ones, with only three dads there without mums. Dads being responsible for their kids is still rare, even on the weekends when dads aren't at work.

It looks like we are so surprised to see six dads at this group, that we somehow didn't see the much larger number of mums on their own with their kids. A salutary lesson in confirmation bias[35].

Dads are becoming increasingly present in their children's lives compared to decades gone by and they say they want to do more. But we are still very far from equality in the amount of time spent by each parent with the little ones. This problem is only amplified during the working week when very few dads get more than a few hours in the evenings with their little people.

They don't get the practice and the experience of being around their baby, doing the baby stuff like changing nappies and feeds. But more importantly they miss out on getting attuned to the needs and wants of their offspring that are needed to lay the foundations of a closer relationship as they get older.

Baby time and shared parental leave

When shared parental leave (SPL) was launched the government had the fairly low bar target of an uptake of between 2 and 8% of new dads. Early signs from the government in 2018 were that the uptake could be as low as that 2% figure.

The results of a freedom of information request to HMRC revealed around 4% of new dads are using at least some shared parental leave. Other figures are available. Law firm EMW got some publicity with their figures that less than 1% of eligible dads were using SPL, although they refused to share their methods and data, so we can probably discount that finding.

More convincing are the findings of the Chartered Institute of Personnel and Development (CIPD), the trade body for human resources professionals. An extensive survey they undertook found four fifths of organisations had no new fathers at all asking about SPL. The actual take-up rate was around 5% of eligible dads, so in line with the HMRC figures. Moreover, the Trade Union Congress has indicated that only three in five new dads are even eligible in the first place, suggesting that the figure for all new dads is even lower.

Vitally, the CIPD found that while overall it was only about 4% of eligible dads using SPL, in the public sector it was 13%. This hints at some of the barriers dads may be facing to taking up their rights to SPL. The public sector has always been held to a higher standard for employee rights and the uptake still looks relatively low, with the battle even harder in the private sector where there's less oversight.

However, whichever figures are correct these aren't great numbers. To put it another way, well over nine in ten new dads are unable or unwilling (mostly the former) to take significant time off work in the first year of their babies' lives to care for them. What's more, because of the limitations in the policy and how people are viewing dads and mums differently, without reform, Shared Parental Leave is unlikely to go much further, as we'll see.

This is pretty bad compared to some other OECD countries. Around half of dads in The Netherlands, Luxembourg and Belgium take parental leave. In Germany in 2006 uptake was around 3% of new dads, with fathers only given a basic minimum to cover their lost salaries. Following a change in the law in 2007 that gave parents two 'bonus' months for the dad and increased the leave's pay to cover most of the parent's salary, uptake rose to 30%[36]. So they seem to be doing something right.

Following the trend in Germany, the uptake in all Nordic countries increased when months were reserved for dads on the same basis as for mums, with Norway seeing an increase from 3% to 70% by 2000.

In Sweden, Norway, and Iceland, around 90% of new dads are taking parental leave. In Sweden alone in 2013, 340,000 dads took parental leave. That means around 3.5% of the entire population of Sweden were dads who spent some time that year out and about wearing their babies during the working week[37]. By comparison, around 4% of the population were mums who chose to do the same.

Images of dads bouncing their babies whilst eating a cinnamon bun in a coffee shop on a Wednesday early afternoon have somehow become an expected feature of Swedish life. When visiting Sweden over the summer, I couldn't help but notice the high number of dads looking after their kids on their own during the week, and not one sign that they were thought of as out of place for doing so.

At the other end of the scale, the low uptake in the UK is shared with France, Finland, and Austria, all below 5%. Denmark, surprisingly, is hovering around only 15% of dads. Each of these countries have had some form of shared parental leave policies for at least a decade. Yet their uptake by dads remains low. This doesn't bode well for the UK if we get stuck in the same rut as these countries and struggle to reduce the over 90% of dads unable to get their turn.

But the story about how dads aren't getting their turn in the first year runs deeper than just the choice to take a piece of parental leave. We also need to look at how big that piece is.

Like most of the dads we spoke to, Brian was in the vanguard of SPL users, the first in his company to use the policy to look after his second daughter Annie eight months after she was born. He's taking six weeks after his wife took the first eight months.

When asked if he'd considered taking more, especially after he's been running the home for a month already, he thinks for a second: "I wouldn't mind it. I love spending the time with Annie of course. I'm gonna miss her when going back. But I can't really take that time out. People in the office were already getting nervous about me disappearing for nearly two months. You have to get the right balance and see what you can get away with."

Chris Mason is a familiar face on the telly. He's a BBC political correspondent and occasionally presents BBC Breakfast. He also took shared parental leave when his daughter Ivy was born, but nowhere near as much as his partner. He took the last two months after his teacher wife had done ten. He laughs, "The very fact we're having a conversation about the fact my wife and I split a year of maternity leave ten to two and my involvement is seen as somehow revolutionary tells us something about how big a leap doing what I did is but in the grand scheme of things how small it is."

Chris's reasoning was practical and financial. His wife being a teacher there was a natural break in their year for her to return to work in September. But he was also aware that he wouldn't get paid for the two months he took off.

He explains, "I did this weird thing where I decided that to make it work financially I was going to take on enough extra work in the remaining ten months (before my shared parental leave began) to cover those thirty-two shifts I would be forgoing. So effectively I was almost doing an extra day's work a week and the curiosity of doing that is wondering if I'm robbing Peter to pay Paul here because my wife's at home with my daughter and I'm working in order to have some time off." Chris needed to come up with what he confesses is a weird solution because he's been put in a crazy situation and it points up just why many dads feel like they can't take as much parental leave as their partner.

Out of the small proportion of dads using SPL many are unable to take more than a month, or even a few weeks. Whilst there's no data yet on exactly how many weeks new dads take off work to look after their babies in the first year – again the government review should throw up some decent research – all the anecdotal evidence we've gathered is that mums and dads are very unlikely to be sharing parental leave equally.

From the dads we encountered who had or were about to take shared parental leave, nearly all of them were only able to take a handful of weeks, mostly at the same time as their partner, and almost none more than two months. This pushes down the real split of time shared between parents very far below the 5% eligible uptake figure of SPL.

Sweden in contrast saw a third of the total parental leave available taken by new dads in 2017, and this is an upward trend[38]. But this has been after concerted efforts from the government, and some radical changes to cultural expectations.

Surprisingly, the update of the very basic right of dads to two weeks off on 'paternity leave' just after their child is born in the UK is not as widespread as we'd expect. A third of dads take less than the ten days granted by law, so effectively give up several days of paid leave that they're entitled to spend with their babies and partners.

This isn't taking on full-time responsibility for your kids, it's spending just the first two weeks with your families just after the birth. Almost 90% of dads who don't take any paternity leave and go straight back to work the day their kid is born regret not being able to have taken that time, often citing work pressures as a reason[39].

Dads and older kids

As mentioned in chapter 1, the first year is crucial to forming deep bonds with the little ones, so this lack of opportunity for dads to form those relationships with their babies isn't great. But perhaps the story changes as the kids get older? Unfortunately, the patterns established during those early weeks and months are often set for life and dads of older kids are also often deprived of responsibility and time with their kids.

According to detailed research into the activities of parents carried out by the Equal Opportunities Commission, dads spend less than a third of the amount of time caring for their under-fifteen-year-old kids during the week than mums do[40]. On the weekend, this only rises to less than half, putting down the claim that dads tend to get 'compensated' for their lack of time with the kids when they're off work.

Dads spend on average over the week less than 60% of the time spent by mums just 'around' their under-fifteen-year-old kids. That's not even time spent focusing on their kids. This is unsurprising, given that men also spend more time out at work.

In around three-quarters of households, the mum is the main care-giver, with dads in only 6% of families having the role. This is not just for small babies, but for kids up to the age of eighteen. Only a quarter of total childcare-related activities are being performed by dads in two-parent households during the week[41].

When we look at childcare responsibility we find a new level of dads taking a step back. Around 4 in 5 dads report that they do not have sole responsibility for their kids at any point during the week. 60% of fathers say that they do not provide any care for their children before or after school. Under 1-year-old babies are left with their dads as 'sole parent' for at least 30 hours a week in only 1% of two-parent households. In two-parent families with 3- to 4-year-olds this number only climbs to 4% of dads[42].

There is a consistent message coming out here, not just from the anecdotes of what we see in families around us, but from the best stats we can find on the topic. Parents are not managing to share time and responsibility with kids anywhere close to equally, from birth to the chicks leaving the roost.

People are making more of an effort, since dads now spend seven times as much time with their kids than they did in the 1970s. We shouldn't ignore this big achievement, as kids, dads and mums have benefited from it. But with dads only spending a small fraction of the amount of time looking after their kids compared to their partners, there is still a very long way to go. We need to get to the root of the problem and why it's stopping dads spending their fair share of time with their kids[43].

Stay-at-home parent?

The term 'stay-at-home parent' makes me chuckle, as parenting during the week tends to result in my tiny person being more persistent at dragging me out of the home than my last boss ever was. But whether they're 'out-of-house-parents', 'home-parents' or just 'parents-who-parent-during-weekdays', they have all left the labour market with the intention of caring for their kids.

When parents decide that one of them shouldn't go back to work after the first year and should become a stay-at-home parent, it is, in nearly every instance, the mum. Let's be clear, if it's financially doable, and a couple feel that it's best that one of them stay looking after the toddler, then this can be a great opportunity, despite the large sacrifices this will have on the carer's career.

But our curiosity should be piqued that it is almost always the mum that takes this on, especially given how many parents believe parental responsibility should be shared equally, and the lack of any evidence for sex differences in our biological compulsion to want to care for kids (as we'll see in Part III). Do mums need to make the stark choice between time with their toddler and time at work? What if dads want to make the same trade?

John Adams, author of *Dad Blog UK*, is the primary carer for his two daughters, Helen and Izzy. "I would like to live in a world where people didn't think it was so unusual for a dad to be the primary carer for his kids, to be the stay-at-home parent. But people still find it weird and unusual so people still talk about it." John explains that the parent-baby groups during the week and the school-gate parent cliques are all mums, with him being the unusual exception. "Dads are just not there in significant numbers yet."

"When I started as the primary carer of my kids several years ago, there weren't any other dads at all. That's changed a little recently, as there are occasionally other dads around during the week looking after their kids. But they're still massively out-numbered by mums, and are often there with their partners rather than looking after the kids by themselves, like nearly all the mums are. Not that I don't talk to the mums, but it can feel a little lonely as the only dad sometimes."

Out of all full-time stay-at-home parents, 96% of them are stay-at-home mums. Numbering just 3.8% of those full-time stay-at-home parents, it's little wonder that John and other guys like him feel like they're in a minority. Around 20% of mums that take maternity leave don't return to work after a year. This is compared to almost no dads after they've taken parental leave[44]. The number of stay-at-home dads is higher now than it used to be. But again we shouldn't pretend that a revolution has happened with such small numbers.

Stay-at-home dads are still very rare, and tend to only be the most committed bunch of dads who had the opportunity to stay at home with their kids at the right time. Ideally, every couple, free of peer and work pressures, should be able to choose who will look after their kid following the first year.

Since we know that just as many dads hold that parental instinct as mums, the question is why more dads aren't able to be the ones that choose to stay at home. It harms women's careers, which for some mums can lead to resentment and frustration later if they feel they want to go back to the workplace. For the dads who might really enjoy it, it's just not an option for them, not even something they consider because what is expected of them, to work and not be a full-time carer, is so deeply ingrained.

7

POPULAR OR NOT

WHY IS THIS A GAP?

Not all good ideas are popular, and not all popular ideas are good. However good it may be for dads to play a bigger role, if people didn't want to do it, then it's unlikely we'd get very far. None of the figures in the last chapter matter if everyone thinks that's the right way to do things.

A quick Google search will throw up plenty of articles claiming dads just don't want to look after their babies. You'll be surprised to learn that many come from that home of equality *The Daily Mail*, presumably written by journalists who think only a few people drive a Porsche because everyone else actively prefers a cool and stylish Ford Mondeo.

Remarkably, such articles are nonsense. The new model of fatherhood is not only good for everyone involved, it's also increasingly popular – in theory at least. You can take your pick from a range of surveys showing a significant proportion of adults wanting more equally shared parenting. Dads want to spend more time with their kids, and play a bigger role in their upbringing. More and more mums want to share the burdens of raising the kids, continue with successful and fulfilling careers, and not have the constant pressures, judgement and guilt of being seen as the only responsible parent.

One government-backed survey from 2015 showed that public attitudes towards caring for children are seriously at odds with how things tend to play out. When people were asked who should be the main carer responsible for children, 53% said responsibility should be shared equally between the two parents, with a further 4% arguing dads should be the main carers, and 22% saying that couples should be 'free to choose'. That leaves only one in five thinking that mums should be running the home alone or with dads as backup[45]. That's telling a very different story to the real involvement of dads at the moment.

The good thing about this 2015 survey is that it didn't risk asking people what they already did, but what they wanted to do, what they thought people should be doing if there weren't limitations. And the interesting thing about these 'what if?' results is not just that it was a lot higher than many people would have expected, the results were actually higher amongst dads, with 56% of dads thinking parenting should be shared equally, and an additional 7% thinking dads should be the main carer. The results are also spread pretty evenly across regions and classes around the country.

A study undertaken by the Equality and Human Rights Commission showed a similar trend, with over half of parents feeling that their childcare arrangements were not taken out of choice but out of necessity. Over 60% of parents felt that fathers should be spending more time with their kids than they do now, with only 5% saying they spent enough or too much. 60% did not believe childcare was primarily the responsibility of the mother[46].

People's understanding of a man's role in the family is changing. In 1987, half the country believed that it was a man's job to earn the money, and the woman's to look after the kids at home[47]. By 2013, this had dropped to 13%. That's a pretty big shift in just two decades. With the twin tools of argument and example, opinions about what's normal can move and they can go a long way in a relatively short space of time.

What dads want

More recent research shows that, in addition to this changing understanding of what men and women should be doing for the family, dads are increasingly seeing a conflict between their family life and their career, and that the former is more important.

Alex, a first time dad, works in strategy consulting and has a nine month old daughter, Anna. "I really want to get on at work, and to do that you need to be willing to sacrifice everything if the client wants something or changes their mind... Late night and weekends happen all the time, that's just life. But I really hate not being around Anna more. I missed when she started crawling and I think about her a lot at work. You've got to wonder sometimes, are the long hours really worth it!?"

I bumped into Alex grabbing his morning coffee on the way to the commuter train a month after he had explained his desire to spend more time around Anna. He had just received a job offer from a public relations company that promises better family-friendly policies and a good work-life balance. He's considering taking the offer, explaining "I want Anna to remember me being around when she's older."

Almost half of dads in the UK[48] said that they would like to reduce their hours or think about a less stressful job because of their families. A third were even willing to take a pay cut. This pro-family-time sentiment is stronger amongst younger dads, with just under half of dads under thirty-five ('millennials') willing to lose some of their income to spend more time with their kids. Of course, a lot of this sentiment may be because we feel work is expecting too much from us, but dads are increasingly making a connection between spending too much time in the office and missing out on the joys of being with their little people.

In the past, bringing home as much money as you could was the best way a man could look after his family. But modern men are beginning to see that they can do things differently. We can dispute whether holding a sick baby or trying to get a reluctant toddler into the car is more or less annoying than trying to get someone to stop being an ass in the office.

But blokes are increasingly realising that chasing their kids into play tunnels and tickling them into hysterics might just be more rewarding than finishing a project for your boss. Your building a human being at home, and helping them learn how to walk, talk, and invent, holds the sort of life satisfaction that isn't matched by whatever you're building in the workplace.

But this isn't necessarily about dads not wanting to work. Many blokes still want (not to mention need) to carry on working and building their career. This is about dads wanting to find a better balance between their career and time being responsible for the kids. Blokes are increasingly seeing the fun of being an active and engaged parent, and wanting to be a part of it. Whether dads can have it all though remains to be seen, but there is a clear call for it.

Thoughts from mums

While slightly less supportive overall of more equal parental responsibilities than blokes, women are still very keen. That slightly lower figure may be in part due to women's concerns that if men get more rights to parental leave for example it would come at the cost of hard-won maternity rights. That's a factor we have to be aware of as we formulate proposals to improve things.

We've already looked at how shared parenting could be beneficial in reducing the incidence or the impact of post-natal depression. Shared parental leave can help reduce stress for mums too. As it stands mothers have to take two weeks off after birth and are encouraged to stay at home for at least six weeks because they are entitled to 90% of their normal pay in that time. Inevitably, even if a couple decide to split SPL fifty/fifty, the physical demands of labour mean the mother will likely take the first stint.

Returning to work at the end of any stretch of maternity leave, or just any prolonged period out of the workplace, is daunting. Any parent that has gone through the rigmarole of settling a child with a childminder or nursery knows how draining that can be. But if a mother sets off for her first day back knowing her child is with its father that removes a huge mental burden. She can commit to and enjoy her work without having to worry.

It's something Matthew at British Land clocked when he took SPL in 2017. "My wife was able to go back to work earlier, her transition back to work was easier because she had the confidence that she was leaving the children with someone who knows them and knows how to look after them. There was less pressure on her having to try and get them into nursery, all that sort of thing and that gave her the headspace to focus 100% at being at work."

Half of mums believe that parenting should be shared equally, if money wasn't an issue. In fact, only one in five mums believe that mums should be the 'main carer'. This is a surprising result considering popular myths often claim that mums have a 'special impulse' to care for children that men supposedly don't have[49].

Paternity gap – getting stuck

Just before Shared Parental Leave came in, 83% of people said they'd definitely or probably consider using the leave for their next baby or would have considered using it for past kids. So a lot of parents are keen on the idea of letting Dad play a bigger role in the first year of their baby's life. The idea of Dad having his turn looking after the kids is no longer an unusual fringe experiment pushed for by a tiny number of 'radical' parents. It's become what people want and expect. But the actual uptake of the new parental leave options is low, and dads are still not getting their share of time and close relationships with kids as they get older. A clear gap is emerging between what people want and what they are getting. Roughly how big is this gap?

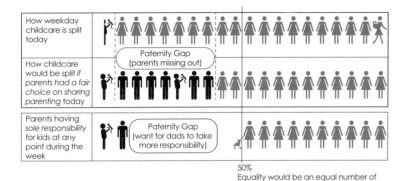

How weekday childcare *is* split today		
How childcare would be split *if parents had a fair choice on sharing parenting* today		
Parents having *sole responsibility* for kids at any point during the week		

Paternity Gap (parents missing out)

Paternity Gap (want for dads to take more responsibility)

50%
Equality would be an equal number of dads to the left as mums to the right

Figure 1: *Different ways of seeing the Paternity Gap across the population of two-parent households*

There are a lot of ways to measure the gap, but they all involve the difference between how parents *do* split childcare and responsibility, and how they *would* if equally shared parenting were a real option for them.

As one way to look at it, picture taking your toddler to the parent and baby group at the local library. Twenty parents turn up with their little people in tow. There are no couples today as it's in the middle of the week and spouses are at work. In an ideal world, if parents could do what they thought was best, we might expect to see around eight dads and twelve mums singing *Wind the Bobbin Up* and trying to imitate cow noises whilst the toddlers were straying into the box of toys and musical instruments in the middle of the room. In a few months, some of those dads might swap with their partners and vice versa.

Coming back to reality, we have to take seven of those dads out of the room. One dad at most and nineteen mums. Seven mums who are likely to have preferred to be back at work, and seven dads missing out on the chance they really wanted, to spend their turn with the kids. That's a lot of parents in the population at large falling into the gap.

Figure 1 shows two examples of how we could roughly measure the paternity gap. The top two rows show the gap in dads being at baby-cinema or rhyme-time during the week, with the last row showing the gap in dads taking responsibility for the kids.

The other thing worth thinking about with the paternity gap is that, as more dads start to play an active role in parenting, people are likely to expect more equal parenting. So the numbers of people wanting more equally shared parenting is likely to rise, as has happened in Scandinavia.

So we can see a big gap emerging between what people want, what they believe *should* be the case, and what they are doing in the real world. Only 22% think mums should be the primary care-giver alone, but this is the case in over 76% of families. The vast majority of families that want equal parenting aren't able to get it. This is the paternity gap. The rest of this book will ask why it's there and how we can solve it.

8

SHARED PARENTAL LEAVE

A 'STARTING POINT'

For too long, mums have been told their place is at home with their child, while dads return to work. I want parents to choose for themselves.

Nick Clegg, Deputy PM

The changes to the law are really helpful, but real change requires more than just the law, it requires people changing the attitudes that they take for granted.

Sarah and Max

Only in 2003 were dads given two weeks' paternity leave compared to a woman's right to a whole year off. Fathers were entitled to more leave, but they wouldn't get paid for it. Then in 2015, building on reforms in 2009, came Shared Parental Leave allowing parents to divvy up a year of time off as they saw fit. Such a big step to allow dads to use any maternity leave that mums hadn't could have revolutionised the role of fathers and gone a long way to closing the paternity gap. It might still do. But not without being seriously beefed up.

Not that long ago, the answer to the paternity gap would have seemed obvious. Dads had no rights as parents. After the birth of their baby, dads had to go straight back to work. Indeed not that long ago dads were at work during the birth of their baby. The solution to fixing the problem would have been to give dads more rights.

During the 2000s, dads were granted a few days of paternity leave which slowly increased to ten days. Compare this to (also not very impressive) maternity rights, with new mums able to take a year off work with the right to receive the best part of their salary for a few weeks, and a basic income for up to nine months. The imbalance in parental rights was pretty big.

Then in 2010, during the last days of the Labour Government, a law was introduced that took a real step in the right direction. Dads were given the right to take up to six months Additional Paternity Leave if their partner returned to work and donated their maternity leave leftovers. With the law on their side, dads were now able to take on the responsibility of the household without losing their job (provided their partners let them). Was a revolution beginning?

Spurring on the march, in 2015 the Liberal Democrats in government introduced 'Shared Parental Leave'. It meant that, following the first two weeks together, couples were able to share the next fifty weeks, almost a year, between them however they liked. For the first nine months, however it was split, the parent looking after the baby would be entitled to at least a statutory minimum pay. Both parents have the chance to be there to watch their babies learn to roll, gabble, crawl, walk, and start to talk.

When she became a minister in 2012, the Liberal Democrat MP Jo Swinson took on the task of making shared parental leave law. She told us it was not straightforward. "There were lots of battles about how it would happen, how long it would be, whether there'd be loads of exemptions and stuff – these were the fights we basically had with the Tories about it, some Tories. There were some Tories who were fairly positive, including Theresa May to give her due, but also plenty who were rather less so and just kept blocking things and didn't really understand the policy and it was very frustrating."

The politics of the time helps to explain why we got the policy we have today. Jo admits there were some 'dinosaurs' in the business community but that the politicians put in hard yards to win them round. "I got pushback within government... sometimes it was painted as 'oh well the cost to business would be ridiculous, they couldn't possibly manage.' Some of that I found quite sexist in itself because the assumption was that business couldn't possibly manage if MEN are going to be out of the workplace when these are issues they are already dealing with in terms of women. The subtext of that is that men are more indispensable than women. So although some of it was painted as economic really it was a feeling that this isn't really the thing for men to be doing."

She returned to parliament in 2017 and she's no regrets about not being more radical. She told us, "I feel very proud, it's my proudest achievement from government. I don't think it's a job done as in it's a really good step, a starting point, and I don't think we could have got it further when we were making those policy decisions and discussions in 2012/13."

That first step is often the hardest, as anyone, male or female, who has looked after a baby and watched it start to walk can attest. But now it's time to take more steps, to walk confidently and move to a position where men can strut confidently behind a stroller.

Some might like to say the struggle for parents' rights is now over. Just like when all women got the right to vote in 1928, many people assumed the job was done and equality would come about in quick order. But the paternity gap is still there, and it's likely to grow. In over 95% of families, dads are still not taking part fully.

The problem is the struggle really isn't over at all. A century on from women's suffrage we're still having to fight for sexual equality by looking at values, attitudes and culture, more than legal niceties. In the same vein, fixing the legal barriers and protecting dads' rights regarding fatherhood doesn't automatically address the other big social barriers to dads taking on their role as carers.

Many couples do not qualify for shared parental leave, perhaps around 40% according to the TUC, perhaps because one partner is self-employed for example. Out of those that do, parents are still having to deal with similar problems to twenty years ago[50]. It may not be the biggest problem, but family finances are frequently cited as the main reason why shared parental leave is a non-starter for most families.

Money, Money, Money

When your first little treasure is on the way, it's fun to head to the shops (or online) and start preparing. What will they wear on the way home? What will they sleep in when they get there? What type of car seat will they use? Do you have enough nappies and clothes ready for the first few weeks? And probably the biggest expense is the pushchair or pram: this can be close to the cost of a second-hand car. Then the first year starts moving on, ever more clothes, bottles, baby food, blenders, and more nappies. Then the swinging chair, the bouncing chair, the baby carrier (always worth the extra cost for what it saves your back!), the jungle gym and the play mat.

The newborn books, beakers, baby toys, toddler trinkets, and walking trolleys, and of course more nappies. Your toddler needs to learn how to build with blocks, paint pictures, and use pencils. Your once organised and adult living room is now overwhelmed with train sets, dismembered dolls, and dinosaurs. Not to mention the need to fill every gap under the sofa and coffee table with bits from the Lego sets you paid through the nose for. Then computer games and the computers themselves, smart phones, and train tickets to see their mates.

We may disagree how to get our babies to sleep, and how to deal with our kids if they get back home too late. But all parents agree that kids, from start to finish, can be expensive. The Centre for Economics and Business Research estimates the cost of raising a child from start to finish approaches a quarter of a million pounds[51]. Nearly 60% of people found that they were struggling with the costs of paying for their kids.

But the £230,000 figure hides a bigger financial problem for families as they start to grow. Who's going to look after the little ones? In nearly all working-age couples, before kids both will be working. Long gone are the days where marriage meant a woman was expected to leave the labour market. Why have one income and one career when you can have two? More often the question is can we get by on one income, and increasingly the answer comes back a resounding no. This generational change has increased women's financial security and independence, and made the economy more productive. But things change when baby arrives.

When you arrive home from the hospital with your first kid, both parents are given a few weeks where they get their usual income, plus child allowance comes on tap. Though no-one would describe it as generous and these days it only pays out for the first two children, it does help to cope with the bump in baby costs. But longer term, every couple needs to figure out who's going to look after the baby, at least until school starts when they're five.

When the baby's a bit older, they may go to nursery or a childminder but, in the vast majority of cases, a parent will be taking time off work to look after the new family member. After the first few months, if a parent is looking after the baby, then their contribution to the family income will drop, if not disappear altogether. If they go back to work, their income may be largely swallowed up by the high costs of childcare. So families get faced with a double hit to their finances, where they have to pay for ever more things at the same time as losing a chunk of the household income.

Smart families will try to minimise the burden of having kids. We all know kids will cause the household a financial hit, so it's just rational to minimise that where you can. If you have to make a choice of who will lose their income, it should probably be, at least over the longer term, the person who brings home less pay.

Jess Phillips is a Labour MP, author of modern feminist text *Everywoman* and a member of the House of Commons Women and Equalities select committee. She sums it up thus: "The fundamental thing that makes you make the decision, as a set of normal human beings, is whether you can pay your rent. The gender pay gap exacerbates the problem."

If we follow some of the optimistic headlines in the press – "more women than ever before are the family breadwinners" – the problem is that the headlines, again, mistake a small relative shift in responsibilities for a revolution. If we take out single-parent families, then blokes are still the highest earners in around 78% of families[52]. The gap between what men and women earn is still persistently high at around 10% for full-time earners[53] and around 18% overall[54].

Laura and Jake are expecting their first kid in a month's time. As far as progressive credentials go, Laura and Jake's are pretty high. They both work in the charity sector and have been long-standing campaigners for gender and racial equality. But when asked whether they'll be taking shared parental leave, Jake looks down and Laura gives the most common response I've heard to this question: "we can't really afford it. Jake earns more than I do, and they won't cover his salary after I've taken my part of the maternity leave."

Jake is stuck, he explains that he's going to be there and ready to do his part when he's at home, and this is going to be an equal partnership. But Laura will have to spend most of the time with the baby because there just isn't the money to do anything else, even referring to the parental leave system as 'middle-class privilege'. "It's great if you can afford it,", says Jake. As the conversation progresses, he realises that, despite wanting the parenting to be equally shared, because he can't afford to do it it's just not going to happen in practice.

Emma worked as a nurse for almost a decade before baby Abigail arrived. Emma's husband, Derrick, is in charge of groceries at a local Asda. Derrick was keen to take some time off to look after Abie when she arrived, and Emma enjoyed her job. But Emma's job paid around £25,000, and Derrick's around £31,000. In practical terms, Emma staying at home rather than Derrick meant the family could be better off by £80 every week, and around £320 every month. That's pretty close to offsetting the costs of the new baby. Needless to say, Emma and Derrick decided they couldn't take that financial hit for too long. Derrick took some extra leave to 'help Emma out', but Emma took the full year of maternity leave to look after Abie and let Derrick keep putting food on the table.

The number of couples who have fallen into the paternity gap and tell us a story similar to this is shocking. There are at least a few of those dads being kept away from baby-rhyme-time or tot-cinema, wanting to get their turn with their little person, but to do so would strike a hefty blow to the family's finances. This is not really a free and fair choice.

The other gap hurting parents

The gender pay gap has a lot to answer for, but its role in keeping the paternity gap open is clear. There is a gender pay gap where women generally earn less than men, and alongside it there is also a parenting gap, where men get less time with their kids.

Both of these gaps are two sides of the same coin, both feeding off each other and punishing women and men.

If the woman is earning less in a mixed-sex, two-parent household, it becomes difficult to let Dad take his turn looking after the babies when the pay protection for him to do that is so weak.

The gender pay gap has its causes, and far from insignificant is the fact that employers expect women to take a large period of leave from work, or even quit entirely, when they have kids. The pay gap, as we highlighted in Part I, increases massively once a woman has kids.

It's still not uncommon to hear talk about how women at work are of 'childbearing age', meaning you think they'll disappear any minute to have babies; or even – something I've rebuked a colleague for in the past – talking about the fact that a woman has kids at home, which might weigh in on work opportunities and 'commitment' to the company.

The pay gap is one of the reasons British Land introduced their enhanced shared parental leave offer. Matthew Webster, adopting his future-proofing hat (and if you haven't seen a future-proofing hat you really should) is honest that there's an unconscious bias when deciding who to hire or promote or to assign to a certain project: "When women get to a certain age it's almost expected that they are going to have children and need to take time out. By having this policy in place eventually it would be just as likely for men to take time out as it would for women so it levels the playing field a little bit."

In most workplaces the vicious circle is unbroken. Women miss out on jobs or promotions because employers know they'll take on nearly all childcare responsibility and have to leave the workforce for years or permanently. But because mums are paid less than dads, it makes financial sense for most families to make dad keep on earning when the babies come.

9

SHORTCOMINGS OF PARENTAL LEAVE

A PATCHWORK APPROACH

As many as two in five new dads are probably ineligible for parental leave[55]. This is pretty unfortunate for a policy that hopes to give more parents the option to share parenting, with 40% of families excluded from the off. This also disproportionately impacts lower income families, where parents may have less secure working arrangements and incomes such as zero hour contracts.

One of the most comprehensive assessments of dad-only time with kids across the world, *Fathers on Leave Alone*, argues that "the condition of continuous and secure employment excludes the growing number of British fathers in precarious employment situations", citing ONS figures to argue that this problem will only increase with time[56].

Although a significant proportion of couples can't use shared parental leave, for the remaining families that can, the first nine months are given financial protection. If Derrick, who we encountered in the last chapter, opts to take four months of shared parental leave to look after Abie, the government will stump up statutory parental pay, currently around £140 a week. That's an annual income of just over £7,000. Whopping. And if your income does approach the low level of £140 a week for whatever reason, you lose your right to the SPL pay anyway[57].

The average annual income in the UK is around £27,600 (four times the pay protected by SPL), so around £507 a week[58]. So for the first nine months the government would cover only a small fraction of your income if you chose to take the time off to look after your baby. This really doesn't make taking months off work for Derrick to look after Abie much less of a financial blow. The low level of pay protection means families are still faced with a similar choice to before: let Dad take his turn and face a bigger loss to family income, or avoid both.

Ben, who works in the media, took three months off to look after his first baby. He says he would have done more but for the drop in income. And he's since pondered the message that sends, "We live in a world where we ascribe value to things. If we ascribe the value to a man doing shared parental leave as £140 per week then it's clearly not that valued." Of course men were less bothered about that value when it didn't apply to them and only women were the ones receiving that small amount of money.

This compares pretty poorly again to leading countries. Note, there are plenty of countries in the world that have poor parental leave policies – Iran, Angola, and the US for instance. But that's not company we should want to keep. We shouldn't be comparing ourselves to the worst performers; we should be comparing ourselves to the best because, in ten years' time, that's where we want to be.

In Germany, dads are paid two-thirds of their normal salary for up to fifty-two weeks. In Sweden, for sixty-five weeks, parents can take parental leave on 80% of their income. As figure 2 shows below, a decent protection of Dad's salary is an essential pre-condition for increasing take-up amongst eligible dads. As we'll see later, incentives for dads to take the leave are also needed.

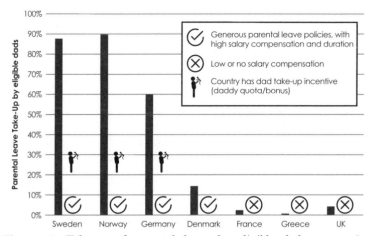

Figure 2: *Take-up of parental leave by eligible dads, comparing generosity of parental leave and dad incentives*[59]

Anders Malmberg, living in Stockholm with his wife Eva, took seven months of parental leave after their daughter Alba was born. 'I didn't even think twice about it. Of course not. I wanted to do it, and it would have been silly not to!' He was a little baffled by my question, about whether he felt pressure not to take it because he earned more than Eva. 'It was only a very small drop in money each month. Nothing to worry about. We still had both of our incomes. Plus, it's my responsibility to care for our daughter, just as much as Eva's, and I really enjoyed doing it.'

Anders, along with other Swedish dads, feels very little pressure not to take their right to parental leave because doing so won't hurt the family finances. 'You're more likely to be asked why you're not taking it if you don't, than when you are if you do,' Anders explains.

This is in stark contrast to the financial blow that taking parental leave can cause in the UK. With low uptake, and over 80% of families believing that the financial limits of shared parental leave are the main reasons stopping them from considering it[60], we should probably do better.

Enhanced pay

But credit where it's due. A number of companies in Britain voluntarily top-up the first few months of maternity leave pay, and some of these have offered to share the benefit with dads, allowing either parent to end up taking home their normal, or close to their normal, pay for a limited period.

British Land is just such a company. It's a commercial property firm in the FTSE 100 and some of its landmark projects include the Cheesegrater skyscraper in London, the Meadowhall centre in Sheffield, and the redevelopment of the area around Paddington station. In spring 2017 they announced they were levelling up their parental pay provision with male and female employees entitled to six months of full pay.

Matthew Webster has the unwieldy title of head of wellbeing and future-proofing in the company. He explained that there were commercial and ethical drivers behind the decision. "It was quite an easy decision," he explains. "There's been an understanding in the business that diversity and inclusion is a really positive thing and can help us do better business by reflecting the people that we're serving, better reflecting our customers.

> "Current maternity leave policies reinforce existing gender stereotypes. So women are often seen as the childcarers and men as the breadwinners. We think we've come a long way on maternity rights, so protection against discrimination, maternity pay, increase in flexibility and opportunity when coming back to work. But that didn't really challenge gender equality, that helped women maintain their stereotypical roles as someone that does everything."

Matthew had first-hand experience of this. He was one of the first in the company to take advantage of shared parental leave. His description of how it affected him and his relationship with his Swedish wife (yes, we've spotted the pattern that men with Scandinavian partners – including one of us authors – are FAR more likely to take SPL) could come straight out of a textbook on the concept of mental load.

> "Our relationship has always been pretty level in terms of domestic chores. It's often me that does the ironing or the hoovering but this shared parental leave made me understand it's often her that does the thinking and the planning. And suddenly there was this moment where I had to think about what I'm going to give the boys for lunch. It's really helped me move on in that respect."

But you don't get to be a FTSE 100 company without being hard-nosed capitalists. And profit hunters don't put in place policies just because they're nice. "We did a very detailed financial position on it and basically the senior team thought the value far outweighed the cost of doing it," adds Matthew.

He's clear that enhanced SPL is a route to attracting and retaining the best people. Keeping talented women in the company creates a more diverse workforce which Matthew claims has been shown to be a more successful workforce. And people who are happier and more engaged at home tend to be happier, more engaged and, crucially, more productive at work. That's Matthew's experience. "I certainly feel more engaged, grateful and therefore loyal and proud and I think all of that adds up to me being more productive."

British Land are not the only blue chip company to enhance SPL and other big firms are now tapping up Matthew to ask about the firm's experience. But he accepts that British Land would have been unlikely to equalise its offer to parents if it hadn't been for the introduction of Shared Parental Leave as a legal entitlement.

This speaks to the line between how much government can achieve through legislation and how much comes from culture change. But it's clear that the change in the law was the spark for the good work that voluntarily followed.

British Land are one of the trailblazers. And an exception. Around a quarter of companies don't offer any pay enhancement for mums and, out of those that do, the policies can vary widely from a few extra weeks of almost no extra pay, to six months on full pay[61]. So the impact is far from even. This leaves many families still being forced to have one of their incomes take a nose-dive when baby arrives.

Out of the companies that top-up maternity pay, few extend this to dads. Less than half of companies that offer enhanced maternity pay offer the same deal to dads on parental leave. About the same number offer only the statutory minimum to dads. And the organisations that do offer dads enhanced pay on the same terms as mums either tend to be in the public sector or very large private companies with both the cash and the vision to take a chance.

The fact that take-up in the public sector, according to the Chartered Institute of Personnel and Development, is almost three times that in the private sector points to a clear conclusion that if you reduce the financial penalty, take-up will rise.

But this still leaves a large chunk of companies, well over half, that either don't offer either parent any enhancement or encourage mums to take the time off to look after their babies, but expect dads to get back to work sharpish, with no or only limited pay enhancement. What's more, over 90% of these companies have no intention of reviewing their dad pay policies in the future.

Setbacks

Unfair? Surely, if mums are entitled to enhanced pay, why shouldn't dads be on the same footing? That's what David Snell thought in 2016. Network Rail gave new mums a generous half a year on full salary. David, excited about the opportunity to use the new shared parental leave he was entitled to, decided to split the first few months looking after their new baby with his wife, also an employee of Network Rail. Given that Network Rail would offer a woman parental pay top-up, why wouldn't they do the same for the bloke in the same company?

They didn't. Network Rail decided that childcare was really a woman's job, and that they weren't going to encourage real men who worked for them to be doing the childcare that their female workforce would get paid properly for. It was better to keep David's wife out of the workforce for twelve months than let her swap with him. David Snell felt this was wrong, and took Network Rail to court. The law (and common sense) were on David's side, and he won the case. Network Rail tried to argue that by encouraging mums to take six months off work to look after the baby, but telling dads they couldn't, they had a good 'family friendly' policy, and were championing the cause of keeping women in the workplace.

Well Network Rail, you weren't. To keep women in the workplace and retain their talent, you also need to give dads the opportunity to take more responsibility at home. You need to give dads the chance to take care of their kids.

Now imagine a kid in the playground who was caught pulling a girl's hair because she had told him to stop throwing mud at her. In response to being told off by a teacher, rather than apologising, he walks off in a huff, tries to push the other kid over, and then schemes at how he can get his own back. Not nice behaviour from a kid. Even worse from a large public service company.

Network Rail was that petulant kid. As if trying to stick their tongue out at the fairness that David Snell brought to bear on them, Network Rail cancelled its top-up for mothers. It claimed that its new 'family friendly policy' was now fair again, because now neither parent was entitled to anything more than the bare minimum.

To top this off, an Employment Appeal Tribunal in 2018 decided that if a company tops up maternity leave for twelve months, it wouldn't be discriminatory of them to do nothing for shared parental leave, in what appears to contradict the Network Rail ruling[62]. Why? Because they believe that the real purpose of maternity leave is the mother's health, not childcare... Well since most mums (C-sections to one side) are given a clean bill of health and asked to leave hospital the day after baby arrives, and maternity leave lasts twelve months, isn't taking care of your baby also a pretty important reason for baby-related leave?

To argue that a dad should get nothing on shared parental leave whilst a mum in the same company is entitled to full pay at month twelve is discrimination, and it harms women as well as men. The main purpose of maternity, parental, and adoption leave is to look after and bond with your child, even if the weeks around childbirth also need protected maternity leave for the mum's health. Companies top-up baby-related leave voluntarily for months after birth because they want to retain talent and allow parents to take care of their kids, not because they believe that a healthy mother needs to be kept away from the dangers of coffee machines and office gossip six months after her tot arrives.

These developments are not a great sign of things to come, and it certainly stops us from too much wishful thinking that one day all companies will voluntarily just top-up the minimum for mums and dads equally.

Why even pay enhancement doesn't help dads much

But here's the bigger problem with companies deciding to top-up pay. Even if we were lucky enough for more and more companies to offer pay top-ups that could be shared with dads on the most generous terms available (covering the first four to six months), the voluntary top-up pay is still likely to be used up by the mums anyway.

In Sweden, when faced with how the two parents should split up the first year, most of the conversations go something like this:

Mamma-to-be: We should probably have the first few weeks together, as that's likely to be tough.

Pappa-to-be: Couldn't agree more.

Mamma-to-be: And I'd like some time to recover after birth and not have to go back to work too quickly. Plus, I'd like to try breastfeeding.

Pappa-to-be: Well, it's probably best if I take my Pappa-Leave when little Sven is six months then, giving you a little time to breastfeed and all that before you head back to work.

Many couples in the UK might feel the same. But that doesn't work if the enhanced parental leave pay only applies to the first few months, as it often does in the UK. Most pay enhancement on parental leave is per baby, not per parent. That means once a mum has used up six months of maternity leave and pay, the other parent also loses those first six months, and any statutory or enhanced pay that comes with it.

By the time it gets to Dad's time to take his turn, after six months or so, Mum has already had to use up the enhanced pay. He then only gets the minimum salary for a few months before that drops to nothing. So even if a couple are faced with the best of circumstances – they're both lucky enough to have jobs that offer enhanced pay on shared parental leave – they're still likely to face the financial cliff question when it comes to Dad's turn. And if Dad's earning more, it continues to make a lot of sense for Dad rather than Mum to keep on working. Back to square one, despite pay enhancement.

To break out of this dead-end for parental rights, we need to change what we're doing and how we compensate dads for taking time out to look after the babies. Shared parental leave, the way it's set up at the moment, doesn't do that. Even superficially, ignoring those big social pressure problems beneath the surface, it simply fails to offer the financial conditions that most families can find acceptable to allow Dad to take his turn.

10

FIXING THE PROBLEM OF FAMILY FINANCES

HALFWAY THERE

The most obvious way out of the family finances problem is to make the pay gap much less important to a couple's decision on who's going to look after the baby. As Anders says in his sing-song Swedish accent, a dad that could take some months off looking after their new baby on next to full pay would be "silly not to".

Looking at where dads have had significant success at taking their turn, adequate pay protection has been vital, protecting 65-100% of pay for not just a couple of weeks as in the UK, but for months. In the case of Sweden and Norway, both parents are able to share just over a year at 80% of their pay. Germany allows parents to share twelve months at 65% of pay. To recall, these countries have much higher uptake of parental leave by dads, with the Scandinavian top performers, Sweden, Norway and Iceland, at around 90%.

Anders and his wife Eva in Sweden split their parental leave down the middle to look after Alba. Eva went back to work after seven months, and Anders took a further seven, with little impact on their family finances. "I feel I got the better side of the deal in a way, teaching Alba to walk and start to talk. And it didn't really cost us much at all… It didn't cost my work very much either because we're paid out of the social insurance we pay into beforehand. My employer offered to pay a little extra but if they hadn't, we still would have done exactly the same. So it's all fair and sustainable."

Since the global financial crash, governments seeking to balance the books have tried to cut less 'productive' government spend. Well-paid parental leave has fallen into the basket marked 'optional extras that would be nice to have, but we really can't afford right now'.

How have the countries that pay the most into their parental leave – Sweden, Norway, Iceland, and Germany – done? What do their budget deficits look like? When was the last time you heard that Sweden and Germany were wasting their tax money and driving themselves into debt?

It should come as no surprise that these countries, despite Iceland being hit very hard by the financial crisis, are doing pretty well. They all have nearly balanced budgets, and went out of their way to increase spend on leave for dads, whilst still keeping very low budget deficits. Greece, on the other hand, not spending a cent on dads, is still in serious budget trouble. We're not saying it's cause and effect, but clearly spending money on letting dads take their turn is not demolishing national budgets.

If you're faced with some people pretending it will be almost free, and other people telling you it will cause bankruptcy, the first question you have to ask is how much it's really going to cost. According to the OECD, the total parental leave costs in Sweden are around 0.8% of GDP[63] to cover around 80% of Dad's salary *and* a generous childcare system. The parental leave policy is used by nearly 90% of Swedish dads. If we matched this in the UK, it would still be only a tenth of how much tax we spend on pensions. At the moment, the UK spends only around 0.1% of GDP on giving its parents peanuts if they opt to look after the baby.

But the UK actually spends a lot more than 0.1% of GDP anyway, with many companies that choose to voluntarily top-up the costs of maternity leave (some even parental leave) not being included in the 0.1% figure. The big difference is that in the UK people with good enough jobs to top-up their maternity pay packages will have access to this, and the companies that do so will take nearly all of the costs, making the system inherently uneven and unfair. This doesn't even include the costs to the economy from lost talent as many mums leave the labour market involuntarily.

In Scandinavia, people working for less forward-thinking companies get the same advantages, and the lower individual costs are spread across all companies. Much fairer. There is also no significant difference in fertility rates between the UK and its Nordic neighbours. This suggests that well-paid parental leave hasn't led to a bunch of deluded adults committing to eighteen years (at least) of caring for a kid just because they think they'll get some extra paid holiday, as some have argued it might if we did the same in the UK. It has however contributed to increasing the number of women in the workplace, well above what it is in the UK, with all the broader benefits that brings.

But there are a lot of good ways to cover the costs of better parental leave, even if we don't look at the big net financial benefits this would bring to the economy. We could for instance just increase taxes. The increase really wouldn't be that big. Overall, it would cost people roughly an extra 50p a day to match Sweden, with large companies and wealthier people paying a little more than this, and people on lower incomes paying a lot less. If 50p is too much, then we could meet Scandinavia halfway.

This is small change given how much we earn and spend on a daily basis, and well under the cost of a cup of coffee or what Network Rail are costing us in rising commuter fares (despite their backwards parental pay policy). This is really small considering the relief you'll get when it comes to the first year of childcare costs! And when more women can retain their talent and role in the workplace.

So it's not going to change a country's credit rating, and in fairly quick order the social and economic benefits outlined in Part I will start to add up and are likely to cancel out any costs involved.

But there are other ways to look at it if governments are worried about the cost to the Treasury. Several countries in the EU run what amounts to an insurance scheme for example. Here employees pay into the insurance when they're working, and just as when your home insurance provider pays out when your house is turned upside-down by that leaking pipe that sprayed water over all your furniture, the insurance fund pays out to parents whose house will be equally imperilled by the arrival of kids.

If you earn more, then you've paid more in, so you are given more back to cover the cost of you taking the leave and to make sure your life isn't (financially) disrupted too much. It turns out this is fairer and more sustainable than the way we do it in the UK.

So the cost to your pocket, whether through a slightly higher tax, or a small insurance contribution, could very easily make properly paid leave for both parents utterly affordable. But there are other costs!

What about the costs to companies when men, those people employers thought would always stay in the office even when the baby arrived, start regularly taking six months out to look after their babies? As we know from Part I, this is a red-herring. Companies, and so the wider economy, also benefit from more equal parental leave, as women take shorter periods of leave, and dads feel the benefits of having a better work-life balance and more time with their kids.

Even if both parents take nine months or even a year off, bear in mind firms manage to cope with a woman leaving the workplace for that length of time. As Jo Swinson points out, "there's an inherent sexism in the idea that a man on parental leave is a bigger hit to a company than a woman on maternity leave".

We can recall that the benefits of parents being able to share parenting more equally are likely to boost women's participation in the labour market, increasing talent, productivity, and competitiveness in the economy, as well as leading to a happier workforce.

When we weight the possible economic costs and benefits of introducing proper parental leave, we find that, because it's a 'productive' form of spending, the 0.8% of GDP a fully-funded version would cost to introduce would be more than paid for just by the growth to the economy. This might hint at why it's caused no harm to the prospering economies of Northern Europe.

The higher female labour market retention alone following from more widely available and used parental leave in the UK could lead to benefits of between 5% and 10% increase in real GDP over the next decade, according to the OECD[64]. And these benefits are shared across both families and the companies they're employed by. That's better for business, and better for creating sustainable jobs.

Notably, if there are some costs of voluntary dad-friendly policies for individual companies, those costs will disappear when all companies can rely on everyone taking part in proper and well-funded parental leave. If only one company did it, they might have their dads taking six months off, but the mums who have partners in more stingy firms might still need to take twelve months off because their baby-daddies can't. But if everyone has to offer these benefits to dads, then more mums will also start to take shorter lengths of parental leave.

This is a classic case for government intervention. Voluntary parental leave top-up by companies is not good enough. If we are to get the full benefits of parental leave, it needs to be full and it needs to apply to the whole country, not just to a few firms who dare to make the change. If government boosts the bare minimum enforceable by law, firms that want to attract the best people will have to go even further. We can go from a vicious to a virtuous circle.

But we're not here to just make an argument about the money. The benefits of giving dads the real option of being able to spend more time with their babies is more valuable than just increasing how much they might be able to spend on cars, furniture, and holidays. Arguably the bigger benefits are dads being able to have the really free choice of spending that time with their kids without ruining the family finances, and for mums to feel they can share the responsibilities of childcare.

The 'daddy quota'

Reserving a fixed portion of parental leave for dads would without a doubt allow dads to get more involved. All the evidence points in that direction. Every country where the daddy quota of parental leave has been introduced, the uptake amongst dads, unsurprisingly, has shot up.

Jeremy Davies, Fatherhood Institute

So if we just make it about being affordable for dads to take their turn, is the job done? Recalling the words of one of the dads we spoke to, "people in the office, they're already getting nervous about me being gone for two months". Dads and families don't just face the financial barriers against them taking the opportunity of shared parenting. They also face pressures from work, from friends, from family, from strangers when they take their kids out during the week, and from what people around them expect from dads.

The picture is very complex, but the breakdown is simple: by and large, society doesn't expect Dad to be a responsible and fully involved parent. When most people think of who to call when a baby or a kid needs help, they will go to the mum. Dads are either seen as irrelevant to childcare, incompetent and in need of womanly supervision, or, at best, a capable assistant to the 'main' parent, Mum. This is not an easy thing to fix, as Part IV will show. But the closer we get to dads, family, friends, TV, magazines, and the stranger on the street looking at a dad on paternity leave quoting Anders' "he'd be silly not to", the closer we'll be to fixing it.

One popular move for governments in Scandinavia has been putting aside a little parental leave just for dads. In Sweden, this has just gone up from one month to three. In Norway ten weeks are reserved for each parent. In Germany, on the same lines, if couples split their parental leave, they get two 'bonus' months, allowing them to share some extra paid leave between Dad and Mum. These all break down to the same thing, parental leave should be seen as being for both parents – not a way to look 'politically correct' while in fact still just being *de facto* for mums.

The opponents of such a move have argued that reserving a little leave for the dad imposes shared parenting on couples. It's not government that imposes parenting on a man, it's making a baby that does that. And clearly there must be flexibility built in to the system. Even three months being reserved for Dad in Sweden still leaves ten at 80% pay for the mum to take if that's what the parents want to do – more than both parents get paid for right now in the UK.

If we want expectations to change, we need to start somewhere. Gently making it easy for more dads to get out there and being seen to be the responsible carers they often want to be, is going to be the easiest way to start progress on that front.

That's where daddy quotas can start to help. If we see the daddy quota as a 'free' few months of parental leave, just for dads to take if they want, employers, friends, strangers, and family start to look daft for pressuring dads not to take it. But at the same time, if they really don't want to take it, and they don't fall into the paternity gap, then they are free to turn it down. No-one's making them do anything.

Expectations on dads start to change. Employers that make dads looking after babies sound exotic, weird, and risky start to look a little silly. They begin to sound like someone discouraging their workforce from taking their annual leave entitlement. It's just daft. If a dad wants to take a few months off to look after his baby, why wouldn't he?

What's the evidence on the daddy quota really bringing out the dads though? We already know that the Scandinavian countries that introduced the daddy quota and Germany all have much higher participation rates from dads. When it was introduced in Germany, we even saw an increase of dads taking parental leave from 3% to well over half the population of new dads! This wasn't the 80% needed to close the paternity gap, but it also wasn't a small jump, and it looks like it was largely prompted by the bonus months that parents get if dad takes a turn at baby care.

Denmark also has a reputation for being dad-friendly. But whilst they make sure they cover Dad's salary when he's taking parental leave, they don't reserve any leave for Dad alone. Although there are still clear paternity gaps in Norway, Sweden, and Germany, they are much smaller than Denmark's. Still only around 14% of dads are taking parental leave in Denmark[65]. Given the impact that the reserved months for dads have had on Denmark's European neighbours, part of this low uptake number is likely to be linked to not having a daddy quota.

Figure 2, on page 85, shows just how important it is for parental leave policies to incentivise dads, through things like daddy quotas, to defy cultural norms and not leave his partner holding the baby.

Nearly all families in the UK are faced with either jumping off a financial precipice to reach their goal of splitting parenting, or biting the bullet and letting Mum take nearly all the leave. This is not a free choice for one of the most important decisions parents can make. Better paid parental leave and reserving a good chunk of the leave for dads doesn't offer the whole solution, but it is a really good start.

But it's not only money and parental leave policies that sit underneath the paternity gap; it's also the significant cultural barriers and expectations that make it harder for parents to break social conventions and divide parenting responsibilities more equally.

11

STUBBORN EXPECTATIONS

PARENT TRAPS AND THE CAUSES OF THE PATERNITY GAP

A mum turned up to the parent and baby group on her own yesterday with her little boy. At first we thought it must be her day off work and she was giving the dad a break, but she said she was there full time. We all told her what a great 'Mrs Dad' she was, helping her husband out and babysitting the little one for a bit. What an amazing mum bringing her little one to play group all on her own! She should be really proud of herself.

Although, makes you wonder a little bit, how can she manage the little one all alone, and how could the dad manage to go back to work! I would be too worried thinking about my little guys all the time to let that happen. The 'Mrs Dad' idea is great, and mums can be a great help with the babies, but let's be honest, it's not quite the same as having dad around.

The one advantage they get I guess is that there's no danger of being kicked between the legs when changing nappies, although difficult to imagine a woman changing a nappy right of course! They'll probably get the wrong size and do it back to front. She complained that the only changing station was in the blokes' toilet at the station. I said she should just ask the guys to leave and use it anyway... Doesn't seem practical to have too many changing stations, and besides, dads change nappies more.

Mums are great during the pregnancy and labour, but everyone knows there's a special bond between a father and his child, and that it's best for him to look after the baby. It's all natural you see. It's all about paternal instincts. I read a book recently explaining that dads are better at parenting than women for so many reasons, it sometimes feels a bit daft that people are trying to fight their biology and get women to do more childcare.

There'll be a time when the little guy just wants daddy and they're going to have a real problem when dad's working instead of caring for his own baby.

Andy mentioned to the mum that she probably had really clear instructions from the baby's dad, otherwise how would she know what to do! We noticed she gave the baby some canned baby-food (not organic!), but I can understand since it's probably really tough as a Mrs Dad and she's trying her best.

But of course it must be hard for her as well taking on the man's role, 'playing dad' for a bit, when she'd probably prefer to be working and bringing home the bacon. Think how weird it must feel for her to be a 'Kept Woman' now. Jim suspects she lost her job and ended up having to stay at home while the dad was forced to carry on working. Come to think of it, it must be pretty defeminising to know she's not the one supporting the family at the moment!

My wife wanted to take a couple of weeks off work to help me out with the little ones, but her boss made it clear that would be bad for her career, and we really need her to get promoted soon. Plus we couldn't really afford it since I won't be working for the next few years with a growing family.

From Mr Mum to Mrs Dad, Switching Perspectives
D Freed, Dad's Turn blog[66]

There are plenty of people who see a dad out with his baby and declare that he exemplifies the 'modern parent'; that a man changing a nappy is 'the way it is nowadays'; and that a dad holding his toddler's hand shows 'just how much things have changed'. The thing is, as the role-reversal above shows, we're really not there yet. There has been a lot of change in the last decade that shouldn't be ignored, but there is still a long way to go. There's an underlying pressure on mums to be the main parent, and for dads to be seen as secondary or even incompetent to the parenting thing.

Stay-at-home Dad Blogger John Adams explains that a mother of four kids once started to have a go at him for 'getting attention' for doing the same thing that she'd been doing for the last fifteen years, parenting. The woman was upset that she had received no recognition for her efforts, whereas John was becoming a minor celebrity. "She had a point, but it's important to realise why people think what I do is worthy of press attention. Not because I'm better at it, I'm not, but because it's so unusual. It's really weird for a dad to be the primary carer so people write and talk about it because they're curious. It means that if you're going to do it as a guy, you're going to be challenging what people are expecting from you."

It's a familiar feeling for those of us that do our fair share of childcare. I (Dave) have been invited to talk about my experiences of parental leave and childcare on Radio 4 more than once, on a breakfast show and even the News at Ten. I'm an average parent as far as caring for my son goes, but the fact that I split responsibility with my wife got the media interested.

I (James) was dubbed a 'hero' by Rebecca Asher in her book *Man Up*. That's a word that comes up laughably regularly. Ben, who works in the media and who took three months of SPL, laughs, "I find this hilarious, where you do something as a dad that a mum does every day and suddenly you're a hero. Which is brilliant for a dad because you can go 'Yes, I am a hero!' If I really wanted to be a hero I should've done a year."

As soon as a dad does take his turn, people are surprised enough to comment. It might sound nice to get these compliments but, by not holding dads to the same standards as mums, people are expecting less from dads. Despite the widespread want from men to play a bigger and more responsible role in parenting, those low expectations on dads often pressure them to play a more passive role at home.

Parental expectations – 'that's just how it's always been'

The flip side of people expecting so little in terms of parenting from dads, is that it remains the norm that dads are kept at arm's length to the parenting deal. People agree what 'maternal' means: mums are thought to be instinctively nurturing and responsible for everything that happens to their kids. This is pushed to the point where if they have a momentary lapse they're seen as a failure.

But why are the things other people expect from parents so important? Rules play a big role in our lives, from keeping us all driving on the same side of the road, to paying the bill after you've eaten out. We need rules to live alongside each other well. They tell us what we can expect from other people, and what they can expect from us.

In fact, probably to make society function, people seem to have an impulse to follow the rules most of the time. This seems to start from early childhood. As small kids, believe it or not, we start to recognise that we're not the centre of the universe, and that we fit into various groups. To stay a part of that group it becomes important to understand the rules and what others in and out of the group are expecting of us, and to follow those rules[67].

Once we've accepted a rule, we also have a 'confirmation bias', which means anything we see that confirms the rule we tend to pick out and let it reinforce our expectations even more[68]. We generally accept these things at the expense of counter-examples that might challenge the rules.

So if we accept a rule about women being more nurturing and dads being bumbling idiots with kids, every time we see a dad stumble and a mum smile at a baby in the street, on TV or in the paper, we take this as 'proof' of the rule.

However, every time we see a mum accidently knock her toddler flying with her handbag and the dad running to comfort the now crying toddler, we don't label it as proof against the rule. We label it as an 'exception'. The mum's action is an anomaly, and the dad's response is unusual and worthy of comment, as John and others found. Confirmation bias means that once we have labelled these behaviours as an exception, we can continue to believe in the original rule.

As we'll see later, kids are actually really good at picking up social rules just from recognising cues from adults and the kids they see around them. The strongest and earliest group identity they tend to pick up is gender, seeing themselves as girls or boys. Like the sponges they are, they pick up all the rules they and others need to follow to stay part of the girl or boy groups. The mere presence of other children pushes them into sticking rigidly to the rules they've picked up[69].

As they get older kids learn that there are some things they're allowed to do: eat porridge for breakfast; and some things that they're not meant to do: throw the porridge at their sibling. Whilst most adults pick up the nuances in these rules and expectations about their behaviour as they grow older, they will nearly all follow the majority of these rules, whether consciously or not. These rules are like a glue that holds society together, although often it can also hold it back.

They are found everywhere, from explicit laws to the more common hints that we get from people around us; the comments of what other people find acceptable, the attitudes and behaviours expressed and imparted to us from our parents, siblings and friends; the subtle hints from people around us nudging us towards a certain accepted way of behaving. We by-and-large follow the nudges because conforming to them is easier than fighting against them most of the time, because pushing against the nudges can come up against resistance and disapproval that we just don't want.

Clearly, when it comes to driving and paying bills, it's a good thing we stick to what we're expected to do. But occasionally there are rules we don't think much about, we accept them because they've been floating around for a while, and we let them nudge us into doing things that aren't necessarily good, and which we wouldn't have chosen to do without the rules.

Dropping the bad rules

One great thing about humans is that although most of us love sticking to the rules, we're also able to challenge them when we believe they're wrong. Challenging these rules isn't easy, but that doesn't make the rules right. The first task is to identify which are doing more to hold us back than hold us together.

We can't change the dodgy rules alone. We need to persuade other people to tear up the rule book and get rid of the rubbish ones that needlessly limit our choices. Scrapping many sexist and racist rules has allowed us to treat each other with more respect, and allowed minorities to have a fairer range of choices about what they do with their lives.

Parents are in a weird position. The rules mean we give Mum a privileged place in the home, and Dad a privileged place at work. But they also mean Mum gets more pressure and judgement at home, and has less room to make mistakes. Whereas Dad is not expected to be responsible for the kids, and is nudged away from it and back into the office. All the time, this pushes us away from doing what we want to do: what might be the best choice for us and our families. We need to know where these rules come from.

The sources of limited parental expectations

Some people claim there's some sort of deep-rooted basis in our biology for why Mum should be the main parent, and why Dad belongs outside the cave on a hunting trip. In the past they made references to God's design for the sexes. More recently they claim that "it's always been like that" and make some vague reference to 'hormones' and 'maternal instincts', and the incompatibility of parenting and the 'male brain'. The more sophisticated ones will show you pictures of brain scans with dots on them and explain that a man can't cope with things like soothing a baby because of some dots on the left side of the brain.

People who believe that dads are 'naturally' ill-suited to childcare will often throw in an argument from evolution, as if this justifies it; something like: men aren't built for looking after babies because when we were cavemen we needed to go out hunting. So we're better suited to killing things. Whereas women evolved to tidy the cave and protect the babies. These explanations are pish (that's not a scientific term). They assume we're still living in caves (broadly untrue) and critically undervalue just how brilliant an organ the human brain is. It has evolved to be much more flexible than they give it credit for, as we'll see.

These ideas are offensive to active dads (not to mention many neuroscientists), offer a cop-out for ones who don't want to be involved in their kids' lives, and, most importantly, are nonsense. Yet they run deep in society.

These ideas about the biological nature of the traditional sex-split of parenting seep into our everyday experiences, from people we bump into in the street, to books we read, to the programmes we watch. They remind us what the rules about parenting are, that mums do it, and dads at most 'help out'. They limit the expectations we put on ourselves as men, and nudge us away from life choices that we and our families could have benefited from. They help drive a firm wedge into the paternity gap to keep it open. Part III will look at how these myths have been busted and show just how ludicrous they are.

Changing the stubborn expectations on parents

If you demolish the biological arguments for why only mums should be responsible for the kids, there will be other people waiting to explain that it still doesn't matter. That's always been the split between the sexes, so why should we change it? The argument that it's always been that way, so we should leave it alone, is even more daft than the biological one. That's not how we should be treating social rules.

For millennia, people used leeches to 'cure' most illnesses, they practised slavery, and they acted on the belief that the world was flat. When others said, "hang on guys, maybe this isn't such a good idea, how about we do something else?" they were treated to the same arguments. That we've 'always used leeches', or that one group of people's ability to dominate another was 'best for everyone'.

When the social rules got challenged and changed, and people's expectations on what people should be doing changed, things like modern medicine, equality, and not living in caves became accepted. And hopefully we can agree that in all these instances it's a good job they did change as things have turned out for the better because of it.

We haven't survived longer as a civilisation because social rules expect dads to play a backseat role in parenting and place all the responsibility on mums; we have survived as a civilisation because we adapt and progress. Challenging these rules now and giving parents more choice can only be a good thing, and the evidence discussed in Part I makes it clear that these are expectations we really should be changing.

But if the majority of parents think parenting should be shared equally, then why do the expectations society puts on parents continue to prop up the old fashioned view of how parenting should be done? This is the real challenge behind the paternity gap.

The simple answer is because social rules are 'sticky'. They tend to take a lot longer to change than people's personal opinions. It also doesn't take many people to make comments about how "dads are always daft and hopeless when it comes to knowing how to change nappies" to have a disproportionately big impact. These ideas stop us from genuinely believing that dads are just as capable as mums are at parenting.

Three big problems in the social rules that tell us how we should relate to our families remain, even if dads are expected to be around kids more than they were fifty years ago. These are: the lurking belief that the traditional sex-split of parenthood is built into our biology and so challenging it is somehow anti-scientific; the low expectations people place on Dad, or the 'babysitting handicap'; and the heavy expectations on Mum because of her 'maternal instinct' and the ever-haunting reminder of the super-mum.

These rules and expectations weigh heavily on who they should treat as the 'real parent', and how dads and mums feel about parenting. They trap dads and mums into performing parenting roles that fit social expectations. They limit parents from being able to freely choose how to split parenting in a way that works best for the family. Even if we remove the financial and workplace pressures to allow dads to take their turn, perhaps the biggest challenge of all will be changing these expectations to allow parents more genuine choices about childcare.

Before we take on the problems of the babysitting handicap and the myth of a maternal-only instinct, we should address the popular idea that there are genetic differences between the sexes that justify this social segregation.

Part III

BIOLOGICAL MYTHS OF MOTHERHOOD AND MEN

Why childrearing is not sex specific

12

MYTHS OF BIOLOGY

WHY OUR SEX DOESN'T MATTER WHEN IT COMES TO BEING A GOOD PARENT

Shared parental leave? Can we not. I mean seriously. Just no… A new baby needs their mother… It's basic biology. It's instinctive. It's fact… I believe that's why they come out of us after all. They are for that first year, often an extension of us. And that's completely natural

A Mum Track Mind[70]

Most active parents would agree that we want to be good at a number of things to be the best parent we can be: bonding; understanding our kid's emotions; being the sort of person kids like; being able to cope with the paraphernalia of childcare while staying on top of it all; and lastly, enjoying (most of the time) looking after tiny versions of ourselves.

But listen carefully and you'll hear that these traits are not shared equally between mums and dads. There's a continual hum reminding us that the ability of 'mums' to outperform 'men' in parenting is part of biology.

For as long as we can remember, people have been keen on explaining the 'natural' differences between the sexes. We find newspapers, TV programmes, books, and, above all of these, casual conversations, about how men and women behave completely differently because of their innate biology. This idea around the biological difference of parents underpins all the other expectations that pull dads away from playing their full part in parenting. There's no point in fighting the inevitable pull of biology, we're told.

In 2017, James Damore, an engineer at Google, wrote a memo announcing that science has proved some fundamental and unchangeable differences between the sexes, and that he can reveal to us what they mean for how adults should fit into the roles tradition had granted them. His words hit the global press, touching on a popular nerve on whether or not the differences between the sexes are 'natural'.

Despite trying to soften his diatribe by explaining how the differences weren't all that big, he nevertheless goes on to explain that women are better at empathising and don't like high stress jobs compared to men. This means they shouldn't be leading companies, and instead prefer being at home getting to know their kids (clearly this guy has never tried raising a toddler or caring for a newborn with colic). Men in contrast care little about work-life balance, so are better suited to the rat-race since they're less likely to understand human emotion.

The ideas in his memo have been spouted by people ranging from sex columnists to psychologists, all arguing that they have science on their side. They weave themselves into everyday conversations about how we should treat people from the opposite sex.

There is a vocal minority in every country that believes that mums are always better parents because of biology. In the UK one in five parents think that mums should be the main carers, and half of these believe it's because mums are 'naturally' the best parents[71]. Out of the majority who don't think this, the chances are pretty high that at some point we'll repeat 'mum knows best' and 'it's in her hormones' platitudes without thinking about it.

A lot of neuroscientists roll their eyes at the nature vs nurture debate: are these things 'biological' or 'social'? It is increasingly apparent that the way we behave is a mixture of our biological programming, and how that programming responds to the world we live in. Social rules and expectations have a direct biological impact on how we feel and how our brains (and hormones) respond to the world. There are of course physical differences between men and women. However, the question remains whether these have any significant effects on how good we can be as parents.

Science has found that there is such a thing as mummy brain; women's brains are changed by the experience of looking after children. Science has found that there is also such a thing as driver brain or being-on-holiday brain or sitting-on-a-bee brain. Experience alters our brains; whatever our sex. The plasticity (or malleability) of male brains is no different to that of female brains so when men look after children their mental chemistry is altered in a similar way. To suggest that women alone have some in-built ability that separates them from men is putting the cart before the horse.

People who believe that dads are 'naturally' ill-suited to childcare will often throw in an argument from evolution, as if this justifies it. Something like: men aren't built for looking after babies because when we were cavemen we needed to go out hunting. So we're better suited to killing things. Whereas women evolved to tidy the cave and protect the babies. The same logic says humans are not suited to living in houses because, well, caves.

We're not talking about gestation, clearly. We're talking about the ability to bring your child up in a loving, safe, and stimulating environment. Women carry their babies in their womb for nine months, and many women offer breast milk. But neither of these seems to matter when it comes to the ability, success or rewards of being a fully involved and responsible parent.

Popular books, from *Men are from Mars, Women are from Venus*, to *The Male Brain* and TV shows like *Why men don't do the ironing*, have tried to plaster a veneer of modern evidence-based respectability to the age-old quest to justify why women are better looking after the kids and men are better in the workplace.

They each pull out some brain scans or some studies into how monkeys or rats behave, and declare that they have proved beyond doubt that dads just aren't 'biologically' up to responsible parenting, and it's better if us men don't worry our pretty little heads about something that's only really suitable for women.

It's bog standard bad science really. They ignore the evidence to the contrary, and then argue that it's all in our 'biology' and anything we learn about how men and women are meant to behave just reinforces the natural order of things. It's all about hormones and 'hardwiring' that we can't control. Men just aren't built for raising kids and caring.

These kinds of arguments mean that when a dad says he's going to look after the baby on his own people can make comments about how mothers have a special maternal instinct (that he won't have), that her hormones will go wild, and that he'll probably struggle because he's not built for it. He's odd because he's going against society *and* science.

One look into the impact of these sort of sex difference studies and how they're reported showed that even when these studies don't infer differences about parenting abilities, when they're reported by the media parental difference suddenly appears[72]. The researchers argue that "traditional gender stereotypes were projected onto the novel scientific information, which was harnessed to demonstrate the factual truth and normative legitimacy of these beliefs".

This pop science of innate differences is at the centre of the paternity gap. When a researcher says "if society departs too far from the underlying sex-dimorphism of biological predispositions, they will generate social malaise and social pressure to drift back towards closer alignment of biology"[73], most people won't have a clue what he's talking about. But then a newspaper or magazine reports that a dad has 'done real damage' to his daughter because he didn't have the 'natural' maternal abilities of his wife when he looked after her for a couple of months, vaguely alluding to some dodgy innate sex difference science to back this up[74].

The bad-dad isn't just reported in the media as an inadequate parent; his poor performance is tied to innate differences between the sexes. It doesn't take a stretch of the imagination for readers to conclude that it must just be *'the way it is'*; add some references to hormones and you've got a sciencey full house.

How the media reports science is critical in forming our expectations of parenthood. When people are shown articles explaining differences between the sexes as 'biological' or innate in origin, they are significantly more likely to support stereotypical roles about what men and women should be doing. In contrast, when we're told about the impact culture has, we are unsurprisingly more ready to challenge those limits and ponder whether the alternatives might be better[75].

Don't get us wrong: if science is really telling us something important around whether men or women are 'better' at raising kids, we should look into it. But because these sorts of statements have such a big impact on people's expectations of themselves and each other, we should really put them under proper scrutiny.

There are better places to run through the weaknesses of sex difference 'science' in more detail; that's not the purpose of this book. Ben Goldacre's *Bad Science* is an excellent primer on how to spot bunkum, and for stuff specifically on gender you can't go wrong with Cordelia Fine's *Delusions of Gender*, or *Brain Storm* by Rebecca Jordan-Young. But here we can summarise the most used research and where it leads us on the innate parental abilities of humans, and whether dads really do have a disadvantage deep inside their brains compared to mums.

Baby bonding and preferences

Even in the dark of night, [Baby] Blake knew which parent was bending over his crib to take care of him. But Tim confessed he couldn't help feeling jealous that Blake seemed to want his mom more. Tim was discovering, for fathers, early on, it's hard to match the biological force of the love bond between mommy and baby.

Louann Brizendine, The Male Brain

Despite being based on lots of things that are true, the real evidence for maternal-only rather than a parental bond is pretty weak. Babies probably do feel comforted hearing a heart-beat because it reminds them of the womb. They do connect closely to their mums (whether their birth mum or their adoptive mum). Breastfeeding can (if it works well) encourage a close bond with a baby. Mums of course do feel a yearning to care for and comfort their babies, and, as the baby grows, they will understand more about their little ones than nearly everyone else in the world. But so can dads.

None of these things need a female-biology mysticism to be true, nor do they need to keep out dads. Women can make brilliant parents, but not because they are women, because they are human.

It makes sense that if you carry your growing baby around for nine months in your womb, and you're overwhelmed by a loving and protective instinct when they're born, that you conclude that these feelings come from them having grown inside you. But just because a mum feels that's happening when she has a baby, it doesn't mean that dads aren't also overwhelmed by the same feelings when they see their little people.

It may sound unfair, but nine months' gestation is simply not the only route to developing a deep parental bond with your baby. Nor is there any reason to think that the bond is inherently stronger in either parent.

Clearly, dads aren't going to start breastfeeding any time soon. Active dads are occasionally even asked whether they wish it was possible for them to breastfeed. I've been asked this twice, with the assumption that, because I enjoy caring for my toddler during the week, I must have a longing to be more female... No. Dads don't wish these sort of things.

Someone who claims the only real way to bond with your baby is to let them suckle you hasn't tried bottle-feeding their baby. Holding them close to you and looking into their big eyes whilst they stare gratefully right back at you doesn't just feel like the same sort of bonding that breastfeeding gives; the evidence suggests that both sorts of bonding experiences are just as good[76].

In fact, whereas breastfeeding does trigger bonding with babies, for those who don't breastfeed eye contact and physical closeness seems to have just the same effect. This is not a breastfeeding vs expressing vs formula debate. It's just not relevant to a discussion on how we feed and bond with our babies.

Studies into how newborn babies bond with their parents have shown that there are several routes to the same goal. Dads, adoptive parents and bottle-feeding mums rely more on holding their little ones close to them, eye-contact, and interacting with them. These bonding experiences release hormones in both parent and baby, and, as we'll see shortly, start changing the way parents think and act around kids[77].

Another popular idea is that there's an innate preference within babies for women. If so, shouldn't we just give the little bundles want they want? Dads should clearly just hand them over to Mamma and leave the room. At three months old, babies are shown to have a better response to women's voices than men's, and to prefer women's faces.

The study into female voice preferences missed out how to deal with one critical response that most adults, men or women, have when confronted with a baby: baby-talk. The babies did have a preference for higher-pitched voices, but inexplicably, when we talk to our little bundles, dads have an uncontrollable urge to raise the pitch of their voice[78].

This can be embarrassing when we hear ourselves chatting with our newborn babies on the home-videos taken just after birth, when the normally low-toned manly bravado of even the hardiest tattooed and bearded man flies out the hospital window to be replaced by something out of the *Teletubbies*. But there's a chance that we do this instinctively because newborns prefer the familiarity of the higher-pitched tones they heard in the womb.

As for preferring female faces, rather awkwardly, other studies have shown that babies also prefer the faces of Chinese people... So this raises some serious problems for those of us who aren't Chinese and want our babies to like us[79]. Predictably, these were babies that grew up in China, and the babies were actually just showing preferences to things that were more familiar, whichever ethnic group they spend their first few months around.

In fact, when babies predominantly cared for by women for the first three months were excluded from the data, the remaining babies who had their dad as the main carer were more favourably inclined towards men[80]. This should be a sobering lesson for any dad who wants his baby to pick him over Mummy for cuddles once in a while: you need to get in there.

So babies are happy with being raised by both parents, and can bond equally with them both too. But what about parental abilities?

Different brains

Testosterone... the more you have of this special substance... the less your brain is tuned into emotional relationships.

Simon Baron-Cohen, The Essential Difference

This implicitly tells us a story about suitability for parenting that pop psychology feeds on. It implies that, since women are better at empathising, they will be better at nurturing kids than men. It confirms what people see around them when there are so few dads at toddler rhyme-time or baby cinema. It gives a half-baked legitimacy to the paternity gap.

Simon Baron-Cohen (he's Ali G's cousin; hopefully it bugs him to be introduced like that) tells us that there are reliable brain scans that show men and women use different hemispheres to perform the same task. He goes through the importance of women using both halves of their brain for language, and men using only one. He tries to argue that this means women are probably better at empathising, hoping that we'll just assume that if you can speak you can feel (try looking sad or happy at a six-month-old to see how they react and you'll realise why this doesn't make sense).

He even manages to drag up one study that shows boys have "more right-hemisphere brain activity, and girls more left-hemisphere activity" when matching faces to emotions. He doesn't argue that there is a difference in the outcome of either though. He then throws in there that "almost everyone knows that the right-hemisphere of the brain is more involved in spatial abilities such as route-learning". He hopes that we'll take these two fairly unrelated assertions about different functions that happen to occur in the same *half* of the brain, and assume that because girls are on average a little ahead in learning language, the woman's brain must be suited to "concern, appreciation, understanding and comforting", whereas a man's is not.

If you feel his trail of reasoning is difficult to follow, you're not alone, as plenty of neuroscientists also have trouble with his inductive leaps. Ali G could probably do a better job biggin' up the West Side Staines Massive than his cousin could with explaining the importance of the right-hemisphere in parenting abilities. But let's be fair, the reason he can't explain it convincingly is not because he's not smart (he's very smart), it's because the evidence is underwhelming.

The different brains theory is a nice story but, as countless neuroscientists and endocrinologists are keen to emphasise, when it comes to the hard science, we still have "not got an inch closer" to working out how different brain states lead to different behaviours[81]. The way we use brain scans to detect differences and how we interpret these is still very much a developing area of research, and there is almost no neuroscientific publication that doesn't heavily caution their use. What is reported one year is frequently overturned the next.

Moreover, we're told time and time again by scientists that there are many ways to skin a rabbit, and they all have the same results. Because a tall person uses more of one region of the brain to sneeze than another, and a shorter person uses the reverse, it doesn't mean that they are not both sneezing. Nor does it even mean that they're not both using the same regions to some extent (something the neuroimaging pictures often hide). Men and women can predominantly use different parts of their brains to respond to an IQ test, but they can get exactly the same results[82].

The average woman may predominantly use different parts of her brain to care for a child than the average man, and the average man may use predominantly different parts of his brain to solve an engineering puzzle compared to the average woman. What this does not tell us is whether either way is better or even if either way is significantly different in its outcome. It also doesn't tell us if these differences are 'innate' or just caused by the different ways men and women are treated.

The human brain is, much more than other animals, exceptionally flexible or 'plastic', and responds hugely to its environment[83]. When exposed to other people's opinions, rules, and expectations, our brains change what they're doing. Given the huge range of rules that push mothers into childcare and fathers into the workplace, regardless of what they might prefer, it becomes pretty plausible that these are going to have an impact on how we think, and indeed how our brains work.

After undertaking a wide review of the available research into sex differences in the structures of children's brains, Barnett and Rivers argue that "there is surprisingly little evidence of innate sex differences... It's not true that boys have brain structures that girls don't possess". They draw from extensive research showing that for nearly every study reported in the press indicating some innate difference between boys and girls, there are other studies showing no difference or even the opposite difference[84].

Empathy and natural nurturers

One popular myth is that women are more suited to caring roles because their lack of prenatal testosterone makes them better at empathy. The boy-hormone in contrast has given men an inbuilt social ineptitude.

A huge testosterone surge beginning in the eighth week will turn this unisex brain male by killing off some cells in the communication centres and growing more cells in the sex and aggression centres.[85]

Despite the quote above being widely read as part of the popular literature on sex difference, when examined researchers can't find any actual science behind it. In fact, one researcher even explains that 'if anything, existing data suggests testosterone might grow the structure most strongly associated with recognition of faces and emotional expressions, the amygdala, though this is from research in rats and monkeys'.[86]

Another widely quoted study by Jennifer Connellan tried to argue that there is an innate empathy difference between the sexes. She found that newborn babies had different tendencies to look at faces rather than mobiles, depending on their sex. The idea being that newborn babies haven't picked up any social rules around them, and, even if they could, they don't yet understand that they are future mummies or men. Thus, any difference found here in behaviour must be innate and carry through to adulthood.

Girls looked at Connellan's face 49% of the time, and boys less, at 46% of the time. Let's be honest, a three percentage point difference between boys and girls may only just be statistically significant, but it is certainly not grounds to argue that "these differences are beyond reasonable doubt, in part, biological in origin".[87]

The other problem was that this study was a case study in poor science. For example, the experimenters could spot the sex of the baby before they started the test, so they could easily encourage baby girls to look at their faces more than the boys. Researchers that repeated the experiment without the design flaws found no significant difference between the genders at all[88].

In most scientific disciplines the study would have been consigned to the rubbish bin by now, but not so a study that ticks the boxes for confirming sex differences and confirming that boys and men understand people less.

Simon Baron-Cohen argues that differences are innate because there is evidence to show that they are caused by different levels of testosterone in the womb. Testosterone essentially stops men being empathisers. But Cordelia Fine takes him to task on this, showing that, through the research he used for his assertions, different levels of testosterone prior to birth do not seem to be related to different levels of empathy.

What was shown was that mothers report higher levels of empathy in their baby daughters than in their baby sons. But this was not related to more or less testosterone in the womb, so it could just as well be parents reporting their own expectations on their babies. When tested on a more objective measure of 'empathy' for kids being able to read emotions looking at people's eyes, there was a higher level of empathy with lower levels of prenatal testosterone, but there was *no* significant differences between the sexes[89]. This is an awkward finding for Baron-Cohen who argues that sex is the big divide.

Studies showing women have a significantly higher level of empathy than men on average, tend to rely on self-reporting of empathy or asking parents what they think[90]. To test if this is good science, imagine talking to a group of women and asking them, "are you good at feeling how others feel?" The woman that stands up and says, "well, I'm not very good at it" is pretty brave, and is more likely than not to get some judgement from her peers.

Now imagine asking a group of men the same question... The brave guy suddenly becomes the one who says "yea, I'm great at feeling!" He'll probably notice some of the other guys staring at him, picking up what they're feeling no doubt: "He's like a lady (and that's a bad thing)."

Other studies with a little more sophistication have tried to drill into the idea that women are more empathetic, to understand why. When given better and more objective measures of empathy rather than just self-reporting, the difference between the sexes drops to become negligible[91]. Some even give the contradicting message that women are less adept on average at reading people. The more scientifically controlled studies that try to rule out environmental pressures show practically no difference in empathy between men and women at all.

The well-used and imaginatively named *Reading the Mind From the Eyes Test*, and Baron-Cohen's own version of it, showed some difference. But the differences were very modest. For instance, in the first of these, the average woman scored twenty-three out of thirty-six, whereas the average man got twenty-two. One point difference doesn't make you noticeably worse at understanding someone's emotions. They are also referred to as the "hurried person in a burka" tests, as they only show participants the eyes and not all the other signals we use to understand other people.

But sweeping all the claims that only women have the sensitivity needed for raising children to one side are studies that have shown that, when a child is involved, there appears to be no difference between Mum and Dad[92]. When the average dad is focusing his empathy on a child, the average mum has no advantage.

Dads that get hands-on and active become more sensitive and responsive to infants, as substantial research has shown. It is difficult to square this with the essentialist arguments of Brizendine and Baron-Cohen, since there appears to be in fact no sex difference when it really matters. Yet their ideas are still pervasive in the expectations we place on each parent. So every time we hear that mums are 'naturally more nurturing' than dads, it's worth challenging this gross representation of the facts.

Childcare skills

The second set of differences popular writers claim are innate are the skills of men and women. Women are better at multi-tasking and doing fiddly things. According to generations of grumpy old men, women talk more and the more talking babies hear the quicker they learn to speak. The last of these is nonsense, as there is no significant difference between the average number of words spoken by men or women, mums or dads (both around 16,000 words a day)[93]. But the other skills deserve a little attention.

Multi-tasking

Women, it's claimed, are able to perform several tasks at once, essential to good parenting and household management, whereas men are more likely to prefer focusing on one thing at a time.

This one runs deep. It's also cobblers. When doing one thing and asked to do another at the same time by my wife before parental leave, I would have said it has to wait and invite the inevitable comment about being bad at multi-tasking. To which I would respond tongue-in-cheek, pretty unfairly to her I admit, "at least I can do one thing well rather than several things badly".

But parental leave changed that scenario. From the first week I was comforting my son in one hand whilst preparing food with the other, shutting the dishwasher with a foot and talking to the broadband provider to fix the internet (again). Could it be that we tend to do the number of tasks that we need to do at once, rather than passively rely on our innate sex-hormone distorted brains to tell us what we can and can't do? Could our brains instead adapt to the conditions we're faced with?

Yes, basically. In some ways mental load is just a trendy term for multi-tasking. Women take on multiple tasks at once, especially in the home, because traditionally they've been forced to do so. Men have just the same capacities for this.

Whilst there are reported sex differences in multi-tasking between adults in the home, there are in fact no differences in the ability to become a multi-tasker. The Fatherhood Institute has looked closer at why. Jeremy Davies explains that in household tasks, including childcare, the woman often fulfils the role of 'manager', seeing what needs to be done and delegating or doing the jobs. In these instances, men often take on the role of 'employee', and await their tasks to be allocated, not thinking about the 'bigger picture' of what needs to be done and multi-tasking to get it done.

However, in couples where the men took on the mental load of the household, and were the dads who made themselves responsible for thinking about whether the kids were ready in time for school, or making sure that the family had the right food for dinner, they became the 'manager' themselves. They acquired the ability to multi-task[94].

Similarly, a study for the Swedish government looking at the benefits that more paternal involvement can bring to the workplace showed that when dads get back from parental leave, they are better at multi-tasking than before. So if guys ever get jealous of their partner's ability to do several things at once, just take some ownership for running the house and it'll soon come naturally.

Nurturing

Boosting his sex difference arguments, Baron-Cohen explains that mothers are superior at nurturing because of their brains' hardwiring. He lists traits that show why women are more nurturing and in tune with their kids, whereas dads are in their own worlds failing to connect and nurture. The argument goes that if they can connect with and nurture their kids better, they are biologically better at parenting.

"Mothers are more likely to follow the child's play topic whilst fathers are more likely to impose their own topic"; and "mothers fine-tune their speech more often to match what a child can understand… whilst fathers tend to use unfamiliar or difficult words".

One study he quotes got parents to describe a picture to their six-year-old kids, and then the kid had to pick the right picture based on the parent's verbal description. Mums did better than dads! So they must be more skilled at nurturing and 'tuning in' to their little people.

But the studies are horribly flawed by the same issue we found in the mummy-face preference study above. These tests are like letting one contestant in the 100m sprint run the first 20m before firing the starting pistol. *Of course* the parent that has spent the most time with their kids is going to be more tuned in to them.

Because of the expectations we put on parents, in an overwhelming number of cases, the mother is around their kid and taking on the main responsibility for childcare. This no doubt does make her good at nurturing and picking up her baby's needs.

In fact, when tested, it is apparent that there is again no difference in the capacity of either parent to provide intimate and nurturing care[95]. The key ingredient is that the parent – dad or mum – needs to get involved if they want to develop the nurturing skills.

The fiddly things

Women are shown to have better fine-motor skills than men, so not only do they have neater handwriting, but they, so we're told, are better at doing the fiddly things in childcare[96]. Does this mean that men are more clumsy when it comes to the staple tasks of childcare and so probably can't be trusted with looking after the little ones on their own?

You can imagine a poor helpless dad struggling and failing to assemble a milk bottle while his baby is screaming. He's probably also being taxed by the challenge of clipping the toddler into the car seat correctly, only for him to wriggle out of the dad's clumsy job when they're already in the middle of the motorway. Then there's the dad with his stubby and poorly coordinated fingers trying to write a note to his child's school teacher.

But these differences are found in kids aged two and over[97], and so, as with differences in multi-tasking skills, could just be the result of how the kids have been brought up, and changeable as a result. We are in fact much more ready to do things for little boys when they just grunt at us, compared to the higher performance we expect from girls of the same age, when we expect them to communicate what they want, and then do it themselves[98]. But, more importantly, these differences don't seem to carry on into adulthood to any significant degree.

13

FAULTY INFERENCES AND SMALL DIFFERENCES

Arguments for mums always being the 'main' parent when the little one arrives:
1. *Because of the 'maternal instinct'*
2. *Because she was the one who was pregnant*
3. *Because of hormones*
4. *Because of the special bond with the baby*
5. *Because she needs to 'rest' rather than go back to work at the beginning (for parents who think this makes sense, we're jealous of your first experience of a newborn)*
6. *Because mums' hips are built for carrying babies*
7. *Because mums can multi-task*
8. *Because people will have opinions if she's not the main parent*

Equally daft arguments for why dads should always be the 'main' parent when the little one arrives:
1. *Because of the 'paternal instinct'*
2. *Because she was the one who was pregnant (if you carry them around for nine months, the least I can do is carry them around for the next nine months)*
3. *Because of hormones (if we use it for mums, we can use it for dads)*

4.   *Because the dad needs to form a special bond with the baby*

5.   *Because the mum should have a 'rest' by going back to work at the beginning. If she just went through pregnancy and labour, it's now his turn to go through the early morning cluster feeds and change every nappy until the baby turns two, at least*

6.   *Because dads are physically stronger and so can lift, carry or suspend babies, nappy bags and other tot-paraphernalia for longer*

7.   *Because dads have better spatial awareness for nappy-changing, pushchair navigating and baby-planes*

8.   *Because he doesn't have to deal with mum guilt, and everyone will be praising him just for being a parent*

Let's be clear, these are tongue-in-cheek. But they show that nearly all the 'reasons' we give for mums being head parent aren't as clear as we might think they are when we first hear them. For every reason we have for mum's being 'naturally' the only active parent, there is an equally daft one for dads being the 'natural' parent. It turns out the word 'natural' is frequently misused to mean something we feel is right because of social rules, and what people around us expect, but doesn't relate to anything substantial past that. This isn't fair on dads, but even more so, it isn't fair on mums.

Not so different
D Freed, Dad's Turn blog[99]

How big are these purported differences? Not very big at all. The differences just aren't big enough to imply that we can in any way predict someone's childcaring ability according to their sex. 46% of boys are better at understanding emotions than the average kid, compared to only 54% of girls[100], with the differences shrinking with age. These biological rules aren't really rules if they're not hard and fast.

There is an awkward impression here that we are writing off a huge chunk of men because their male peers happen to perform slightly worse on these tests than the average woman. We start equating the 'average' man or woman with *all* men or women. It becomes okay to claim that 'women are biologically better at childrearing', despite the research behind the statement claiming that only a little under half of men (even under these daft tests) perform below the average.

How did we buy into this nonsense? A simple answer is that humans like differences more than similarities, especially if they can be strapped to a convenient label like sex. The world is a complicated place, and any means of making it a bit simpler is going to help us understand it better. Humans like spotting groups and patterns that help us understand how the world works[101]. Since pointing out a difference between the sexes is way more interesting than commenting on what we do the same, it's easier to sell books that argue men are from one planet, and women, like a different species, are from another.

Sex is likely to be the first way kids start dividing up and trying to understand the world. If you're not sure about how much importance our signalling of gender has to our kids, try talking to your two-year-old without continually informing them of their and every other kid's sex: "What a brave boy... I mean kid, you are. Share the toy with her... er, I mean, the child. Be nice to the old lady... I mean person. Let the boy go first and stop hitting him... I mean them, it, whatever." It's difficult and a little hopeless to avoid signalling that gender is important to kids, because learning our language requires kids to differentiate between the sexes, even if just to use pronouns correctly.

The split is then reinforced through a lifetime of pink and blue labels as we grow up. No wonder that when the statistical output of a scientific study says that only 45% of men perform better at something compared to 50% of women, the way to make it appeal to our popular imagination is to declare that "[all] women are better at this than [all] men"! The 'all' is implied when we read about the studies, because we like to understand the world in simple terms.

Imagine if the *Daily Mail* led with the headline "Men and Women are essentially the same in how they care for children". Fewer people are going to find it interesting because it's not helping them organise the world into simple black and white categories. The problem with the human desire to spot differences is that it often leads us to make prejudices, and then reinforce them by expecting people to act in the same way.

This doesn't help freeing people from the expectations about what they can do. So *Men are from Mars & Women are from Venus* is a top-selling book, whereas the more scientifically honest, *Brain Storm: the faulty science of sex difference,* struggles to make it onto the bookshop shelf.

The difficulty is that because these sort of books and headlines about differences fit so readily into what we already expect of each other, because it gives 'scientific' explanations for the rules we already use, it's difficult to convince people they're wrong, as reading them reinforces the limitations we put on each sex of parent[102].

Inferring too much

Putting the poor quality of the gender-difference studies to one side, and ignoring the small size of any spurious differences found, what conclusions do the researchers, and later the *Daily Express*, the Google engineer and others draw from these studies? We're told that the higher chance that girls will look at Connellan's face means that they must have inbuilt empathy skills that make them perfectly suited to leading large groups of people in multinational companies and . . . no, wait, we're told that it means women are naturally suited to childcare.

Boys, because they like looking more at mobiles than Connellan's face, must not be suited to childcare. Because they like to see things that move, they must be averse to navigating pushchairs into tight-spots and cuddling babies. Instead, we're told they like 'systems' and therefore must be better suited to the workplace and roles of leadership. This leap of faith from evidence to explanation is present in all science. We have to explain our results in a way that makes sense for them to be useful. But in few areas of science is the leap so far and so fraught with difficulties.

This is a problem that plagues all sex difference writers. They take a weak result of something that's not so important, and take a huge inductive leap to land squarely where they wanted to, declaring that they have found incontrovertible proof that men are suited to one thing, women another.

Because boys at age five can't articulate their feelings so well, they're supposedly less suited as adults to becoming responsible and active dads. Instead they should stick to the office, the factory floor or the board room, where nobody has feelings. This neither matches up to the science that shows we talk to baby boys differently nor to the experiences of dads and women who choose to ignore this 'innate biology' argument.

Could the studies not tell us something completely different? Could reading these results lead to opposite but equally valid conclusions?

Empathy is of course essential in looking after kids. When they cry, we should be instantly compelled to help them. But highly advanced empathy skills are not essential. Newborn babies basically either cry or do not cry and that's about it. As they get older their range expands, but there's not a lot of interpreting required to provide loving and high quality care for them. Dads with lower emotional intelligence are not all psychopaths. They can also understand and feel distressed when their child cries, just as women do.

Why shouldn't we claim that dads clearly have an innate biology, with the 'systematising brains', to manage childcare? Babies, unlike adults, are pretty systematic in how they need to be deal with. In the early days, you need to figure out the mechanics of everything from nappy changing, bottle-feeding, trial (and error) of building sleeping patterns and routines, to the careful practice of building motor skills and speech. Then there's working out the different pitches of their complaints, assessing how tired they are, or whether they're just getting hungry. According to the dodgy evidence presented by sex difference writers, these are systems that dads are built for.

Could they also argue that the 'dad's brain', able to focus fully on the baby and block out unnecessary interference (such as the unsolicited advice and judgement thrown at all parents by strangers), is uniquely able to give his baby his undivided attention. And, let's face it, when your kids are throwing a tired-angry tantrum, ostensibly because you didn't let them play with that knife or jump in the duck pond, it could be useful to have some of that 'understanding systems' part of the brain that Baron-Cohen likes to talk about so much. Someone with a 'more right-hemisphere' brain, as Brizendine argues men have, is clearly better suited to bringing up children.

The woman's brain, in contrast, is more suited to dealing with dozens of different issues simultaneously. So staying on top of emails, corporate politics, people's complex emotions, meetings, briefings, making multiple decisions, and leading companies and countries are tasks that women's special skills are better suited to. She can also quickly connect all of these things together, and not separate them like the dad's brain does when he's looking after the baby.

Men also report having a higher pain tolerance. In an economy dominated by the service sector modern work tends not to require a lot of physical labour[103]. The modern workplace (hopefully) doesn't really require a particularly high tolerance of pain, in contrast to the physical rigours of dealing with the bundle of hyperactivity known as a toddler. Ever stepped on a Lego brick in bare feet?

Together with the broad shoulders of men that make them especially suited to giving piggy-backs and carrying babies freestyle or in baby-carriers, not to mention lugging all the baby paraphernalia around, we can clearly demonstrate that there is yet more 'evidence' to show that there is an inherent part of a dad's biology that makes him suitable for childcare. This means that the woman is suited to the more cerebral domain of the modern workplace.

These inferences are of course nonsense. Our sex doesn't make us better or worse parents; our abilities as parents and people do that. If we set ourselves different expectations about who should be the 'natural' parent, we can continue to use the same spurious evidence to draw the opposite conclusions from these sex-different writers.

This could go on, and, if you have a free moment, it's worth trying it with almost any 'innate sex characteristic' argument you find. Do men's better spatial-awareness skills make them better at steering construction equipment, or do they make them better at navigating difficult angles while carrying a wriggling kid, or squeezing the buggy into that tight spot on the bus whilst not waking up the sleeping baby?

Women being better at communicating complex ideas sounds pretty essential in the office, especially in the service sector. Less essential in talking to a baby, who surprisingly doesn't need an advanced vocabulary, just a lot of talking hot-air about the world (something dads and grandads are also rumoured to excel at).

The idea of parental sex difference looks more and more silly. When we see examples around us that appear to confirm the popular ideas about the biologically special status of mums compared to dads, we need to ask ourselves whether it is really sex genes we're talking about. Perhaps that particular guy just hasn't had as much time around his kids as he'd like, or, crucially, maybe he just does things differently.

14

BABY-BONDING HORMONES

DADS HAVE THEM TOO!

Hearing a baby cry makes her hormones go wild
Mothers form special hormonal bonds with their babies
Men are naturally more aggressive because of their testosterone
Mothers can't focus on work for a year after having a baby
because their hormones are 'all over the place'

If there's one form of abused science that invades almost every discussion on whether it's right or wrong for dad to take his turn with the kids, it's hormones. These little do-gooders, some just for men, others just for mums, we're told, get everywhere.

When it comes to childcare, we have a long list of hormones that mothers get in preparation for and focusing their brains on childrearing, from oxytocin and prolactin to estradiol and cortisol. When baby is born, lots of warm fuzzy hugs and suckling starts pushing up the levels of these chemicals in Mum's brain. She becomes more nurturing, protective and closer to her new offspring. Three days later the hormones all piss off again and the baby blues is the result.

There are very few parents in the developed world who haven't been told this. Hormones are generally something women have, and which are portrayed as pink, fluffy, and believed to be slightly irrational things.

In contrast, what does a blue man hormone look like in the popular imagination? It's thought to be impolite to imply that men have hormones, as blaming behaviour on hormones is often reserved for patronising women. If a man does have a hormone, it needs to be the most manly of them all so that he doesn't come across as feminine. It's got to be testosterone because all other hormones are pink.

In pop culture, the man hormone makes you angry and aggressive, and apparently more stupid too (unfortunate). In short, the way we use it in everyday conversations, testosterone turns you into an angry caveman. The lady hormones in everyday conversations in contrast make you nurturing, prone to mood swings, compelled to make sure only you get to hold your baby, and great at looking after them.

If someone asked you what hormones men get that help them with childcare, you'd be forgiven for answering "none", or even "get your man hormones away from my baby". With the way hormones are spoken about in pop literature on sex differences, and by certain Google engineers, we get the impression that men don't get the chemicals that mothers do to bond with their babies.

If we assume that mums are nurturing because of hormones, we end up labelling the responsible hormones 'maternal' or 'female' hormones in the way we talk about them because this fits with what people are expecting. If a dad is nurturing towards his baby or kids, people don't talk about his hormones or instincts 'kicking in', because that would imply him getting a jolt of testosterone. We comment about how unusual it is and what an amazing dad he must be (for what, fighting against his natural instincts to eat the baby or sell it for beer money?). These expectations need to change.

Science talk about hormones

Research into hormones began around a century ago. Scientists discovered that part of the way we behave was signalled and controlled by chemicals (nicely called 'secretions' at the time). As far as we know, these hormones control a lot of things: they regulate things from our temperaments to how our hearts react when we're faced with stress or hugs. They give us physical urges and reactions that impact our behaviour when we see, feel and do certain things. They also play a role in shaping how our brains form.

As we showed earlier, the small differences between the average man and average woman might be caused by something 'innate', something in their sex genes, or it may be predominately caused by social rules and the things that we're trained to do. On the face of it, hormones look like they can help convince us that it's the former that causes these small average differences.

Right from the start, the study of hormones has been obsessed with sex. It's where it all started, with early endocrinologists thinking of the main hormones as "chemical messengers of masculinity and femininity"[104]. In reality, there are around fifty hormones that we know of, all doing many different things at different times; many of them seemingly doing something similar to other ones. Between five and ten hormones for instance might be involved in making all humans feel happy. Something we often don't realise is that, despite each sex having higher or lower levels of a few of these hormones, both mums and dads have all fifty running around their bloodstream[105].

The thing is, following the pleasure of using science to explain differences in simple terms, and the ancient obsession with wanting to split people down sex lines, the popular understanding of research into hormones continues to label them as 'male' or 'female'. As science is trying to move beyond this, the popular impression of hormones remains divided along sex lines. Four small hormones, testosterone for men, and oestrogen and progesterone and perhaps even oxytocin for women, have crept into our popular imagination.

We're told that "girls not boys come out wired for mutual gazing" because too much manly testosterone has "killed off cells in the communication centres"[106]. So the 'man' hormone destroys all the parts of the brain that could prepare us for loving and relating to our kids and even other people. We're also told that the sole function of the 'female' hormones is to prepare a woman for looking after her kids.

But these are not the only hormones, and they are not as restricted to one sex or the other as we're often told they are, nor are they apparently the only ones that are needed to carry out the things that make us good parents.

Dad hormones

Recently a number of studies have identified the neurochemical causes for why dads get goose bumps when faced with their kids. Holding on to your baby as a guy for as little as fifteen minutes after they're first born shows a rise in the level of dad hormones in the bloodstream. This paternal cocktail appears to promote bonding, trust, and sensitivity towards little people[107].

The change in hormones appears to start well before birth too as dads hover around their pregnant partners. It's possible that this is to get the dad ready for the biggest change in his life, as he moves from footloose to doting dad. Then when the baby's born, the dad hormones kick in and start the bonding between a father and his infant: that's the feeling dads naturally get every time they handle and look after the bundle. There could be nothing more natural about that.

The hormones flood his veins when he holds the baby and stares into its eyes. Evolution and nature sees the need for a man to look after his baby, and it starts changing his hormones to make that happen the best way possible. He's now ready to nurture, empathise, and protect this tiny thing in a way he didn't think possible before. The feeling he gets from the daddy hormones (and a little testosterone) makes him want to bin his midwife's copy of *The Essential Difference*, while continuing to firmly keep hold of the baby of course.

This doesn't stop there. The more time he gets babbling with his new tyke, carrying, changing and feeding it, the quicker and higher his dad hormone levels rise [108]. His neural pathways, his dispositions and his feelings start to change and his world and happiness start centring around the alien shaped creature in his arms.

Because these hormones weren't spotted in dads first, they're associated with only mums in the popular imagination. So the hormone that makes a dad bond with his baby and which spikes when he cuddles him is called prolactin, as it also promotes lactation in mums. Since a lot of guys are normally averse to doing something that might raise their lady hormones – just in case their penis shrinks or they start growing breasts – the name prolactin isn't too helpful for a sense of 'manliness' in being a dad.

If a woman is told that successful women in the workplace have more testosterone than other women, she, and most people around her, will believe that because testosterone is a 'man' hormone she is essentially becoming more of a man. A lot of women don't want to hear that, and so may be more reluctant to do things we label as 'testosterone driven'. It's implying that she must have 'the balls' (actual testicles) to be that confident at making the big decisions in the workplace.

Equally, if men are told that their testosterone drops, and prolactin, oestrogen, and oxytocin goes up when they get more involved at being dads, they risk hearing that they are being told they are *losing their manliness and becoming women*. As we'll see in Part IV, this has some big costs, and it pushes men away from wanting to look after their kids.

The first step is to accept and talk about dads as having 'manly' hormones that make them better fathers, and that talking about a man's hormones also means talking about the critters that makes him a nurturing and caring dad, not just ones making him a Neanderthal. The next step is to realise that, despite what we've been taught about hormones, the ones we get to bond with and bring up our babies are parental, and not sex specific. Indeed, mums too get the daddy hormones.

In one study based on brain scans, scientists found that whereas mums used more of the brain that helped them feel their kids cry, and secondary (back-up) dads tried to work out what their kids wanted, primary-caring and more active dads did both together! Was this the result of prolactin, as it correlated with the brain activity? So if dads take their 'biological' role as the primary carers in their family, not only are they emotionally compelled to stop their kids crying when the tears start coming, but they can also work out how to do it!... *Super-parents?* [109]

No. If we recall from chapter 11, the studies into brain scans can only give us hints about how the brain is working, and they should not be used in this way. But the study reinforces the growing body of research that shows dads' brains change substantially, along with their behaviour and hormone levels, the more they get involved with caring.

When casual conversations about hormones focus on the differences between the different types of parents, we're missing the pretty strong similarities. By obsessing about what the differences are between mums and dads, between male and female, we end up missing the more interesting discussion of what is parental, and what is human.

The sex categorisation of hormones in popular culture puts the horse before the cart. It says women are meant for raising kids, and men for breadwinning, then it finds the chemicals that cause these things to happen in each sex and labels them as male or female, reinforcing the split. It then stops and says "job done, mother and father differences have been scientifically proven beyond doubt". Science doesn't work like this! Science is meant to find something and ask what's doing it, without building in the pre-existing prejudices.

What we're finding with hormones is that they are very complex, that each hormone does several things, they're prompted by different environmental ('nurture') conditions to do these different things, and different combinations of hormones can often result in the same behaviour outcomes.

Until recently, hormones in dads have been largely ignored. But increasingly we are finding that dads are reacting to a cocktail of hormones that's driving how they feel and act towards their little people. It's becoming apparent that hormones in both dads and mums seem to be driving the same sort of bonding and caring instinct when they take on their new role as parents.

Feeding, changing, and tickling your baby, even looking out for them, starts gearing up your male-brain for being the dad you always wanted to be. The chemicals in your bloodstream help you bond with your baby, calm you down to help cope with the inevitable stress of parenthood, tune you into your little person's cries and babbles, and just make you happier.

The slightly awkward fact for people who claim that there's an immense gulf between the sexes is that these hormones for dads and mums are largely the same hormones. They're doing the same things. Both parents get the oxytocin and cortisol that prompts similar levels of tolerance (don't we all need it as parents) and sensitivity to kids[110].

Granted, anatomy means that mums can prompt the hormones through breastfeeding. But dads, adoptive parents, and bottle-feeding mums equally prompt them from staring into their little ones' eyes and holding them.

So when we hear about studies that show mothers wake up to baby cries but fathers sleep through, or that mothers understand their babies' moods and needs more than the dads, we should ask ourselves: do the dads in these studies need more hormone encouraging time with their little tykes to fix this?

If people want to point to hormones as the source of excellent parenting and an inner parental instinct, then we should start challenging the idea that only mums have them. We need to get more comfortable with saying to dad that his hormones let him form a special bond with his baby, that his hormones give him that irresistible urge to tickle his kids into hysterics, that sometimes his hormones are 'all over the place', and even that they give him that special parental instinct to care for and nurture his kid.

15

THE PARENT'S BRAIN

NOT CAST IRON, MORE LIKE PLAYDOUGH

When writing this, I'm sitting in a café looking at a dad drive his baby into hysterics. He's got a huge smile on his face, and it's not entirely clear who, him or his daughter, is enjoying the game more. The mum sits quietly reading her book. Listening to the baby's ecstatic giggles, I'm feeling a warm fuzzy feeling in my stomach. As a guy, I'm probably not meant to wave at her, but I can't help myself. Her smiles and waving back at me make me feel happy. Asking both parents how old she is prompts the dad to stand up with enthusiasm and explain her ten month old noises and her recently changing sleeping patterns.

After a lifetime of being trained not to talk about my feelings, I'm honestly finding it difficult to repress talking about feelings every time I hear a kid giggle like that. Especially when it's my kid. Twenty-five years ago I showed no interest in dolls, six years ago I showed little interest in kids, three years ago I started getting a little broody. Now I'm happy getting the chance to spot a ten month old discovering that she can move her index finger separately from her other digits and then cover her face with her hands. This is of course nothing compared to spending time with my own toddler.

Baby-bonding hormones
D Freed, Dad's Turn blog[111]

A similar message is hopefully coming out of these different studies of parental biology: contrary to what the sex-difference writers imply, the human brain is not hardwired to follow a specific path based on whether we're dads or mums. The brain is way better than that. It is, in fact, the most amazing and flexible organ on earth. Our parental abilities, for mums or dads, are no exception to this.

When a cat, dog or lizard is born, it's full of pre-programmed instincts that let it learn to walk, play, and hunt, all in short order. Within the space of months, its biology means that it is ready to take on the world like an adult. Not so the helpless little pudding that is the human baby, that after several weeks of life can only just begin to understand the presence of its nose and the fact that its fingers are firmly attached to its hands.

This is because we have far less pre-programmed instinct about how to manage ourselves than other animals, and instead have to learn and adapt to our environment. Taking in this information and processing it to become a rational adult takes a lot longer, but in the end the flexibility and evolutionary advantage this learned approach to life-skills gives us is immense[112].

The slow learning process in the human brain allows us to react to our environment in a way that no other species has managed. The mole's brain is like sending a football team onto the pitch against the same opponent using the same tactics game after game, unable to change your pre-programmed tactics. You might know how to match that team and beat them. If, however, a different team comes out to face your guys with a whole new strategy, you might be screwed. And if you're not allowed to change your team's strategy, then you're destined to lose every game you play against the new opponents.

The human brain in contrast allows you to know who you're facing, and to change your strategy; to adapt to their tactics and them to yours, each game getting better as the players learn new ways to get the ball in the right direction. Unlike what innate sex difference writers claim, after we've lost 1-0 to another team, we don't give up and decide we can't play them again because "they were born to win against us". We think about how we can improve our game and get back out there. We adapt, because that's what humans can do better than any other species.

The worst of the sex difference authors point to some minor difference then ordain that men can never really relate to childcare, and that women will be compelled to be the only responsible parent. But, in truth, the brain just adapts to its conditions. A dad being put in charge of his baby triggers hormones and changes his brain, just as it does in mums. It changes their brains in a way that makes them parent better and enjoy it more.

Getting involved – taking on the mental load rewires your brain

If you can take one thing away from this chapter it's that the thing that makes us into better parents, or feel closer to our kids, is not dependent on our sex, it's dependent on getting involved with childcare. This is critically why, even if (and it's a big if) there are minor average differences between the sexes, this does not mean that one sex or the other is 'innately' better at parenting. It only means that more women are given the opportunity to develop their parenting skills.

The behaviours caused by our hormones do not neatly divide themselves based on whether we have one Y or two X chromosomes. There are multiple complex functions in our bodies that mean that when we are presented with looking after a child, when we're given the responsibility to care for them, that through some very complicated and weakly understood routes, we all as parents start to feel similarly about our kids, just as the extract above shows.

We need to think less about how men and women have different 'hardwiring' in their brains, and more about what humans do that prompts a 'rewiring'. This is good news for adoptive parents for example and it's good news for dads, and every other family member that becomes involved in the upbringing of their kids.

Dads aren't becoming more feminine or emasculated by their new hormones because those are not female or male hormones, they are parenting hormones. They're the chemicals that we get as humans when we become responsible carers so that we find it easier to bond with our kids and make the sacrifices we need to when we become parents. That's not dads thinking like mums, it's dads thinking like parents.

So we've shown that the sex-difference theories that imply women alone are innately built for childrearing, and men need to stick to the workshop, are scientifically unreliable. They still get press not because their research is robust but because they play on popular ideas. They also offer evidence that we can very easily use to reverse the inferences that they make. On top of this, the studies themselves don't even indicate very big differences between men and women, and imply that there are many women who could perform better at the 'man' skills, and many men who could equally perform better at the 'woman' skills.

It's somehow seen as right to talk about 'maternal' instinct, 'maternal' hormones, and 'maternal' feelings. Only half of the science of parenthood appears to have seeped into the popular psyche. Instead, we need to start recognising that human biology means that being given responsibility for a baby makes us become better parents, and that these instincts are neither maternal nor paternal, they are innately parental.

Part IV
THE BABYSITTING HANDICAP

16

LIMITING EXPECTATIONS ON DADS

Security Guard:	*'So you're babysitting today?'*
Dad:	*'No, I look after the little bear full time'*
Guard:	*'So where's mum?'*
Dad:	*'She's working'*
Guard:	*'Oh! Very nice for her [laughs awkwardly]. As long as you don't have to change the nappies, women are built for that sort of thing!'*
Another random bloke:	*'Yea mate [laughing], wouldn't touch that!'*
Dad: [forces a smile]	*'Do you have a baby-changing room in the building? Preferably not in the women's toilets'*

Limited Expectations on Dads
D Freed, Dad's Turn blog[113]

'I look at the stay-at-home dads and I think, the thing is, you're just a bum. You're looking after the kids and doing nothing all day. I always think that they're not capable of doing a day's work'

Mum quoted by Jasmine Kelland

The number of dads who have told us how annoying it is to be told that they, as the father of their children, are 'babysitting' is strikingly high. Before you say that they're 'overthinking' a one-off comment about childcare, it's not the odd comment about babysitting itself that causes the problem, nor how pissed off the parent receiving it gets. It's that it's symptomatic of the expectations people are placing on dads.

These comments from strangers and co-workers, and impressions from books and TV, tell a consistent story: a woman should be the main parent, and a man should not. When a dad is parenting, he has been delegated this privilege by the mum, and doesn't hold it in his own right.

The term 'babysitting handicap' of course doesn't just refer to comments about babysitting, but all the hints and nudges that imply dads can't really hold responsibility for their kids. It's when a worker is told he's 'helping out' his wife by doing the school run, or even asked "why can't your wife pick them up instead?'. I'm probably told I do 'daddy-day-care' more often when I explain that I look after my son for two weekdays... No, my wife is not delegating childcare responsibility as if to a nursery. As a parent I already have that responsibility. I'm just looking after my son. A stay-at-home mum is not babysitting, 'helping her husband out' or doing mummy-day-care during the week, she's just parenting.

These expectations are important in how they limit us and add stigma to the choice of more equally shared parenting. There are two relevant theories from psychology here: the human desire to learn and follow rules, as we discussed in chapter 9, and stereotype threat.

On the first of these, just like the naff arguments for a maternal-only biological readiness for nurturing, the assumption that 'mums and not real men' are the only people who hold proper responsibility for kids builds up a solid picture about what society expects, and influences what we expect in our own relationships.

Stereotype-threat kicks in when someone recognises that they are acting against a stereotype. They are uneasy about doing that thing; not only are they likely to perform less well at it than they are in fact capable of, but they are also likely to be pushed away from doing it[114].

On my first day of parental leave, I decided to take my son to a weaning class run by the local children's centre. I arrived alongside some mums, and the group was led into a playroom covered in toys. The two professionals running the class commented on how brave I was heading out with the baby on my own to 'give mum a break'. When I told them I was on parental leave and my wife was at work, one of them joked that she must have given me detailed instructions on what to do. With the other one chiming in to ask whether my wife had passed on any questions...

No, I went to the weaning class entirely because I thought my baby would start weaning soon, and, like most first time parents, the idea of them choking terrified me. No instructions were sought from or given by my wife because I was taking, like any other responsible parent, sole charge. By welcoming me into parental leave by trying to explain my sex and the absence of my wife, these professionals were propping up the impression that, as a dad, I was doing the mum a favour. That I was just helping her out, rather than being the responsible parent.

John Adams, owner of *Dad Blog UK* and stay-at-home parent, explains that there's a big difference in the way people out and about react towards dads and mums. "I've had GPs tell me it's nice that I'm babysitting when I take the girls in for a check-up, and a nurse look around for my wife when I took my youngest in for her vaccines. I've even been told by a librarian that I was a 'brave dad' just for taking care of my own child! Would you go up to a working mother to tell them that they're brave for their work-life choice? No, because it would be patronising and sexist."

Mums don't get that attention, but people think dads need to be patronised when doing a 'woman's job'. Not to mention the fact that being 'brave' implies that it must be more difficult for the dad than the mum to do the same job.

It's easy to write off these comments, as many dads try to, explaining "I'm sure they didn't mean anything by it", or "it was just a joke". But, as Jasmine Kelland explains through her research into the forfeit that involved dads face at work, "years on, people were still recounting these stories to me, so actually maybe it is deeper than they thought".

These nudges we get from the babysitting handicap have an impact. One stay-at-home dad explained that he "feels excluded [from a lot of parenting activities]. It's difficult to pinpoint how much is my fault, I did withdraw a little, I felt self-conscious... I see women forming groups but I don't get invited. I've never felt legitimate to be part of it."

There are signs of change, as more people are making an effort to include dads in kids' activities, books, and talk about kids. Not just as curiosities, but as equal and responsible parents. But the babysitting handicap still dominates what expectations are placed on dads.

When a boss questions a dad for leaving work early to pick up his sick kid from school, he can ask why the guy's wife isn't able to do the pick-up duty instead. This would sound like nonsense if a boss said the same to a mum, asking why the dad couldn't nurse the sick tots.

Parents, and nearly everyone else for that matter, think that kids have at least one person in their lives who's fully responsible for them. If they're lucky, they'll have two. If you drop your kids off at school, or let a relative look after them, you're trusting the new carers to take care of them. But you're not giving up that ultimate responsibility.

There is no-one in the world with a stronger vested interest in their kid's happiness than the parent. It's a deep responsibility that can be at times a real burden, and at others the best feeling you can get. Parenting doesn't just mean looking after a kid. It means taking on that responsibility with all its ups and downs: being the one who stays up late worrying when they're getting back or dealing with the poo-explosions in the baby-grow. You just understand that's the other side to all the fun stuff you get as a responsible parent. This is true for single or co-parents, it's true for adoptive and step-parents, it's true for gay or straight parents, and it's true for mums *and* dads.

Dads get these limitations, these hints that they don't quite belong as responsible parents, foisted on them from TV, advertising, family, and, probably worst of all, the workplace, where being a responsible dad can cost you dearly. It's these nudges that contribute to keeping the paternity gap open. If you're not fully certain of the social role you have, people implying that you're doing something they don't think you should be doing makes you feel less secure about it. If someone at work says you're probably "not well suited to your role", it's likely to shake your confidence a bit, or at least make you question what you're doing a little. That's only human. That's us responding to how people see the rules and expectations on how we should be behaving. This isn't men being oversensitive; it's people responding to negative stereotypes.

Research into stereotype threat has shown that when we feel the weight of other people's expectations going against us because of a stereotype, whether our gender, race or nationality, we divert mental resources away from where it's needed to focus on worrying about how we're performing against the stereotype. It makes us think we're less capable of doing something than we would think without the stereotype, and that pushes us away from those options.

Comments about dads not being the ones who are 'meant' to be responsible for their kids, that they are voluntarily babysitting them, are never thrown at mums, but they are frequently thrown at dads. We've even had someone say that she didn't understand what word she was meant to use when seeing dads looking after their kids. If she saw a mum looking after her kids, the words 'looking after' or 'parenting' or even nothing at all would have felt pretty natural. So stick with one of those.

17

PATERNITY RIGHTS WHEN BABY ARRIVES

GETTING THE RIGHT START

Work is probably the most obvious place where you can find the babysitting handicap, and where it has the most direct impact on the paternity gap. Here, new dads are expected to return to work as quickly as possible, whereas new mums can often come under the opposite pressures, being told that it must be 'difficult being away' from their kids. Mums are expected to leave the workforce for as much as a year, and often end up not being able to return when they want to. Dads asking for more time off to look after their kids and work flexibly to accommodate a new family arrangement can often come up against a brick wall or face workplace stigma.

As we've seen, the most obvious barriers to dads taking their turn out of the workplace are the financial ones. But they are far from the only challenge. Many couples will find a relatively surmountable financial barrier to Dad taking his turn, but will also come across a range of other social or personal barriers and will summarise all of these challenges to outsiders as "we couldn't afford it".

Jo Swinson piloted shared parental leave onto the statute book, and in the course of that process she has concluded that financial considerations are acting in combination with other forces. She explained to us: "I've seen research where lots of people say they would take SPL if they could afford it but separate research where you say 'have you done the calculation?' Lots of them haven't and so there's a kind of immediate view that 'I can't afford it' and there will be couples where that is the case but also I can't afford it for what period? So they might be able to afford it for four weeks."

She explains why exhausting the process of pursuing at least some shared parental leave matters: "For Dad to spend more time [than the minimum two weeks] that's still valuable. And if you're the first person in your organisation to do it and you take four weeks it's easier for the next guy to take six weeks."

Not that long ago, after the birth of their baby, dads had to go straight back to work. Employers expected it, as did work colleagues. Dads weren't seen to have a role in looking after babies, and in many places they still aren't.

John Watts, now fifty-four, remembers asking his employer if he could have a week off work, unpaid, after the birth of his first daughter, Charlotte. In return, he received a letter giving him his employer's warmest congratulations on the arrival of his baby girl. They 'generously' granted him a few unpaid days off, but made it clear that, if he ever asked for this again, he should not bother making the trip to work the next week. His employer was mostly worried about his 'commitment' to the job, and what sort of a 'precedent' this might set.

That generation of fathers were more likely to leave work at 5pm sharp compared to the longer hours many face today. But when they got home to their stay-at-home wife they did not expect to have much to do with their offspring. There's a best of both worlds set-up – leaving work on time, spending time with the children – that we seem to have missed out on.

Now, unlike a few decades ago, if the dad is still in the picture he's practically as expected to be at the birth as the mum is. 86% of fathers are at their partner's side for the big event. We're reminded of this not only by all the couples that turn up to prenatal classes getting ready for labour, but also by the countless harrowing scenes on TV dramas where the dad bursts through the doors of the labour ward in the nick of time to share that special moment at the start of his new family. Yeah, like that's how labour actually works...

There has also been some hype in the press over recent years about how the uptake of Paternity Leave (the two weeks dads are entitled to directly after their birth) has gone up. Almost 95% of new dads on one estimate take 'at least some' time off work after the birth of their baby[115]. Yes, less than half of these take the full two weeks, and many are forced to use annual leave instead of Paternity Leave, but a clear majority of workplaces are not expecting Dad to abandon his responsibilities to his new family and turn up to work the day his sprog arrives.

There are also workplaces that are trying to lead the change. The charity Working Families runs a benchmark for companies that want to improve their family friendly policies given the productivity gains they can get from it. But these are not the majority of companies, and the problems faced several decades ago still persist for many employees. A week with your baby after they're born is great, but parents are now wanting much more. Evidence shows that the prejudice that dictates that men 'belong' in the workplace still exists in most modern jobs.

If we want to have a fairer and more family friendly workplace, workplace culture needs to start being more open to dads taking half a year of parental leave, and to be more prepared for part-time working for both sexes.

This has progressed a lot for women, but many mums find, whether coming back to work full- or part-time after having a baby, that they are expected to feel bad about not being around their little person. From "why would you even bother having a baby?" to the more subtle "you're so strong, I just couldn't leave my little one that long when they're so small", mums are put under pressure to return to work.

Dads don't get any of this pressure. Can you imagine a dad returning to work after a few months on parental leave and being told that they must be "so strong to leave your tiny babies with someone else", or another bloke saying "I just wouldn't be able to come back to work so early"? No. Instead, dads face the opposite pressure.

Whether conscious or not, people are expecting dads to work more or less the same after they have a baby compared to before. In fact, having a 'family' somehow makes a man look more respectable, settled down, and more likely to be relied upon. Working fathers receive over 20% higher wages on average for the same work compared to those without kids by the age of forty-two[116], and being a father whilst applying for a full-time job boosts your chances of getting an interview. This is what employers and companies expect from fathers. Their children are not an obstacle to being good workers, but rather prove that they have someone at home to provide for.

The odd thing about this 'fatherhood bonus' is that whilst employers may think it's because the dads will work harder than the non-dads to provide, real higher productivity from dads only explains a tiny fraction of the higher wages.

Unsurprisingly, the opposite is true for mums who return to work. Wages for mums over the longer-term are 9% lower than for non-mums, and they're less likely to get interviews and are given lower scores in job applications.

The picture is pretty clear: employers are expecting mums to be responsible for the kids, and to always have an eye on the household and be less good at their job as a result. They have the opposite expectations on dads. They expect new fathers to be more committed, more focused at work, and on the hook for longer hours. And if dads don't fit into these expectations and instead ask for several months of parental leave, request part-time work or take on more family responsibilities, they are often penalised[117].

Tony became a dad towards the end of 2015. He works in a popular high street bank and enjoys his job. But like a majority of new dads now, he wanted to play a bigger role in his baby Arya's early years. He approached his boss about taking some time with his baby under Shared Parental Leave. "I thought it was best to talk to my manager directly, rather than talk to HR first, since I knew what my rights were. I get on really well with him and thought he was quite 'liberal' too". His boss hadn't had the HR briefing though.

"He started by just looking at me which made me feel a bit weird about it. Then he starts explaining that it was a 'nice idea to have some extra holiday with your wife and child'. I was already quite nervous asking him and when he said that, I didn't really know how to react. So instead we got stuck on the fact that I didn't want to take it at the same time as my wife, but just on my own."

Tony's boss then went on to explain how he doubted Tony's wife would let that happen, since his own wife had barely let him hold his kids. Like many sources of fatherhood stigma, Tony's boss seems to have taken Tony's actions as an implicit criticism of how he raised (or delegated raising) his kids, and then tried to justify his actions by explaining it was his wife's choice not his.

When Tony raised the issue of taking off more than a few weeks of 'holiday' (according to his boss), he was treated to a relatively common reaction that dads get when they raise the idea of exercising their rights to take proper responsibility over their babies: "Well, this isn't going to be good for your career, so you and your wife will need to think about that in the round." Tony left the conversation feeling awkward and deflated.

'You've got to think about your career'

Men and their partners are often worried about the impact of childcare on the guy's career. Understandably, just look at the impact looking after a baby has had on women's careers and long-term pay – this is not a small problem.

Not only has maternity leave had many decades to settle in, there is also an assumption that mums, being the only real responsible parent, must sacrifice their jobs to look after their kids and will be judged for taking less than the full maternity leave allowance. Implicit behind the reaction to dads taking even a small about of time to do the same however is the assumption that dads are doing something 'optional' to help out the mum.

Parental leave is often seen as a slightly exotic, and sometimes even 'lazy' option for new dads[118], but essential for mums. If a woman at work tells her boss she's pregnant, her boss might congratulate her, and normally immediately starts planning the six-month maternity leave absence she has requested, and for the possibility that she may extend this to a year, or even not come back to work at all after it. The boss is unlikely to turn round and say, "oh, that's great. Your partner must be looking forward to his six months with his little one".

As recently as 2013, research has shown that managers and older employees have more traditional attitudes when it comes to what role their male staff should be taking on at home, when compared to younger co-workers[119]. Considering the importance of having an understanding boss in the workplace, this isn't going to be great for giving a lot of dads a stigma-free choice.

Parents are treated differently from other work colleagues. Employers often assume traditional family roles when told a child is on the way. However, when employers are faced with fathers who choose to share childcaring and breadwinning responsibilities with their partners, managers can often react negatively because their traditional expectations have been challenged[120].

In many organisations this can show up strongest when dads extend their paternity leave and opt for parental leave. When Ali's second child arrived in 2016, he was the first person in his public sector organisation to apply for parental leave. He requested three months for when the baby was six months old. Whilst HR were keen to get their heads around the new system and eager for a guinea pig, Ali's management were less than happy. "My line-manager didn't want me to take it and explained that it would be difficult to cover my workload. But I pointed out that there wasn't really an option. The law says I can take it after all. Eventually he backed down, but said that, rather than taking it in two chunks, I had to take it 'all at once or not at all'.

> "My boss was particularly unhappy with the whole thing, and asked why, if my wife couldn't do it, why couldn't we find another relative, like one of our mothers, to help out. Not to mention that my mum was no longer with us so it was a little insensitive, but I didn't think that was really the point. I wouldn't have asked her to do it instead of me even if she was around. I'm the parent!"

But it's not only bosses that can have an impact on how we feel about taking parental leave. Co-workers have a big role to play. Jacob, working alongside Ali, at forty-two and with two teenaged daughters, believes firmly that we should "leave unto Caesar what is Caesar's, and unto women what is woman's". He's not only showing off his biblical education here (along with a strong dose of sexism), he's pointing to a deeply held belief that dads are meant to be working, and not taking care of the children.

Jacob considers men who want to take time out looking after their kids are not really committed to their job, and can end up 'letting down' colleagues because their 'mind is on their children, not on the job at hand'. He believes that, to be successful, your family life always has to come behind your work.

Jacob's outspoken views may look antiquated, but many dads who have fallen into the paternity gap have reported this sort of pressure at work. Few co-workers are as outspoken as Jacob, but it doesn't mean that other people in the office don't hold similar views and make their views known to friends in the workplace.

Looking back to Ali's move to take on a bigger role in parenting than he managed with his first daughter, when he returned to work after only three months on leave, something had changed. "I got quite a few comments, not just from my boss, but also others like 'oh, back now are you?', or 'how did you enjoy your extra holiday?' which were meant as half jokey, but they made me feel uncomfortable. It wasn't just what they said but also the tone, like I was free-riding on them. It made me worry about what they thought and what they had been saying whilst I was gone."

Mums have had to put up with ridiculous comments from co-workers about how 'lucky they are to get this free holiday' for many years. Now, dads are getting the same flak, but mixed together with the expectation that they're in some way deviant for opting for a bigger role in parenting, with the undertone that they should really be getting their wife or mother-in-law to do the job. As Ali explains, "It makes you feel like you shouldn't really be doing it."

The dads that end up taking parental leave are already the few that are determined enough to ignore these social pressures and push on regardless, or the lucky ones who work in the small number of organisations that really are undergoing a successful culture change to support dads taking their turn.

Ali was clear that "the push-back didn't make me feel great, but I mostly just ignored it. I wasn't going to let this stop me spending more time with my baby." But it's not surprising that many dads will be more responsive to these pressures, and either give up on taking the leave, or scale back on their parental aspiration to fit in with their workplace expectations.

This fatherhood stigma isn't only impacting dads that are considering shared parental leave. It's also taking its toll on couples that want to share the burden more equally when they're both back at work.

18

WORKING DADS 1

PAST THE FIRST YEAR AND FLEXIBLE WORKING

> 'What the f**k is your Mrs doing so much that you have to keep
> slopping off to get the girls?... You need to man up and tell Jas
> to get her arse home'

> *The boss of one dad, quoted by Jasmine Kelland*

So the first year is up. The little person starts to copy words
(including the occasional expletive), toddle around, demands
to be chased and tickled, and starts having opinions and
preferences (many of which are impossible to address) about
almost everything. In many ways, this is one of the most fun
times to be a parent.

Somebody needs to look after the little one. Some parents will
choose nursery or childminders, full-time or part-time, whilst
they both go back to work. This can be really expensive, especially
if you have more than one child under school age.

What if one of the parents really wants to spend more time with
their kids during the week? Should one parent go back only part-
time before school starts? What if both parents want to do this?
What if the child gets sick? Who drops them off in the morning,
and who leaves work in time to pick them up every day? Most

working parents have sat in a traffic jam or on a delayed train in fear of 6pm – that's usually the time that nurseries and childminders start whacking on the fees for late collection.

The paternity gap starts to firm up when parents start answering these questions. Dads who wanted to get more involved with their babies have had to fight for it or been discouraged from it for the first twelve months. But now maternity leave is used up, there should be an opening for them to step in.

The problem is that, regardless of how couples want to split it, they're going to find pressures, beyond the financial ones, that again seem to stop them doing what they want to. In almost every family, couples are nudged into a one-size-fits-all solution. The dad carries on working full-time, and the mum takes on all the necessary childcare duties.

Not only are fathers far less likely than mothers to make flexible working requests, and, specifically, requests to reduce their hours, but the remaining dads are twice as likely to have their requests rejected[121]. While around a third of mothers worked part-time (less than thirty hours a week), only one in twenty dads had managed to get the same deal[122].

We encountered Justin, working in the creative sector (not what we might call a macho work environment), and his partner Chloe in the first part of the book. Justin wasn't able to take shared parental leave. But, determined not to repeat the lack of a father figure in his life with baby Josh, Justin wanted to play a more active and present role in the early years of his kid's life. His veins rushing with parenting hormones and excitement about his new baby, shortly after taking two weeks' paternity leave, he raised this issue with his manager.

"I wanted to work four days a week, maybe with compressed hours, flexitime or something else. And the company is run by women, including my boss, and most of the people who work there are women, so I thought they'd be sympathetic. The mums are given flexibility with how they work, and seem to always have their flexible working requests accepted, even if this might not help their careers. But I was shot down really quickly. My manager said 'we don't really do that', but I know they do for the mums who work there. There wasn't even a willingness to discuss it. I felt pretty shot down so I backed off."

With Josh approaching his first birthday, Justin tried again more recently. "I was feeling that I really want to spend more time with Josh because he wasn't really connecting with me like he did Chloe, and I was really missing it. So me and Chloe came up with a plan of how it might work. I would go part-time and the money they saved on that would be used to pay for another person to take on some of my work. It would have been really useful for the company because they could build up more skill and it could even cost them less to do. Plus I would be a much happier worker. But I was told that I 'shouldn't concentrate on that sort of stuff'. I 'shouldn't be thinking about taking a pay cut, but instead on getting pay rises and pursuing my career and becoming more senior'.

> "It was weird that she was telling me what I should find important, and that I should put my career above time with Josh, but she wasn't really open for talking about it. But having kids changes you. I feel really different about work now and I really love spending time with my son. It's really important in these early years."

When asked if it was different for dads and mums, both Justin and Chloe jumped: "Completely! Women in the same division are offered a lot of options when they get back from maternity leave, the company's really proud of it." Justin was keen to add that "friends working in other companies also feel the same, that management get weirded out and annoyed when dads ask for flexible working for caring reasons where mums don't. We're just given the impression that since we're blokes, we shouldn't be concentrating on looking after our family, but earning more money and working harder.

"One woman also working under my manager was allowed to reduce her hours and move to Greece to work remotely to look after her mother. That sort of flexibility is really good, don't get me wrong, but my manager wouldn't even have listened to the idea if a guy had requested the same thing. It's part of the idea that men aren't really meant to do caring roles, whether it's for a child or an elderly relative. Not when there's a woman who's able to do it instead. It's just sexism in another guise. When I asked for an arrangement that was much easier for the company to accommodate, she shot me down."

This idea that men aren't seen as the 'natural' caregivers, and that women are, runs deep, as we'll see later. When it manifests in the workplace, management and work colleagues will start applying the pressure to men, nudging them, or in many instances just barring them from taking on a bigger parental role. Justin nicely summarises this as: "when we want to take on a caring role, we're just not taken as seriously as women are. We get judged badly by other guys and even by our employers". That's bad for dads who want to get involved and it's equally bad for women who want to get back to work and shake off the presumption that they'll like full-time childcare and just want to do it.

Dads are frequently penalised for part-time or flexible working arrangements because implicitly it is not seen as 'legitimate' for a father to reduce his working hours for childcare in the same way as it is often expected of mothers.

Research undertaken by Jasmine Kelland shows that the 'normal' expectations in the workplace when parents are working full-time are that mothers will be 'a bit flaky', whereas men are going to be 'more reliable'[123]. This chimes with Jason's experience as the manager of the start-up we came across in Part II, with an expectation that once a woman becomes a mum, she can no longer be relied on, regardless of what role her partner plays in childcare.

In contrast to 'working mothers', dads are seen as men in the workplace and not 'working dads'. When they deviated from this and were more honest about their commitments at home and their role as dads, many reported stigma from their colleagues and management.

Studies report fathers in this position receiving comments about whether they're prioritising their work any longer, and their commitment to the job is questioned. After returning to work part-time following shared parental leave, despite the relatively pro-family culture of the workplace, I received similar comments about my 'priorities and ambition' since I'd 'become a father' in my first few weeks back. I'd been a full-time working dad for six months of my wife's maternity leave, but that wasn't a problem at all. A few working days into a completely new role, and it was made clear that my decision on childcare arrangements somehow implied that I no longer cared about my work.

Kelland's research drew out a clear message from several of the managers: "think the child, think mum". Part-time working dads were asked where their baby's mother was, in a challenge to why she wasn't taking on her duties and why he wasn't living up to his. These dads also report a loss of status in the workplace, and a drop in confidence. The revealing finding was that, whilst many of these stigmas came explicitly from managers and co-workers, when they didn't, responsible dads reported them in more subtle reactions in the workplace to their childcare choices, feeling they were being viewed with more suspicion and a sense that they no longer had the 'ambition' that they had before.

One study asked groups of managers about prospective applicants to a part-time job. They were shown equally qualified parents of both sexes. The women seeking part-time work were greeted with the belief that their kids were their natural priority, so working part-time made sense: "I like the idea that she's recognised herself that she wants to get her home-work-life balance."

Dads in the same position were treated with suspicion: "I wonder why he's applying for a part-time job... I just wonder", or "I just think, lazy bastard. He's obviously up to the job, but is he a high flyer?"[124] An HR manager with thirty years of experience backed up these stigmas, explaining that dads opting for part-time work would experience "a lot of piss-taking, like being told that their wives 'ruled the roost' or that 'she wears the trousers'", especially when childcare is involved.

And there it is, the babysitting handicap manifesting itself in the workplace: the mum is balancing her responsibilities, the dad is shirking his workplace duties so he can free up some babysitting time off. Childcare is not 'meant' to be his thing.

Mums working full-time reported comments asking what their partner was up to that could have forced her back to work 'so early': "why isn't he providing?" Given how strongly and from such a young age it's drilled into men that they are meant to provide for their families, this can sting and make many dads feel inadequate.

A study by Opinion Matters of over 1000 dads showed that around half of them want to reduce their hours to spend more time with their kids, in line with what we'd expect from the paternity gap. But seven in ten believe there is a social stigma attached to dads working more flexibly and improving their work-life balance, with a quarter worrying that such a move would have a damaging impact on their longer-term career plans. It would be difficult to argue that this stigma does not have an impact on keeping the paternity gap wide open[125].

Other studies report that fathers who move to or even request more flexible working arrangements receive comments about whether they're prioritising their work any longer, and their commitment to the job is questioned. Co-workers frequently voice frustration that a part-time father is not in the office for the full week, because such a practice challenges their normal expectations of a father's role[126].

Out of all parents, twice as many believe that flexibly working dads are seen as less committed than flexibly working mums, and twice as many believe working flexibly will have a more negative impact on a dad's career than a mum's[127]. Of course, it's bad for both parents, but perceptions around what dads should be doing is playing to their fears and helping explain why they're more cautious about getting more involved in parenting.

The extent of these workplace barriers varies significantly across sectors. Studies have shown that the problems faced by Justin can get predictably worse in male-dominated workplaces, with fewer options for flexible working being offered[128]. Jeremy Davies of the Fatherhood Institute explains that there is a macho-culture in many male-dominated professions that says commitment to a company has to be shown by staying later and not getting 'bogged down' by your life outside of work. "Men in these sectors say that showing a 'softer' side and wanting to take on traditionally more female tasks such as childcare doesn't go down well."

Out of those dads that do request flexible working arrangements, like Justin, twice as many are turned down compared to mums[129]. To top it off, those dads that decide to challenge their employer rejecting their request for flexible working face stricter criteria for having their appeal accepted than mums[130].

Mums facing discrimination for their flexible working requests can argue that they are being discriminated against indirectly because such a refusal "particularly disadvantages women, as they're more likely than men to care for their children"[131]. All they need to show is that it's a problem personally because they can't find alternative childcare for their kids.

Dads on the other hand need to prove direct discrimination, which is much harder, and they need to show that a mother in the same role doing the same work was given a better deal. The fact that they may need and want to look after their kids rather than their partner don't feature as relevant, nor does the fact that they can't find alternative childcare.

This is discrimination against dads, but also against mums, who, at the other end of their partner having his flexible working request rejected, then needs to cut down her working hours to fall in line with what other people are expecting them to do.

The reason given for men having worse grounds for requesting flexible working arrangements is women are "more likely to do childcare". This is quite simply a self-fulfilling prophecy, and has no good justification.

And while employers and co-workers are more accepting of women taking on flexible working arrangements, they tend to lower what they expect from women who become mums, limiting their career prospects and their salaries. For the sake of all parents, and indeed anyone who wants to sensibly improve their work-life balance, this situation needs to be improved.

19

WORKING DADS 2

WORRIES ABOUT WORK AND WAYS FORWARD

One strong message to come back from all the dads in our interviews was that, regardless of how others reacted in the workplace, there is a deep expectation on ourselves of what we should be doing. Max, who took five weeks of parental leave alongside his wife Sarah for their second son explains that "as a man you're under more pressure, possibly self-imposed, in the workplace to prove that work comes first. You're more wary about how you're perceived.

> "I'd feel like I was taking advantage if I took more leave than I did... It'd feel wrong if I wasn't pursuing my career as best as I could. I already felt guilty about taking the parental leave that I did because it's nice for the family, so I feel guilty about taking advantage of my employer's generosity."

Max's wife, Sarah, adds, "I'd never feel like that. I want my career to progress, but I would never feel guilty if I have to take time off to look after my kids. It's just what I need to do. For mothers, it's a well-trodden path, and we know that people just expect it more from us and understand that family has to come first." Max adds, "for dads it just doesn't feel the same yet".

Simon, author of the Real Fatherhood blog, who prepared for parental leave for his second child but later turned it down, explains this angst and feeling of guilt about taking time off to look after his own child. "It's having a deeply ingrained need to work and earn the money. When I had kids, that feeling, that need to be even more present in the workplace got stronger because now I was providing for my family. I know that I need to try to do the best I can in my career because that's what men do, especially if they've got dependents. It's very difficult to take a step back from that."

Simon's company, working in the property sector, tried to promote shared parental leave with workplace seminars for new dads and dads-to-be. "Most of the dads that took part showed a lot of enthusiasm for shared parental leave, and really wanted to do it. But when it came to it, only one of us actually took it in the end… And he was a Swede. They have a completely different attitude there. The guy even said that he didn't really care about what other people thought, which I'd say is pretty unusual. Since him, eight dads have had kids, and none of them have taken the leave."

Despite backing down from taking shared parental leave, Simon did manage to change his working hours and take a more equal responsibility for looking after his kids when his wife went back to work. "Leaving early to pick up sick kids from work feels difficult the first times you do it as a guy. Superficially, people seem fine if I do it. But you don't really know what they're thinking, and I've heard people talking about other guys who have left work early some days for whatever reason and I worry that they might think the same about me."

For Simon and Max, their sense of self, like many dads, means that they need to come across as fully committed workers, as people who work hard and are there to get on with the job. These are admirable traits, but there's an underlying belief that doing more on the childcare front can cost them here; that they should feel guilty for not staying late or leaving before five, or needing to pull out of a meeting because their kid needs to be picked up early from school; that they are abusing their company's generosity if they take 'too much' parental leave or ask for flexible working. And these are guys who despite this are taking a bigger responsibility for their kids' upbringing.

When parents were asked who would find it "easier to leave work if there is a childcare issue", twice as many dads are likely to say their partner. So, at the very least, dads feel that they face stronger pressures than their baby-mums to stay stuck to the office or workshop. But mums were nearly three times more likely to say that they would find it easier to leave work for childcare reasons than their baby-dads[132].

There is no obvious reason why it would in fact be different for companies if a woman or man had to leave at short notice, but many parents seem to think that employers will be more understanding towards mums. Coupled with half of dads not feeling confident that they could raise the issue of reducing hours or working flexibly, this suggests that workplace expectations on dads may be ruling out options for childcare responsibility before they've even been properly voiced in the workplace.

For the new dad with the financial option to take a day off work, or share emergency childcare cover with his partner, he has a lot to consider. His employer is expecting him to work harder, and, importantly, put his job and work commitments first. His partner is facing the opposite expectations, given hints that she'll be less committed now because she's got a kid to look after.

When a dad goes against these expectations by opting to work part-time for family reasons, he comes across confusion in the workplace, and more than a little resistance. Out of the dads that go against these pressures, nearly three-quarters believe that there is a serious stigma attached to men working part-time for family reasons, with half believing they were seen as the 'weaker' partner because they were taking a more active role in childcare, and playing a smaller role in bringing home the bacon[133].

For men who are brought up to feel that these sort of stigmas challenge their masculinity and make them seem less in the eyes of others, these are not good things. For men who want to play that bigger role as dads, these are barriers that are pushing back and stopping them from making the choices that are best for them and their family. Workplace expectations on parents put mums between a rock and a hard place, and pull dads away from their kids.

Practical steps for part-time parents

The evidence is mounting that shorter working weeks or shorter working hours increase productivity at work. And it seems pretty clear that if people feel they have a better work-life balance with their family, they're going to be happy and more committed workers over the long term.

But the truth is that, for many parents, the option to go part-time at work or even share childcare days during the week with their partner isn't there, or it comes with significant costs. If women don't want to stay out of the workplace for too long, or want to come back for four days a week rather than three, or want to come back full-time when their leave is up, then we need dads to be able to share their turn in parental responsibility.

If parents feel that they should only have their baby in nursery for three days a week, it should be possible for them each to move to four-day working weeks, rather than expecting or requiring the mother to give up both days. The current rules on allowing part-time working for both parents are not overwhelming. Employees have the 'right to request' new working arrangements. But in practice employers can dream up almost any reason to reject this and dress it up as harmful to their business.

More importantly though, if your boss turns you down and it's not clear how an appeal would play out, most people are very unlikely to push. Dads are likely to get the brunt of this, especially when employers still hold the view that the man should be finding a woman to pick up the childcare duties instead.

Leo and Ivy both work in retail, both in the head offices of two well-known high street companies. After Ivy went back to work following twelve months on maternity leave looking after their baby Abie, Ivy discussed coming back for four days a week with her employer so she could have one day a week to look after Abie on her own. Leo wanted to go for the same option, so Abie would only have three days a week at nursery.

Leo explains, "I felt I missed out a lot with Abie during the week in the first year, and I know she still liked me, but she's a mummy's girl… She never goes to me when she's upset, and even if we're playing, if Ivy comes near she wants to go to her instead… We agreed it was probably because I didn't have enough alone time with Abie, so I really wanted to have that day a week. But when my director turned it down, I didn't really know what to do.

> "They said it was because my job needed five full days a week, and it couldn't be justified on 'business grounds', whatever that meant." Ivy jumps in, "It was so stupid because my company is smaller than his and we do roughly the same sort of work. They just made it work for me and it was never a real problem. Leo's managers just couldn't be bothered to even try."

Asked whether they considered appealing the decision, Leo continues, "but I really like the people I work with and I enjoy what I do. I already felt bad enough about asking for the four days a week. I would have just have pissed everyone off and probably not got anywhere anyway." Leo didn't appeal the decision and continues on five days a week.

These barriers to flexible working are bad for mums too. But at the moment it looks marginally worse for dads, because, not only do they have to overcome the outdated views of a lot of employers on flexible working, but they also come up against the expectations from their bosses and co-workers that they, as men, shouldn't be working part-time. The law in this instance doesn't offer adequate protection.

In Sweden, by stark contrast, both parents returning to work are entitled to reduce their working hours by up to a quarter. Dads are two to three times more likely to work part-time compared to in the UK, and women are more likely to be working.

Has this brought Swedish companies to their knees? No, Sweden is still one of the world's most creative and successful economies per capita in the world. With lower working hours leading to a rise in productivity[134], one might argue this is *because* of its pro-family work and equal parenting laws, not in spite of them.

This law opens up more real possibilities for Swedish families around how they can choose to arrange childcare after the first year. It lets more dads take a bigger responsibility in their toddlers' and kids' early lives, and it allows mums to return to work when they want to, on terms that work for them and their families. There's no obvious reason why we couldn't have a similar law in the UK.

Government support and advice is crucial to allowing change, especially for smaller companies who are scared or ill-informed about how to allow and support part-time working. A government agency or charity could fill the need for these companies to be able to answer questions around part-time working, whether it's showing Leo's boss how easy it would be to allow him to work flexibly, or provide parents with the support to put forward strong cases for part-time working.

Working Families has promoted the idea of 'flexibility champions' in business, leading the way for other companies and managers to adopt better, more family-friendly policies. This is a great idea, and should ensure men are targeted to drive uptake across both sexes[135].

We are subjected to nearly every type of training in the modern workplace, from 'management skills' to 'stakeholder relations' to 'constructive communication' and 'assertiveness'. Would it hurt to have a discussion about how we treat flexible workers as part of that? We need to start changing attitudes in the workplace, and the only way to do that is to start people at work talking about these issues, and having their eyes opened to how important it can be for parents, including dads, to have flexible working arrangements.

Finally, it's up to us dads who can and want to work part-time to try to do it, despite the pressures. This is not always possible, and there are costs. But if more dads start pushing for fairer treatment as they take on more childcare responsibilities, workplace ideas about the role of Dad in the family will start to change. The best we can do is push for that change.

20

THE DUMB AND HOPELESS DAD

The moment we leave the office, it would be nice to feel we could leave these babysitting handicaps behind. To get some perspective on the fact that men can also be responsible parents on their own. There are some signs that dads are becoming more recognised as parents in how they're talked about and treated. But the underlying cultural assumptions about what kind of parents dads are broadly still stick to a couple of crude stereotypes. Dad is meant to be the strict parent or the irresponsible and silly one (the Homer Simpson type). Both are capable of earning, incapable of running day to day family life, and certainly not to be relied on to look after the kids.

Imagine a TV show that started out with a woman who didn't know how to tie her own shoelaces, always failed at her job, snuck to the pub after work to get pissed with her mates rather than heading home to her family. Her husband then steps in at the last minute in each episode. Level-headed, calm, patient, and sober, he makes sure she does the right thing and that the family isn't ruined, and the kids are alright. The reasonable dad, the crazy and daft mum. Maybe an interesting new take on parenting?

What if someone else then makes another programme with the same dynamic: another daft woman and sensible man. Then another, and another. Throw in some cartoons and books aimed at kids along with it. Then start looking for examples of these roles reversed in TV, and realise you can't find any. Is TV being sexist?

"Well, it's 1 am. Better go home and spend some quality time with the kids"

"The key to parenting is don't overthink it. Because overthinking leads to ... what were we talking about?"

"Lisa, come back before everyone finds out what a horrible father I am!"

Homer Simpson

The Simpsons can be hilarious. In 2011, it was declared the biggest US influence on UK culture[136]. There are few people in the country that haven't watched at least one episode. While the whole family play their part, Homer is probably the biggest star, and regarded as one of the funniest characters to appear on our screens. Despite trying and mostly getting away with it, he's an incompetent worker, unreliable friend and husband, and a pretty dumb parent. It's what makes him funny. But is he funny because he's a useless dad?

On his own we could just claim that it's not Homer being a dad that makes him a funny idiot, it's just Homer. He just happens to be a dad, alongside being a bumbling moron. Marge is not playing the role of the sensible, responsible, and relatively dull mum, she's just 'being Marge'. Maybe the writers could have equally switched the roles round when they started the cartoon.

But then we get *Family Guy*. Ok, Peter Griffin is more morally depraved than Homer, and Lois has a bit more grit than Marge. But the story is more or less the same. You could point out that *Family Guy* just follows in *The Simpsons'* footsteps, really. Then let's look at Jim Royle from *The Royle Family* to Frank Gallagher from *Shameless*; Phil Dumphy from *Modern Family* to Tim Taylor from *Home Improvement*. The list goes on. A pattern is becoming clear on how dads are shown on TV: they're irresponsible idiots. That's the best way to laugh at them. Is TV being sexist?

It looks like, from Fred Flintstone onwards, TV has stumbled across a stereotype of dumb dads that we can't get enough of. It's a comical combination that pokes fun at a group of people that normally comes out top in most things. The message is clear – dads are best when they're stupid.

But why should we care? A study in 2016 showed that blokes tend to watch more TV than women, and, what's more, they tend to view TV as a more realistic insight into how people work. Expectant and first-time dads are especially open to picking up ideas of how they should behave, what's considered normal, and what people will expect from them, when they're watching TV[137]. This ties in well with the research into how we pick up what society expects of us, and how this plays into the confirmation bias discussed at the end of Part II[138].

The study into dads on TV explains that blokes are being under-prepared for their role as dads. We're being told by TV shows that it's not just acceptable for dads to be the idiot in the house, or the 'extra kid' for the mum to take care of, it's expected. This doesn't (necessarily) prompt new dads to start eating more doughnuts, but it does limit what we find acceptable to do as parents, and it does make the 'easier', if less rewarding, option of being the back-up and unreliable parent the default. And, worst of all, it makes us believe it's normal for dads to be unreliable at the parenting thing, as if it was never meant to be our place to be responsible for the kids.

It fuels the idea that us dads are clueless when it comes to parenting, which kicks off the feedback loop. We pick up these images of a useless dad, and not only do people expect that sort of behaviour from us, we more often than not find it easier to slip into this sort of behaviour ourselves, even if we'd planned and hoped to be more involved dads.

But honestly, parental humour can be hilarious. The well-known 'Safe Baby Handling Tips' cartoons for instance can make most of us chuckle[139]. Where these cartoons seem to be starting to get it right is that, whilst they show dads doing daft things with their babies, they also show mums doing the same.

Examples of 'Safe Baby Handling Tips' cartoons by David and Kelly Sopp[140]

A dad thinking he can carry his baby in his rucksack isn't making dads think less of themselves when it's next to a picture of a mum thinking she should wash her baby with a garden hose. The real problem is that, almost everywhere outside this cartoon, the dad is the stupid one *because he's the dad*, and the mum is the responsible parent. Some more responsible dads and a few more daft mums would go a long way to evening this out.

Kevin: a new dawn?

Recently we have seen a stay-at-home dad appear as a main character on a popular BBC2 TV series. And he's not a terrible parent. With two million views for the pilot episode, *Motherland* was made into a full TV series in 2017. By any standard it has been a hit, from healthy viewing figures to perhaps the more important standard of being talked about at the school gates by parents who get it.

It hilariously homes in on the insecurities and difficulties of modern parenting. I took my son to a kids' party featuring an animal act as the entertainment shortly after watching the series, and waited for the performer to produce nothing but cats, as happens in one episode. I was to be disappointed. (Though not that disappointed – the party did feature a lizard in a party hat. Really.)

The show's success rests on being brilliantly modern – focusing on characters and scenarios missing from previous or mainstream depictions of family. Including a stay-at-home dad. Unfortunately, just like so many shows that have gone before, Kevin the full-time dad is an idiot. Just an idiot of a different sort.

Unlike the lead mums in the show, he's a socially inept prat. Not someone any viewer wants to identify or even be associated with. As a dad, after watching an episode you don't just come away thinking, "I don't want to be like that guy", you come away wanting to make sure that other people who may also have seen it don't think of you as being like that guy. And, since his defining feature is that he's a stay-at-home dad whose wife works full-time, this isn't great.

This wouldn't be an issue if there were a couple of stay-at-home dads with working wives in the show, or even more broadly on TV, and he was just the odd one out. But he is, as far as we can find, the only main character on a popular TV show in the UK playing a straight stay-at-home dad. It's a funny show to watch, but it's the lead mums who can't really be arsed with keeping up the perfect-mum pretences that we're meant to empathise with. Not the loser bloke who decided that being a full-time dad was what he wanted to do.

Of course the show's aimed at women, and the very title shows how far we have to go. *Motherland* remains a foreign country to dads and Kevin is very much an innocent abroad. To be honest, we'd be angrier about it if it wasn't actually funny. But at the risk of appearing po-faced there is a serious side to a show like this.

When we consider the impact that images of dads on TV have on parents, and dads especially, Kevin is holding back the cause of sharing parenting, and nudging dads away from taking on childcare responsibilities. Better to be hands-off and leave the baby stuff to mum than be associated with Kevin.

Hopeless dad

On *Mumsnet*, a post entitled *Dads, why are they so hopeless?* opens with "I would be interested in other people's views as to why dad parenting methods so often wind me and our son up!" followed by some story about a pretty innocuous parenting disagreement. "WHY DOES HE DO THIS?"[141].

Most mums don't view or treat their partners like they're completely incompetent. And many of those that do may well have incompetent partners. The danger comes when people start making generalisations.

If a mum puts the wrong sized nappy on her baby, people will probably laugh it off and forget about it, not announce that "mums, they really are hopeless". If a dad picks his kid up on time from school, he might get a little praise for "being a great dad". This may be true, but the fact that people need to praise him means they're not expecting it.

If the same dad feeds their toddler twenty minutes late, which results in an over-hungry meltdown, the dad is fulfilling the expectation that "dads are hopeless" and might prompt a few words about how he's a "typical dad" due to the slip-up. Because the idea of a typical dad isn't just the dumb dad, it's also that he's incompetent *as a parent*.

Dads might often do things differently compared to the mum when looking after their kids, but if they've had the same amount of time looking after their tot, rarely would they ever do them worse.

It's normal to see dads as incompetent parents, as parents who don't know how to change nappies or how to be fully involved and responsible for bringing up their kids. What's more, people don't prop up the idea that dads are incompetent as parents because they think that a few dads have never had the chance to properly get involved with childcare. They prop it up and repeat it because they believe that it's somehow innate that dads won't know how to look after their kids properly. Because they think looking after kids is somehow innately a woman's thing.

21

SUPPORT AND BABY BRANDS

IT'S A MUM'S WORLD

Schedule 1: for a formula-feeding stay-at-home mum
Schedule 2: a formula-feeding working mum
Schedule 3: a breastfeeding stay-at-home mum
Schedule 4: a breastfeeding working mum
Schedule 5: a formula and breastfeeding part-time working mum

> *Advice on feeding your baby when they're around a year old, from BabyCenter.com*

So dads don't feed their babies?

Baby advice

The number of questions you have when your first baby arrives is endless. As they get bigger, the questions just keep on coming: what's the best way to feed? how do I stop her from biting? why won't he sleep? how do I stop her from throwing herself into every sharp corner that appears? should he be able to add up now? where are these tantrums coming from?

Of course, the internet has all the answers. No, they're not all the right answers, and most of them will contradict each other. But they do give you a lot of ideas on what to do. There are also plenty of books, professionals, and courses available if you need them. But they are only aimed at you if you're female.

Nearly all millennial parents find the internet an essential resource for parenting, with 97% of mums seeing it as a maternal lifeline. Who wouldn't? Within seconds of discovering the latest parenting road-block, you can bring up the advice for how to tackle it from professionals and a few hundred (some a little crazy) parents. The internet is now an essential resource for explaining and understanding what parenthood is.

With the rise of dads wanting to take more responsibility, 93% of millennial fathers also find the internet an essential resource to help them parent[142]. At the moment though, they're not navigating a world aimed at them.

You know that feeling you get when you realised you've walked into the wrong toilet in the pub or at a coffee shop. For blokes, this feeling is a mixture of guilt for not wanting to seem a pervert, and the realisation that women's toilets smell a lot nicer than the blokes'. There is a sense that this place really isn't for you.

Dads looking for childcare advice enter a distinctly mum-focused world. At nearly every corner they turn, they're reminded that they're just 'helping out' the intended recipient of the advice. We're given signals that this is really a woman's job. Most dads will persevere anyway, if simply because they need to find that magic solution to stop the kids waking up at 4 o'clock on the weekend.

But there is the distinct impression that we're encroaching on a territory that isn't really meant for us, and when it comes to making choices about how childcare is split and who's *really* responsible for the little ones, these impressions will have a big impact. They help limit what people expect of dads and what dads expect of themselves.

Interestingly, while mums are far more likely to rely on established parenting advice websites and chat forums with other mums, dads are much more likely to use *YouTube*, with 86% of millennial dads turning to the online streaming giant for videos on how to make baby-mush or assemble the pushchair[143]. That might get a little concerning when the NHS wants to give the latest advice in babycare but forgot to make it appeal to dads, so dads opt for some dodgy advice from the *Dad Fails YouTube* channel.

Research has shown that parenting guides and parenting magazines have started to show more dads in recent years. But not only do mums still dominate, they are also the main target audience for this advice and support. When dads appear, they are often cast in a secondary not integral role, as we might expect, only there to provide support. As responsible and involved dads, we get turned off looking for support and advice in these magazines, and we're not alone.

Working Families has found that, in the workplace, replacing the word 'mother' with 'parent' doesn't suddenly switch dads on. Networks for support and policies aimed at improving work-life balance, or making life easier for parents are read by most employees as being aimed at mums. Often with good reason. I attended a workplace seminar to promote parental leave after I'd taken it. The room had seven women and one other bloke. Where were all the expectant fathers? They probably weren't members of the 'Women's Network' that HR had used to organise the event.

Ben, one of the dads we spoke to who took three months of parental leave from his apparently cutting-edge media firm, explained that, while he has nothing but praise for the way his company handled his pioneering parental leave request, there was one thing that irked him. "They started this group called super-mums and sent this email round the entire company on which the last point said 'Don't worry dads, we haven't forgotten about you too!'. And I sent an email back saying 'You've got ten points in this email, nine about mums and only one about dads saying we haven't forgotten about you so you clearly have!

> "Then they called me in for a meeting and I said 'I'm not trying to be a dick about this but if you want to make this a normalised thing for mums and dads you can't be running a group called super-mums. Do you not understand how you're entrenching the notion that the mother, the females in your company, are the caregivers and they should be given special treatment?'"

If a young woman was looking at which company to start her career in, and one of the choices only ever showed men in their recruitment material, what sort of signal would this give her? Part of the reason we want more successful women and ethnic minorities to promote their success is because people look for signals about what sort of options are available to them: what sort of paths have people like them trodden? When we see no-one like us being successful in an area of life, we are simply less likely to think we will be successful in it[144].

Positive images of people like us doing things we want to do change other people's expectations on us, and improve our expectations of ourselves. Being a dad is no different. Research on changing ideas about fatherhood argued that dads respond to advice that is focused at them[145]. Expectations are changed, and they feel that this is not just a 'woman's world' but something they can and should be interested in.

This bias of excluding dads extends to the public sector, where we'd hope they'd know better. My wife was contacted about our kid having his two-year check-up where a health visitor comes to your house and makes sure your toddler is able to stack bricks. If you're struggling, that's an opportunity for you to ask for help and see what services there are in your area to help out. I rang them back and gave them my number (which they already had) to call. They ignored it and rang my wife again. When they did get through to her she told them to either call me, the dad, or bugger off because she was busy. They decided that rather than make the otherworldly leap of ringing a dad, they would just give up. We never did get the two-year check-up.

Jeremy Davis at the Fatherhood Institute knows this problem well. "Before we ask them to think about it, many of the support service staff have a fairly ham-fisted view of men. They see them as someone who isn't around, who doesn't really matter to their real client, the mum, and doesn't need to or want to be involved in parenthood. In a very small number of cases that may be true, but in most cases, it just isn't. Dads want to be involved, they're often just waiting, just as mums do, for someone to come and offer support. They're often waiting to be included.

> "A lot of what we do is to ask support services [from child groups to health advisors] to reflect on what they think Dad's role is. You'd be amazed at the stereotypical arguments about the biological limitations of men that some of them come back with at first. It's all that pop science Men are From Mars nonsense that's caused the problems there... But it's also surprising just how effective getting people to reflect is, when you show them the evidence about how important it is to involve Dad. Their client isn't really the mum in most cases, it's the baby or the kid. To do that well you need to reach out to the dads as well."

Baby brands and advertising

Propping this up and looking back to the pre-internet days, parenting brands are still largely keeping Dad out. Nearly all baby and toddler products are aimed at mums: Mumsnet, Netmums, Mum-to-Mum bibs, Mum2MumMarket.co.uk, Mum and Baby Online, from Mothercare to JoJo Maman Bebe, to name just a few. Mum-to-Mum bibs sell at Waitrose, and the company behind them claim that "like most mums we'd had to deal with dribbly babies, reflux, eczema… you name it. So we were inspired to create practical, stylish products that really do work… They work for mums like you"[146].

We don't want to give the idea that Ben the media professional who went off on one about his firm's 'super-mums' group is an angry man, but something he told us speaks to this point too. "I remember going into Mothercare with my daughter when I was on parental leave to buy her clothes and thinking 'How has this happened, what the fuck is that about, how has this shop been allowed to be called Mothercare?' Mother. Care. Parentcare would be a stupid name, true, but what about Babycare? I just remember thinking 'Am I not allowed to be in here then?'"

Looking for baby products on some well-known brand websites, you'll find plenty of pictures of kids and toddlers playing and carried by their mums, but few or no pictures of dads. This is not a one-sided debate, with some companies starting to add a few dads to their branding too, but there are enough mum-only adverts like this to make it an issue. On many adverts there's a token dad standing behind the mum letting her do her parenting thing. These adverts aren't aimed at dads, nor are they aimed at parents in general. They're aimed at mums alone. It's why dads in ads get a supporting or comic role. Playing on the idiot dad is still popular when promoting stuff for both mums and kids.

Showing a disappointing result, reminding us that things don't only go forward, an analysis of *Good Housekeeping* magazine showed that around the year 2000, dads started to change their role, from breadwinner to bumbling fun daddy. But from 2010 onwards, when we'd hope to see a stronger role for dads being shown, dads stop appearing altogether[147].

The problem is that these advertisers aren't looking deep enough. They're seeing what people end up doing and make the mistake that everyone thinks that's the best way of doing it without asking why. They say things like "mums are the ones who buy all the stuff for their toddlers, so of course we should be targeting only women". They don't think about offering other options for how things can work. In fact, traditional advertisers are pretty bad at predicting what even mums want out of adverts, with as few as 12% of mums saying advertisers were getting their preferences right and understanding what parents want to see in adverts[148].

Good ads work because they stand up. Challenging stereotypes can do that. And there are some companies that are trying to offer a more balanced look at the parenting experience. *Mamas & Papas* made the no-brainer move of appealing to both parents in their brand name. Steeped in Scandi values, the iconic *Baby Björn* carrier is shown with both dads and mums carrying the little ones. It's noteworthy that, despite advertising to both parents, these avant garde advertisers are most known for their images of dads carrying the baby. That's what's made them stand out and appeal not just to dads, but to both parents.

Others will be forced to change their ways. In 2017 the Advertising Standards Agency announced plans to ban gender stereotypes from adverts. That includes parents. One of the examples cited was a stressed-out mum assumed to have responsibility for the washing and for getting tea on the table. The new rules and complaints procedure will take time to bed in, and it remains to be seen how robust the ASA will be in enforcing the guidelines. We suspect advertisers will wriggle away from sanctions but they will have to bear gender stereotypes in mind when putting together pitches and campaigns. That's a step forward.

Dinosaurs may grumble about the imposition of political correctness. In fact the regulator will be doing them a favour because focusing on out-of-date stereotypes seems to be a mistake for advertisers.

The internet

You might hope that the brave new world of the internet (we're quite old, the internet is still new to us) would be more egalitarian. It's not. Straight out of the blocks as broadband spread was *Mumsnet*. Plenty of idiots have gone too far in harassing *Mumsnet*, the popular parenting advice platform, for its name. But the *Mumsnet* brand and much of the content on the website is focused just at mums, which only helps to reinforce the idea, for dads as well as mums, that advice should be aimed only at women.

The response from *Mumsnet* was reluctant and superficial. They opened a discussion group called Dadsnet. The site tries to use the word 'parent' in its articles more, but the word switches back and forth with 'Mummy', hinting that even the word parent is just being aimed at one sex.

There are signs that other brands and advice sites are picking up on the trend. But they often think, like *Mumsnet*, that a superficial change will fix the problem. These sites will often focus on how they know what Mum needs, thinking they've ticked the equal parenting box by saying 'parent' instead of mum, or using lines like: "being a parent is the most rewarding experience imaginable [so]… join our Mother and Baby club for exclusive offers". Certainly not inclusive offers then.

One advice site called JustParents sets out to challenge traditional roles with its name. But then starts with "Welcome to motherhood" followed by lots of lovely pics of mums holding their babies, and one lonely dad frowning at his toddler under an article entitled "Disciplining your children".

When dads are brought up, separate from the 'parent' the authors are talking to, he's spoken about in the third person, as someone you should make feel more comfortable with the whole parenting thing you're doing. Maybe even let him have a go now and again.

It puts parenting across as something just for women, and as something that women have to feel innately fully responsible for.

A more successful example is the change of *Amazon Mums* to *Amazon Family*. Prior to the end of 2015, the online retail giant had a membership deal targeting parents. Well, half of parents anyway. The site featured plenty of pics of babies and kids being held by adoring mums. Following campaign pressure from dads groups, the company made the bold move of changing the brand to fully include dads.

They went further than *Mumsnet*, who treated dads like a back-up parent by adding a small empty page that says "if dads really insist on being like mums, then they can click this link if it makes them feel better whilst the rest of us real parents get on with the mum stuff". They changed the brand to *Amazon Family*, changed all references from mums to parents, and made sure that the pictures showed dads parenting as well. Much more in line with what parents expect in the twenty-first century. And they didn't do it out of some sort of philanthropy or on a whim of equality. Amazon makes kjillions of money; if sticking with *Mums* would make them more they'd do it. But they switched to *Family*.

This sort of change is harder, and possibly even more important, when it comes to baby advice sites, which still predominantly focus on women. There are a few sites that have tried to buck the trend by focussing just on dads. The *Dad Network* focusses on dads' experiences and tries to build and 'big-up' a father's role in parenthood, whilst giving dads a real forum to talk about looking after kids and not feel like they're invading on Mum's space.

While these sites, like dad-only playgroups, are only a stepping stone to the same support for both parents, they are an important stepping stone. As recommendations from a number of civil society groups on this show, if we want parenting advice, support, and adverts to capture dads, the first step to break the babysitting handicap, has to be to aim specifically at dads[149].

However, when the belief that dads can babysit their own kids is dead, the ideal is to have one place for both parents to come for advice, and for advertisers to aim at mums and dads together. The more both parents can see that the expectations on them both are equal – that dads are also meant to look for tiny baby-socks when they run out, make sure that their little poppet has the right nappy size or warm enough clothes for the winter – the easier it will be to share parenting more equally.

22

CHANGING WHAT IT MEANS TO 'MAN UP'

We take our signals of what it means to be a guy from others around us. Against our better instinct, most of us do judge that some blokes are more or less manly than others. The bloke that plays football and then drinks beer with his mates after the match is seen as more manly than the guy in drag.

One of the worst sins for a normal guy to commit is doing something 'womanly'. When he's doing a 'woman's job', or 'getting in touch with his feminine side', he's breaking the rules. In a sense he's seen as debasing himself in a way that a woman 'doing a man's job' isn't. To be a 'womanly' man is to be soft, weak, and less than you're meant to be. Even in friendlier circles, people seeing a bloke as being feminine is rarely going to boost his social standing, and we're trained nearly from birth to think that, as boys, we shouldn't and mustn't be 'like girls'.

There is no shortage of studies showing that, whilst women can lightly ridicule guys for not conforming to the hyper-masculine stereotype, and doing things we label as feminine, men are the strictest enforcers[150]. Guys don't like other guys deviating from what they think it means to be a bloke.

Witness the backlash online against anyone who steps out of line. I posted the below on the @GenderDiary Twitter account to make a point about stereotypes. "Grow a pair" came the disgruntled reply from a chap affected by toxic masculinity.

A two-year study following boys from pre-school into school highlighted that one of the biggest drives for boys to start changing their behaviour, to be seen as more aggressive and less empathetic, was when they learnt the rigid rule that the worst thing you could do as a boy was to act like a girl[151]. Femininity, whatever things we're told that includes, is to be avoided like the lurgy. And 'being a girl' can include almost anything for kids, from fringes to jam flavours. But, given the messages we get from society, it will certainly include being nurturing.

This plays to a lot of unpleasant sexism about how 'men's roles' have a higher social status than traditional 'women's roles'. A woman wearing the trousers is moving up in the world, whereas a man working in a nursery is seen as taking a step down on the social ladder because he's doing a caring role that's invariably also low paid and low status.

Few would disagree nowadays that this subtle and often not so subtle hierarchy between men and women's roles is wrong, but it still persists, to the detriment of both sexes. Just as women should not be made to feel imposters when they become firefighters or CEOs, men should not feel their status as a man challenged when they want to become a nurse or even the full-time parent.

Putting the sexism of all this to one side, when 'being a woman' is attached to being a family carer, empathetic, and nurturing to kids, a responsible and fully involved parent, blokes who want to be more involved with their kids are faced with a real dilemma. They can either do it half-heartedly, and leave the real parenting stuff to their partner; or they'll get in there and do what's needed for their kids, but then be seen as doing a woman's job.

The choice is being the uninvolved parent, or being less manly. On the one hand childcare is a womanly thing, and on the other we can't do womanly things without being less of a man. Both of these are problems.

Childbirth is the exclusive domain of women; childcare is not. And yet some active dads are still referred to as 'Mr Mum'. Why the need? Because being a responsible parent is exclusively reserved for women; therefore, if you're being the main carer of a child, you must be 'being a mum'. The 'Mr' is helpfully added to denote the fact that this particular mum is a bloke, even if he's an effeminate one.

But there is already a male word for a responsible parent: dad. Let's just use that, and not prop up the myth that only mums can hold real responsibility for their kids. Nowhere is this emasculating 'Mr Mum' problem more acute than for stay-at-home dads.

Dads as the primary carer

John Adams, a stay-at-home dad and author of the highly successful blog *Dad Blog UK*, talks about getting comments that question his masculinity when people find out he's the primary carer of his kids with his wife in full-time work. It's difficult to see how a guy like John could come across as more masculine without going over the top, but people still see him taking on the role of primary parent and think it makes him more feminine.

Speaking to other dads in the same position as him, with a partner who's the main breadwinner in the family, he finds that he's not alone. He explains that it's "often other guys that will put on the worst pressure, referring to housework or childcare as 'woman's work'".

Jaron and Sarah wrote a piece for *The Guardian* in 2016. Sarah went back to work after seven months, and Jaron took over after responsibility for Coco. Sarah writes that a "female friend recently asked me if we were still having sex now that Jaron had been so completely emasculated. If women still have this mindset, how are we ever going to convince men to change their attitude towards shared parenting?"[152] Jaron also raises the problem of having to rely on money from his wife, something many men feel is demeaning because they're not the ones supporting themselves.

Flipping back to Kevin from *Motherland*, the sole stay-at-home dad on TV, he encompasses exactly how blokes don't want to come across. He's weak, with the occasional joke about how he doesn't drive because his 'wife does that' and that he does the cleaning in their house. Kevin is even caught trying to find ways to convince his wife to sleep with him, which apparently she's not really up for. No bloke wants to identify with a loser with no sex appeal. These are all meant to be funny because they imply that he's not being manly, which fits in comfortably with our expectations that full-time care of kids is naturally a feminine task which saps away your manliness.

Caring is not just for women

There's a consistent message running through these expectations: that caring roles are for women, and, if men do them, they are lowering themselves to the job of a woman and being less of a man as a result. On the flip side we get equally sexist comments about career successful women being masculine: "she has real balls", "she clearly wears the trousers" (yes, most people wear trousers nowadays), "as a woman you have to become a man to succeed". Let's be clear, women can be womanly and succeed, and men can be manly and make excellent carers.

When the 'manly' thing for a bloke to do is seen as earning money and making a career whilst leaving the 'womanly' job of childcare to his partner, parents who want to split parenting more equally come across a pressure, which they shouldn't have to, to fit into the traditional family roles. It is the very definition of toxic masculinity – the strict definition of masculinity forcing men to behave in ways they don't really want to, and that is toxic.

It is not more manly not to feel nurturing towards kids, just as it is not less womanly not to do so. It is simply less parental – and that's okay, because there's a sliding scale of feeling parental and anyone with kids can hurtle from one end to the other in the space of a day.

It turns out that the 'blokish bloke', the hyper-masculine guy who connects more with his drinking buddies than his family, who always finds it fun to avoid going home, who might sleep around if he can get away with it, or bottle it when he gets someone pregnant, isn't really more of a bloke. If anything, lacking those parental hormones, he's less of a bloke because of what he's missing out on.

Just flip to the front cover of this book to remember there's nothing unmanly about looking after a baby when a guy decides to own it.

A new definition of masculinity would include looking after your kids and being a good dad. It's just as manly to change your baby's nappy, cook your kid's dinner, take them to soft play or do the school run, as it is to play football or drink beer. More to the point, it's more manly to be there for your kids than to shirk your parental responsibility, like Michael Gove or the dad who hides at work or goes to the pub rather than be there for his children.

Don't be like Gove, man up and change the nappy.

Real dad, real man

So a dad could be the working but uninvolved parent, or he could be the guy who plays with the kids, but leaves the real parenting to mum, or he could be the guy who helps mum 'do her job', like a back-up parent. If he ends up caring for his own kids, he's getting in touch with his feminine side and 'playing mum for the day'. All of these ways of seeing dad have one thing in common – the mum is the primary carer and the dad is secondary, with all the connotations of that word.

Shifting away from these expectations is so unusual that it needs explaining, even by dads themselves feeling they need to justify to strangers why they are parenting and not their partner. These low expectations on dads limit what fathers can do.

These aren't expectations that dads are blissfully unaware of. On the contrary, dads know them very well. We find them in the workplace, in the family, and on the street, and they have real impacts on our lives. They factor into decision-making, and they influence a lot of dads who might want to be equal co-parents away from that choice.

But, whilst not what most people think about when they think of dads, there are dads who are sharing parenting with their partners, or even being the main carers for their kids, but who are smart, competent and fully comfortable in being a bloke. They certainly aren't 'hands-off', nor are they 'mum's assistant'.

Dads who instinctively spring into action when they hear the more serious fart sound coming from the nappy. Dads who know it's their turn to wake up in the night for their little angel (or rather little devil) at 3am. Dads who have a sense of purpose when they leave work early to do the school run, or at no notice to take their vomiting offspring home. Dads who take the initiative to replenish the endless supply shortage of tiny socks, and spend far too much time on Google finding out how to cook and puree vegetables.

These dads are not less fun than the Homer Simpson type, neither are they 'blokes with no ambition', they are not 'interfering with mum's job', and they are not 'more in touch with their feminine side'. When people make comments that deride active dads, they prop up a world that makes it more difficult for dads to choose to be a more active, tiny-sock-buying type of dad.

If people believe deep-down that mums are really responsible for changing nappies, it becomes reasonable to only put nappy-changing stations in women's toilets. It means everyone's a little shocked when a dad comes to a 'parent'/mum-and-baby group or feels a little excluded by a parental advice forum with 'mum' in the title, or an advert that says, "because Mum always knows best". And it probably makes a lot of blokes worried about asking their boss for flexible working, shared parental leave, or to change their working hours because they have a kid. That's going to stop a lot of dads who want to be the buggy-pushing, nappy-changing, *Hungry Caterpillar*-reading dad from doing what they want to do.

People need to start raising their expectations of what dads can do when it comes to parenting. And if you're not yet convinced that expectations on dads are low, and that we're not yet treating them like equal parents, then think about the other side of the same coin: the expectations we put on mums.

Part V

SPECTRE OF THE
SUPER-MUM

23

PRESSURES OF THE 'NATURAL' SUPER-MUM

We feel this overwhelming pressure to do everything. To raise the kids, keep the house clean, have dinner on the table AND be slim, attractive and fashionable at the same time... Life would be perfect, I would be Super-mum.

I feel a sense of shame. Shame at the fact that I am clearly not the type of mother I wanted or hoped to be.

Super-Mum does not exist, by Kylie Abreu, Huffington Post

The difference between the experiences of being a mum and being a dad appear huge. Obviously neither of us has ever been a mum. But we've both seen one, each working at very close quarters, from which to draw conclusions.

Some scientific differences make sense and really are natural, but these are limited to two things: breastfeeding and pregnancy. Apart from that, the important differences really only exist in the rules other people set us. The last chapter skimmed over how those rules pull dads away from parenting, but the heavier set of rules sits with the mum. Yep, society is dumping on women again.

The biggest difference about being a mum compared to being a dad is that there's no get-out clause for mums. Men can become a father, and do anything from stepping back completely to being fully involved as a parent for every step of the way. Though, as we've seen, the former is easier than the latter.

Sure, he'll be judged if he disappears, but a dad who falls out with the mum does seem to be able to buy his way out of less tangible commitments by paying child support. This type of bloke can skulk off with surprisingly little judgement from people around him. Better bog off than be a poisonous influence.

Mums don't get the cop-out card. Instead, the moment a woman gives birth, and realistically well before, everyone around her will assume that she will be there, 110% in, for the rest of the kid's life. That extra 10% is the unattainable effort she's a failure for not managing to deliver. Mums are expected to sacrifice large swathes of their happiness and comfort for their kids to get even small benefits. A mother who falls short of that standard is judged very harshly indeed.

It's only right that every child deserves someone who will always be there to love and have responsibility for them. Kids need that nurturing and protection, and every human feels the need for it. We instinctively want to protect children no matter where they're from. We send more money to the world's tragedies, famines and wars when we see the impact it's having on a suffering child. The civil war in Syria, dragging on for years, always and understandably climbs the news agenda when a new picture of an abandoned child hits the internet.

A kid's happiness will pick us up in a way that few other things can, and we know that being cared for well by someone who loves them is essential to a kid being happy. As most involved parents will tell you, this has not been an easy burden. It's a lot of pressure on just mums. If each parent put in 60% instead of just one putting in that 110%, many mums would be less at risk of burning out, and the kids would end up with *more*.

The idea that there is a 'maternal instinct' that dads don't get, something in a woman's biology, is a myth. And one we'd do better without. As we saw in Part III, in as much as we can see into what happens in the dad's brain when he gets involved in looking after the kids, it seems pretty similar to what's happening in a mum's brain.

Despite the overwhelming social expectation that there must be something biological in one sex that differentiates their parenting abilities from the other, many decades of scientific research has found nothing of any importance that suggests there is a real difference.

This explains why as a mum or a dad your whole world, its priorities, and how you can be happy start to change the more you get involved with your tiny person. It explains deep feelings of happiness when you see them laughing, and terror and lightning reflexes when you spot them running towards danger out of the corner of your eye.

These are not changes that only happen in women because of their two X-chromosomes and playing with dolls, just as they are not caused by playing with a blue toy truck when a dad was a boy, nor are they changes caused by the Y-chromosome. They are caused by an adult, woman or man, caring for an infant.

But the pressures on mums to live up to this myth of a mum-only instinct and responsibility persist. The idea that she should always be the perfect parent puts pressures on both parents that don't help anyone.

Only a mother knows best? – all parents have their limits

The stereotype is that mums always know what's best for their kids in a way dads just don't, and that this difference in understanding is instinctive. The typical mum is understood as being more tuned-in to what her baby wants and needs, and how to give it to them. This is so drilled into us that this inner know-how of childcare is seen as integral to being a woman. If a dad struggles with parenting or finds something difficult, people understand that he has limitations and like the fact that he's 'trying'. We debunked the pop science behind this in Part III on parental biology, but the impact of it persists.

There's never a shortage of someone around to offer unsolicited advice to the dads looking after their kids who don't seem fully on top of it all. But if a mum struggles in the same way, she can be made to feel that she's a failure at being a mum, and so a failure at being a woman. We know this is stating the obvious but it's still worth spelling out – women are judged in a way men are not.

Dads can struggle with their kids. There are of course many new dads who are worried about being responsible for these tiny fragile things, or are frightened of changing a nappy (yes, if you put it on wrong, you will regret it later). We must have held half a dozen babies each before our first little tots were born, but the moment you hold your own for the first time, you're struck my how helpless and flimsy they are.

There's also no one else around you to take them after a few seconds, or when they start to cry. This moment is both exciting and scary for new dads. And, whilst you can get more confident at holding them, they're still really difficult to look after. It's frightening being a first-time dad.

But it's also frightening being a mum. A rare and lucky few parents will know just what to do with their babies from the word go, others (most) will pick the parenting skills up and develop them through trial and error. Our babies may scream, wriggle and throw themselves into danger; the toddlers refuse, cause a mess or throw tantrums, until we get it right (or sometimes just cope with getting it wrong). But the process of learning to become a parent isn't hidden somewhere in the ovaries; it's something all parents have to go through, dads and mums. That's just part of parenting.

Mums are not born with the knowledge of how to care for a needy baby, a rampant toddler, or a sulky teenager. It's why second-time parents know more about what to do than they did first time around. When humans – women and men – face a new challenge, they get into it and learn how to do it from scratch and get better each time they try. Being a carer makes you a better carer.

Being fully responsible for a tiny person makes you think about what they need, it makes you more connected to their happiness, it teaches you the things you need to know about parenting, and it makes you better at doing these things. Some people learn quicker than others, but when it comes to parenting there is no evidence that this is based on sex. That's just how all humans work.

The spectre of the super-mum: parenting pressures on Mum

This idea that mums are meant to get it right first time and all the time, just to avoid being seen as a failure, manifests itself in the ever-haunting expectation that they should be the 'super-mum'. The words 'super-mum' chimed with every mother we interviewed. The spectre throws a constant shadow over you to be perfect.

The idea that this perfection is in a woman's biology makes it ever more pressing that she doesn't fail, because if she does she's failing at being feminine. Mums aren't allowed to admit that they don't feel the maternal know-how, or may even find themselves facing depression if they are struggling. These are the expectations people have on mums, and they're heavy and often unfair.

Chloe, mother to two-year-old Josh, explains, "With motherhood, you're sort of just told what it's meant to be and that's it. You're not really allowed to change that without a penalty. There are always people who are going to judge you and make you feel bad for whatever you do. People expect you to be this perfect stay-at-home mum and expect you to spend all the time you have with your kids. They expect you to be this super-mum, this parent who does everything so easily and perfectly for her kids. But you can't because in reality it's a lot harder than that, and you have to feel guilty for whatever you do because it's never living up to that mum that everyone's expecting you to be."

The belief in the 'super-mum' runs deep: that you should be someone who knows how to deal with every parenting problem, who makes every possible sacrifice for even the slightest advantage for their kids, and who does this all gladly without showing any sign of struggle.

Kylie Abreu wrote a piece on her Confidently Kylie blog that got picked up and given a wider audience by the *Huffington Post* crying out against this pressure and the impact it can have on many mothers: "I feel a sense of shame. Shame at the fact that I am clearly not the type of mother I wanted or hoped to be. I am tired, I am a mess and the never ending pile of things to do is overwhelming… I had a plan on how I wanted to raise my son. I would breastfeed until he was one year old, I would feed him all homemade, organic food. I would be attentive and loving, I would be organised, and on top of the washing and household chores, the house would be spotless. I would bake and all of our meals would be planned and home cooked from scratch. I would… continue to nurture my relationship and my career. Life would be perfect, I would be Super-mum.

> "However that idea quickly came crashing down, I sit here now in my yoga pants and oversized jumper looking at the piles of dishes that I need to clean and the piles of washing yet to be put on and I can't help but feel like a failure. What went wrong? I was supposed to be super-mum but right now there is nothing super about me. I

look at my son and cannot help but feel sorry, sorry that I am not as perfect as I wanted to be. Sorry that you cannot wear your favourite jumper today because mummy hasn't washed it yet, sorry that I have to give you a food pouch because we ran out of homemade meals and I don't have time to cook some right now…

"… As I speak to other mums, I realise that we all feel this way. We all feel this overwhelming pressure to do everything. To raise the kids, keep the house clean, have dinner on the table AND be slim, attractive and fashionable at the same time. Society expects us to be real life Stepford wives. It is expected that since you are not 'working' you must make up for it. Raising and looking after your kid is not enough, you must show and prove that you are not just sitting on your ass all day (as if that were actually possible), you must make an effort otherwise your husband will stray and you will be put in the bad mum pile to be judged at the school gate. Hell No!" [153]

Kylie and Chloe are far from being alone. A 2015 survey of mums of under-eights found that three in five mums feel that motherhood is too competitive, with pressure to outperform the same people (other mums) who they often rely on for emotional support. Three-quarters argued that they felt it was important to be that perfect mum, with many feeling they didn't match up to the traits they defined as being essential to that role[154].

Some parents are increasingly talking about these double standards for mums and dads, and asking why the bulk of the emotional pressure is on mums. The widely shared comic below by Babble illustrates the point[155].

Double standards for mum and dad: excerpt from 'Going out in public when you're a parent' cartoons by Babble.com[156]

Disconcertingly, this pressure on mums has increased over time, with fingers often being pointed at the growth of social media and its glossy images of 'perfect mothers' for mums to be compared against. But it's all too easy to point the blame at the faceless internet. The expectations people have also play a large role, even if Instagram and Facebook do amplify it.

We can get annoyed at the dad that leaves the mum with the baby and pays the child support, maybe checking in with his kid once a month or so. But we won't be outraged. A mum doing the same on the other hand, with the dad 'left holding the baby', is seen as an abomination. It's not just a little naughty, it's seen as diabolical and unnatural. That's because, at risk of sounding like a broken record, deep in our expectations on parents is the belief that the mum is the 'real' and all-sacrificing parent.

The damage these attitudes can cause is found not just at the home or at playgroup, but, most punishingly for mums who want to 'have it all', it's found in the workplace.

Working mums

The gender pay gap kicks in at around 2% for full-time employees under the age of thirty but when children enter the equation this figure suddenly leaps. According to ONS figures[157] it hits 14% for those in their forties and goes higher for workers in their fifties. And that's just the full-time figure; factor in those doing part-time work too – overwhelmingly women – and it gets worse still, hitting 18%. That means for every £1 a man earns a woman is likely taking home just 82p. The big difference between men and women around that age is that one sex is taking time away from the workplace to bring up baby.

Taking one year out of work is clearly going to have an impact on your career. In fact there's a good chance it'll get you the sack. Maternity discrimination means over 50,000 women are fired every year just for becoming a mum[158]. So just keeping a job to return to is a challenge. Get over that hurdle and return to the workplace and it's likely people will view you differently after having that time away. Taking four years out until your kids reach school age is going to set you well back in the rat race.

A lot of employers will justify overlooking mothers for promotion or salary rises simply because they're seen as the ones who might have to disappear at a moment's notice to look after a sick child or take twelve months out of the workplace to have their second child. This attitude from employers spreads to women of childbearing age, even if they don't have kids, because "it's about that time in their life".

Working flexibly for family reasons brings very different judgements for each parent. Dads face suspicions of being 'lazy', as Jasmine Kelland's research found, while mums on the other hand are praised for fulfilling what's seen as their real responsibility to their kids. However, this attitude comes loaded, with the quick acceptance that, as a mother, she can no longer be ambitious. When she opts for full-time working, she is then judged against the super-mum, with the idea that "it's her kids that need to be worried" when someone employs a mother full-time[159].

With the pay penalty of being a woman and a parent at the same time being 11% on average, compared to the pay bump of 21% received by blokes working full-time once they have children[160] (who don't push for a better work-life balance), the costs of these expectations are clear. People may not be as outraged as they are by watching an episode of *Mad Men*, but this is still sexism of a more subtle type in the workplace. It's made to look legitimate and acceptable because of people's differing expectations on men and women as parents.

Lucy and Kate, both ambitious women who enjoy the rewards of working, explain how when they got back to work after opting for nine and six months' maternity leave respectively, there was no shortage of commentary on their choices. Both were told by their co-workers that it must be 'difficult' to come back 'so early' and how many other mums in the workplace just 'wouldn't be able to manage it'. They were frequently reminded that their choice not to stay at home looking after their kids was seen as unnatural, and potentially harmful to their kids – not too explicitly, but with many little comments all poking at the underlying expectations that the super-mum places on them.

Lucy explains that this sort of pressure is cultural, and doesn't let women feel comfortable about their choices. "I feel I need to be around my kids, but I also want to do well in my career. I don't feel it's really a choice for most women because everyone expects you to stop your career and focus on your family. There's a real culture pushing you to focus only on your family and not your career."

These comments were all the more odd for Kate, whose husband Michael had taken on full-time care of their son at seven months old. "I told them that Michael was looking after his own son and that I really wasn't worried, but they still told me how 'brave' I was and that I was probably thinking about my baby all the time. It made me feel guilty that I wasn't thinking about him all the time, because I didn't feel I needed to. I was just thinking about work."

Ostensibly charitable decisions by managers also play their role. Kate explains, "My manager told me that she thought I'd be really well suited to a big new project that would be good for my career, but that she didn't think it would be sensible to put me on it because I'd only been back from maternity leave a few months. I wasn't happy, and got her to change her decision. I'm pretty sure that Michael wouldn't have been told the same thing when I was on maternity leave. I didn't think these sort of things happened in the office until I heard it myself."

Lucy also points to a sense in which the judgement she was receiving from both men and women was often a way of explaining why their choices about less equal parenting were right. "It often felt like they were trying to justify why they took two years out of work if they were mums, or if their wife took all the childcare duties if they were dads. The implication was that they didn't think I should be coming back to work so early, and that I was casting judgement on them for making my choices. But I really didn't have any judgements about what they decided to do."

The negative pressures also extend to the mums that conform to the expectations and don't come back to work 'early' or opt for flexible working arrangements from the start. Angela became a mum over two years ago. After a year on maternity leave from her law firm, she decided to reduce her working week so that she could spend every Friday with her daughter. "My manager wasn't over the moon about it but totally understood it. The problem is that now I work so late on the four days I'm in the office and on weekends, I end up working five days on the salary of four."

But worse for Angela who loves her work and sees her career as a central part of her identity, despite performing well compared to her co-workers, she was looked over for promotion. "The way my firm works, there's a fixed time each year where everyone who's been there for a certain number of years get promoted to the next level. I was there but I wasn't promoted, and my manager just couldn't justify it. He was all awkward about it, hinting that it was much more intense at the next level. Surely I'm old enough to make the decision about whether I can cope?"

Workplace expectations on dads are radically different, as we've seen. Few co-workers will look at a guy and think: "Is he a dad because then he probably won't want to face the challenge of promotion?"

As we saw in Part I, when mums take long periods out of their careers to look after their kids full-time, their connection to the world of work will obviously suffer. The parliamentary committee on Women and Equalities were told as recently as 2016 by experts that leaving the workplace for more than nine months was a bad idea if you wanted to forge a career and stay connected to the world of work.

So mums who want to get back to work, with the adult interactions and rewards it brings, are not given a free and fair choice. Comments to mums coming back from work such as "I don't know how you manage to leave your little one, you're so brave, I couldn't manage it myself" don't come across as admiring. They come across as passive aggressive, and judgemental. Why? Because too many people's image of the ideal woman is not a successful career woman, it's a super-mum.

If someone sees a kid do something wrong and they want to blame a parent, in almost every case they blame the mum. The responsibility of parenting is squarely on the shoulders of mums in many people's eyes. Just as being a stay-at-home dad or a dad on parental leave means he is 'emasculated' and 'less of a man', a mum going back to work is being 'less feminine', a bad woman, and a bad mum. We see signs of these attitudes changing. They are not the same as they were twenty years ago, but the negative expectations on mums are still very much alive.

If a mum stays at home, leaving her job to care for her kids, the super-mum shames her as being an inadequate woman and refuses to recognise that looking after kids full-time is also working and can be one of the most challenging and thankless jobs. She's failing at her maternal instinct. If she goes to work the super-mum shames her for not being an adequate mum, and refuses to recognise that she can have a career, with happy and flourishing kids too. She's denying her maternal instinct. Rock and a hard place.

Impact on mental health and sharing the load

This pressure may contribute to post-natal depression. Around one in four parents is diagnosed with PND, and the problem is almost certainly more widespread. Bridget Hargreave, who studied the issue for her book *Fine (Not Fine)*[161], told us that many of those with the condition don't get diagnosed because they write it off as baby blues or they find that just getting to the doctors to get a diagnosis can be such a struggle.

Most parents aren't too surprised by these numbers. Taking care of a baby can be a serious challenge at times. Having to do it 24/7 can place a real strain on any person, especially if the little one is ill, has colic or generally descends into a tantrum at the drop of a hat. Throw in possible breastfeeding problems (plus the shame pushed on you if breastfeeding isn't going well), and add in some terrible sleeping patterns, and even the hardiest parent is likely to feel challenged.

Even among those parents who don't dip into post-natal depression there are still plenty of parents struggling on their own for most or all of the week to look after the kids. It's a huge shock to the system when your first baby arrives. If you have more down the road, it can get tougher. Whilst you know the ropes of looking after the newborn and handling a toddler, you now have two sets of different demands to handle at the same time. The mental load is doubled.

With mums in around two-thirds of households being the sole main caregiver for the kids, the anxieties and stresses of parenting fall disproportionately hard on mums. For even in homes where childcare time is technically shared equally it's still the women picking up the bulk of the mental load – that extra work of being on top of chores, admin, and the family diary. Coupled with the pressure of needing to be the ever elusive super-mum while keeping the home together, we need to ask ourselves whether this is really the best way to do things for nearly every couple in the country.

Recently there's been a wave of books, blogs and articles fighting against these expectations on mums. From *Hurray for Gin* to *Parenting the Sh*t Out of Life*, the message is clear: we love our kids, but being a parent can be tough and it should be okay to say that and make fun of it.

It's important and right for all parents to take on this super-mum fiction. If a mum is covered in sick whilst holding a crying baby, struggling to pull a snack together for a toddler who's quickly working himself into a tantrum, at the same time as running late for a much needed meet-up, they can honestly say "this is getting a bit too much". "Good enough is good enough" is a popular parenting mantra. And yet what qualifies as "good enough" for men and women does not seem to be the same.

And this extends to all those less stressful parenting challenges too. The instincts to look after your own baby are not universal and the talent for it seems to be sprinkled among parents at random. If one mum struggles more than another mum with knowing what to do, she is no less of a woman and no less of a mum[162].

There's a flip side to all this with dads. The dad who struggles with knowing what to do is no more of a man than the dad that finds it easier. What makes both of them dads is trying their best to work out how to bring up their kids. We've heard plenty of comments, mainly from mums, that if a dad is managing more than one thing to look after their baby, they are practically "being a mum". This is unfair on dads and it's unfair on mums. This dad is just being a dad who's managing to cope with the parenting challenge well at that particular moment. No doubt coping because he's had quite a bit of practice at getting it wrong first.

In the same way that dads have to learn to get better at parenting, and don't get judged for struggling, mums also, every one of them, have to learn through trial and error, to get better at it.

The idea of some deep and mystical maternal instinct stops dads from taking their turn, whilst piling the pressure on mums to be super-mum and making things all the harder. Just like the nurturing instinct impulses we get towards our kids, the know-how to look after kids is not maternal, it's parental. The know-how is learnt, and it's learnt by all parents who get involved with parenting.

24

GATEKEEPING MUMS AND AWKWARD DADS

THE BUCK ALWAYS STOPS WITH MUM

The other week I was at Story Time at the London Docklands Museum. The kids and toddlers all sat round rapt by the enchanting puppet show… No. Some of the kids were listening, but toddlers being toddlers were also just doing their own thing. One toddler's dad was sitting on the floor near his son, waving at his little guy. The toddler stood up, bumped into a bigger kid and fell over. The tears started coming, and the dad leant forward and slowly began to pick him up to soothe him. Then, as if from nowhere, a woman knocks parent and kid alike to one side to swoop in and pull the child from his father's arms. Is this a kidnapping!? No, it's the kid's mum. She shoos away the dad and takes her son to one side to comfort him, whilst the dad stands there, awkwardly, not sure what to do with his now empty hands.

Picking up my son from nursery I noticed a proud dad walk in with his mother-in-law in tow to pick up his daughter. The daughter, being held by a carer, sees her dad and reaches out to her dad. He steps forward with a grin on his face, and, unbelievably, the mother-in-law does a skilful side swoop under his arm, makes eye-contact with the carer, and the child is steered into her arms instead. The slightly surprised daughter shrugs and accepts her new recipient. The dad's smile becomes a little forced and awkward as he's standing there with open arms and no toddler.

> *The Swooping Parent*
> *D Freed, Dad's Turn blog*[163]

There's a lot of talk about 'gatekeeping mums' (or grandmas): mums that take over full responsibility for their tots and keep dad out. They believe the father of their child will be hopeless and incapable of doing things 'properly' for their kids, and decide to shun them and make sure they have a firm grip on whatever happens.

Mark very recently, at the birth of his son Theo, reflects the views of a lot of dads in this situation when he explains why his wife is the ultimate decision-maker on childcare. "I guess she has a right to that. She can be in charge and get to decide because she was pregnant." Sitting underneath this sentiment is the cultural assumption that something biological puts the real responsibility for parenting on the mum's shoulders, and, as we'll see, compensates the dad by giving him a veto over whether the mum is allowed to go back to work or not.

When wanting to justify why the real choice isn't an agreement between the parents but a choice for the mum to make alone, dads take a step back and explain that they didn't really have a choice. Understandably, a bloke discussing a woman's experience of childbirth is a bit like blokes discussing menstruation. It's not something guys understand: it's something women go through and it's to do with their body, so best to leave it to them. The most we can do is agree it's unspeakably tough and offer all the support we can, because we'll never really know just how much sacrifice our partners are making to give birth.

The thing is that whilst pregnancy is clearly like that (the only thing we can do is hover around in a helpless and often hapless support role, feeling bad that they're the ones doing all the real work), once the baby's out, that's no longer so clear. Especially after birth, the dad taking more responsibility for the newborn could seem much more natural than expecting the mum who's just undergone labour to step straight in.

But in many couples the dad is kept at arm's length, first by hospitals telling them they have to leave their new-born child and exhausted partner when visiting hours are over, and then slowly by the mum. What people often miss is that the solution isn't to shame these mums (there's already way too much mum-shaming), but to understand why they do it.

I accept that I can be a bit of a gatekeeping dad around my son, since I spend more time looking after him than anyone else. You could call it control freakery. My somewhat unjustified concern is that other people just might not know what to do (reasonable) and so things might go wrong (less reasonable).

I've followed family members who are taking my son out, telling them that they shouldn't be giving him milk yet, or that they should be changing his nappy differently (not really reasonable at all). Most parents know the look they get from their own parents when they try to tell them how to look after their grandchildren. A look that says "The fact you are talking to me means I have done this before with some success, you know."

I remember the 'helpful' info I had to verbally download before being able to turn my back on my son at nursery: "I'll be in the café next door" I tell his carers on his first day. "He needs his next milk at eleven and should nap before then. You might have to hold him till he falls asleep if he's sad. He only really likes food if it has tomato in, or is some sort of curry [like a true Londoner, I sniff a proud tear away]. He likes reading the same book over and over again, and will probably want to play with that truck you have there. Ring me if he gets sad, I'll come back. This is very frightening… for him." The child didn't even notice I left.[164]

It makes sense when you've got such an important responsibility that you struggle to trust someone else to do it for you. If something goes wrong, it'll be your fault. The problem comes when parents that want to split parenting start doing this to each other. When they find it difficult to trust the other one to take care of the kid. It means that real responsibility for the kids doesn't get shared, and it pushes one parent into a secondary or 'back-up' carer role, keeping the full burden of responsibility on one parent's shoulders.

In the vast majority of cases, it's the mum who does it to the dad, whether the mum wants to or not. That's because she has the experience of what works and what doesn't. And when her world has shrunk to baby proportions and the control she can exert over it is limited it's entirely understandable that she might seek to exert what little leverage she still has. That gate can represent the last little bit of control a mum has; it's not a surprise she wants to patrol it. Mum will hand over the baby to Dad, only to hover over his shoulder and tell him off if he does something incorrectly.

When the dad isn't fully trusted, isn't allowed the responsibility to fully care for his own kid, then he's not going to pick up the parenting skills and form the bonds he needs to with the little people. For dads to be able to take their turn, they need the space to be able to make the calls, even the mistakes that all parents make, and learn how to care for and connect to the babies. Gatekeeping when it's applied to dads is a serious problem, stopping Dad taking and fully enjoying his turn.

Why mums feel the real responsibility

The biggest push on mums to become an immediate hawk around their baby and question whether their baby-dad can really be trusted with their new wobbly-headed offspring straight from the weeks after birth, is again the spectre of the super-mum. Not only does she put undue pressure on mums to do everything perfectly, but she also reminds them that the mum is the only person everyone will blame if something goes wrong.

This is backed up by the attitudes of the medical establishment. Before birth, doctors regard the woman as the only patient. The man has done his bit and the child is not regarded as an entity. That's entirely sensible from a medical point of view. But it's not smart from a family point of view. It can both exclude fathers and reinforce the idea that the mother is the primary carer.

One father we spoke to, Andy, developed a running gag with his partner when they went to antenatal appointments. As the parents sat in the waiting room but only the women's names were called he'd whisper in his partner's ear "I see dad people", in a reference to the ghosts of *The Sixth Sense* movie. But he took it more seriously after the birth. Having been packed off the night after his child was born, he snapped when post-natal appointments for the child were addressed only to his wife. After he complained his local NHS Trust agreed to look again at their procedures to include fathers more.

Parents of children of all ages are flooded with tide after tide of "if you feed them this or let them watch that or talk to them in this way or that, then they'll be slow, lonely, unhealthy or suffer some as yet unknown psychological trauma". As soon as you've cleared the moral and judgemental minefield marked "breastfeeding", the issue of allowing your children access to screens kicks in and this one goes on a lot longer with the joys of policing social media somewhere down that particular road.

You really can't drop the ball on this, not once, and if you give that ball to someone else, then you're just taking the risk that they'll drop it for you. Because it sells books and magazines, parents, predominantly mums, really are given the impression that micromanaging their babies is not just good for the little people, it's an essential part of bringing them up and preventing future traumas and even imminent death.

When society insists with a nudge and a wink that men are less competent child carers than women, it may feel a risk to let your baby-dad (who ideally you love and trust deeply) take responsibility for your charge. It therefore makes sense to always be hovering over your baby-daddy's shoulder and telling him what he needs to do and correcting things when he puts a step wrong; undermining his confidence, in other words, at a time when he is already trying to overcome a stereotype.

Kids' brains develop mostly on their own accord, so long as they get plenty of love and encouragement. So if you let your kid feed himself tomato pasta every day at twelve whilst sitting in the high-chair and wrapped in a bib, and your partner takes over and hand feeds him toast at one, letting him or her run freely around the living room in just a nappy, then it probably doesn't really matter.

Your kid won't be ruined by your partner taking a bigger responsibility in his or her upbringing (choices about how to do it and all). In fact, they're likely to benefit from the extra involvement and commitment from the other parent in their lives. The choices about how to bring up kids, big and small, can be choices for both parents, for dads as much as mums.

Mum guilt and the phantom dangers of the incompetent dad

Recently there have been articles on dads who don't normally get stuck in with childcare without mum around. Features such as *A day with dad*, or *Being mum for a day*[165], show how these dads, previously oblivious to the full weight of responsibility when looking after kids, step in to 'mum's shoes' and look after the little ones without their partner around. After listing the trials and traumas of the day, along with a few heart-warming moments, the dads explain that they never knew what their wife had to put up with looking after the kids, and that he'll respect her job as chief parent so much more now. Often, they'll add that being a full-time parent is clearly beyond their abilities and praise their wives for being able to do this impossibly tough job.

Hang on. Both of us and our partners could all match each other blow for blow with traumatic tales of those first days looking after our babies alone. But despite all the new challenges you get from your little ones as they get bigger (a new issue every time you get on top of an old one), you start getting into it.

Parenting skills are learnt. If these same dads were left for a week, they *would* start picking up the skills they needed. Caring for others, as we know, changes your brain to be better at caring and forms closer bonds with the people you're caring for. Dads, just as much as mums, just need to be allowed to take on full responsibility and not be second-guessed and micro-monitored by mums, and the chances are pretty high that they'll find their feet well enough to be competent parents.

Unfortunately, this isn't what mums are told with the pressure of sole-responsibility for their little people hanging over them. The mum at Docklands Story Time saw her kid crying, she knew exactly what was needed, and every murmur that kid was making didn't just make her upset because of his distress, it also tuned her into the two dozen other adults (mostly mums) in the room who were expecting her to fix the problem. As dads, we know what the first part feels like, not wanting our little ones to cry, but most mums are weighed down under the extra pressures that everyone else places on them to fix every tear.

Why isn't there a story in the family section of the tabloids about a mum who takes over childcare from Dad for a day, can't cope with how difficult it is, raises her hands up and declares: "Wow, this really isn't for me. Good luck love, you're an amazing dad. I understand that now. Carry on with the good work because I'm not suited to this"?

The answer should be familiar by now: because of people's expectations, dads have a socially acceptable, even expected, opt-out of parenting responsibility. Mums don't, and if they come close to hinting at it, they'll be shamed for failing to be a good mum, for being less of a woman. Such a story would not be a warm-hearted one, it would be one covered in shoddy sneers about the mum's inadequacy as a parent, as a woman.

This gatekeeping problem has started to rear its head with the new shared parental leave system. The law, unlike in Sweden and Germany, starts with the assumption that mums alone have the right to leave to look after their kids. If she decides to grant some of this as shared parental leave to her partner, she can give him the right to take time off to look after his baby. If it turns out she wants to or feels social pressures to stay the gatekeeper of her little offspring, regardless of what the dad thinks, then technically, she has the trump card: she can just say no to shared parental leave.

Jo Swinson explained to us why the policy was designed that way. "One of the early consultation documents had a scheme where mums and dads would each get a period of leave and the rest would be shareable. But of course the downside of that is basically cutting maternity leave... So in the end we went for [a system where] it stays as maternity leave but then couples can choose and the woman stays in control."

It's the same logic that saw family allowance, as it was first known, paid to the mother, for fear the father would blow the money on beer. David Lammy, Labour MP for Tottenham and chair of the cross-party All Party Parliamentary Group on fatherhood, rejects that arrangement. He told us: "I don't recognise the scenario where the men are going to run off with the money.

"I have a problem with the starting point being that you are taking time away from mum. I recognise that it's a critical time to bond in the first three months but it's not helpful to say after that you are taking the time away from Mum. I'd say it's for couples to determine together. Mothers who gatekeep can end up in a position where they don't let fathers do as much, it's easier for them to do it themselves and then the men can just step away."

Of course, ideally most discussions around whether to share parental leave should be agreed on by both parents. But the fact that the starting expectation is that she's the one who should be responsible and that it will be her "giving up her maternity leave" only serves to remind both parents that she's the primary parent, and dads have a secondary role. We're not saying mums should have fewer maternity rights, but there are certainly grounds to explore giving dads full and equal paternity rights to match them. How we leap to equality without reducing maternity rights is a conundrum, for example giving mothers and fathers six months of leave each would be a step up for men but could be seen as a step down for women. It may be equal but would it be fair? We'll juggle the options and come to some conclusions later in this book.

Dad's reaction

The expectation that the buck really stops with Mum is just as deeply held by dads as by mums. There are many hands-off dads who wouldn't think of changing their baby's nappy, let alone picking up their kids when Mummy's ready to swoop in. But even the dads that are challenging the default social expectations about what their role should be can come across a sense that they're not genuinely sharing the responsibility for their kids, just helping Mum out.

Sandeep took six months of parental leave at the same time as me. But Sandeep took his at the same time as his wife Ellen, a step many think is the ideal way to begin life as a parent. When Sandeep and I took our kids to the local park, we let the toddlers explore the grass. Despite Ellen not being there, she was clearly very present in how Sandeep was thinking about parenting. His son, Kian, leant over to grab a handful of dirt and smeared it over his top, angling to put the mud in his mouth, just as a short while earlier he wiped some of his lunch into his hair: "Oh no! What's your mummy going to say, little guy!" Sandeep was really spooked by how his wife was going to react.

As a friend of the family, I'm confident that Ellen would never be concerned about how angry Sandeep might get with her if the situation was reversed. The subtext is clear: if things go wrong, the buck stops with her and it's her that Sandeep needs to answer to when it comes to caring for their son.

Imbued with a deep sense of mothers being the responsible parents, the dads in the Docklands Story Time and at the nursery see the natural 'main parent' step in, and they retreat, feeling like their boss has just pulled rank on them and they've got no other choice.

In many settings, these same blokes would be willing to assert their rights and abilities to make good choices, insisting that they're responsible and that they'll decide how things are done best. But not when it comes to parenting. Implicitly, they look at the social cues around them, the expectations people have on mums and dads, and feel that, however much they may want the buck to stop with them, nearly everyone around them thinks it really stops with their baby-mum.

The couple at the Docklands Story Time was not alone. Mums are frequently driven into the role of gatekeeper to their kids, pressured there not just by the feelings of being a parent, but also by the social expectation that they're the sole responsible parent. Or they may dive into being the gatekeeper, understandably eager to keep a little bit of control for themselves. Dads are reminded that they're expected to be in a back-up role, often prevented or given an easy way out of developing as responsible parents.

The whole family may benefit from dads taking on the responsible role for their share of the time, but expectations on both parents make dads think they probably shouldn't, and make mums worry that doing so would be tantamount to negligence.

Because we're not expected to challenge these expectations, and often don't have the wherewithal to do it, they persist. Gatekeeping mums are kept firmly pinned to the gate, closely monitoring their baby-dads' every move. What's more, because it's so deeply ingrained and propped up by expectations in our culture, it's not always obvious it's happening.

But now we're aware of it, we should be challenging it. If you're a gatekeeping mum who believes that your baby-dad should be taking a bigger share of the responsibility, or a dad who feels they can get shut out sometimes, then why not talk about it? There's little harm in trying to do things differently.

Vetoes in work and childcare

Looking a little closer at how we assume the 'real' responsibility sits with Mum can reveal just how deep the beliefs are that nudge us into traditional roles, even when we try and do things more equally.

When Simon and his wife Sue had their second child, Julia, the plan was for Sue to take the first nine months and then Simon was lined up to take the remaining three. Sue had found it tough for a whole year looking after their first, Aiden, and wanted to split it this time round. She missed being out of the workplace for so long, and it had already led to her falling behind in her career plans, their incomes having been around the same before Aiden arrived, only for Sue's income to have fallen well behind Simon's by the time Julia was born.

But Simon explains that "Sue found it a lot easier with Julia than with Aiden. Julia managed to sleep during the day and had less trouble feeding. So by the time Sue got to nine months, she had decided that she wanted to take the rest of the twelve months, so I dropped my parental leave." Simon is far from the only dad to back off from his plans for parental leave at this point.

Justin, talking about the months just after Josh was born, explains that he "really wanted to be hands-on and involved with Josh. I had lots of ideas about how I thought we should do things but I didn't want to come across as too pushy or interfering to Chloe as she was the one who was doing the main caring."

When several of the dads we interviewed that took parental leave explain what made it possible, they all refer to their partner supporting the decision to allow them to spend their parental leave with their babies. Which is true, since a couple should decide these things together. But when the mums explained why it was possible to share the leave, they didn't once refer to the support of the dads in letting them take their part of parental or maternity leave. They all referred instead to how supportive their partners were in "letting them return to work", some commenting how great it was that their husbands valued their careers just as much as they valued their own.

Steven and his wife Angela decided they didn't want to take the shared parental leave for their first kid. Instead, Angela took the whole twelve months' maternity leave and went back to work part-time afterwards. Angela's income used to be higher than Steven's, which Steven admits he wasn't proud of.

When asked why they didn't opt for shared parental leave, Angela explains that "I don't think Steven would have allowed it! I like my work but my baby has to come first. Steven was uncomfortable with the idea that he would take a lot of time out of work and what that would do to his career, so it was a non-starter." Steven interrupts, "Yeah, but I'm not sure you would have allowed me to take your maternity leave. A few weeks with the baby might have been nice but I totally respect that it's your choice who looks after him."

The dads who didn't take the leave always referred, often jokingly, to the fact that their partners probably wouldn't let them, and then more seriously explaining that it wouldn't be good for their careers.

Chris Mason off the telly, the BBC political correspondent and sometime BBC *Breakfast* presenter, told us: "I thought I was the very essence of the modern man. I said to my wife I think I'm going to take some months off and she said, half joking, 'oh that's my maternity leave'."

And he found more of the same when he did do his two months of shared parental leave and talked about it with other parents, particularly mums. "I was struck by the response it generated was not the wholehearted 'oh what a brilliant idea, I wish I'd persuaded my husband to do that' or 'I wish I'd known about that'. There was that occasional consciousness, I know this sounds absurd, but here I was encroaching on territory usually occupied by others." It's not absurd at all because men taking up parenting are moving into an area dominated by women, one of very few such areas in life, and it's understandable if women are wary of letting men in. We need to be clear that there's a trade-off here: women get access to more options outside the home in return.

Currently we're not looking at an equal agreement or a compromise between parents. As with many couples, because of how the subtle expectations are set up, dads have a veto over their career plans being interrupted. Mums do not. Mums have a veto over sharing their responsibilities over the baby. Dads do not.

There's a number of factors at play here. Women fought for maternity rights; given the story of that struggle and the resistance from men in power to granting things like maternity leave and maternity pay, it is unreasonable to expect them just to give them up. Feminists circling the wagons around those rights are right to do so.

However we, men and women, also have to ponder how far decisions are being driven by deep-seated expectations about who will do what. Just as men may need to be coaxed and cajoled to immerse themselves in the domestic sphere, women will have to be persuaded to let go a little. A scenario in which men and women are entitled to equally big blocks of parental leave would be ideal. And it has to remain the aim. But to get there it may take a little leap of faith for women to give up something in the short-term in the hope and expectation that other women will reap benefits in the future.

Simply leaning back on the old expectations of men belonging in the workplace and women caring for the kids is too easy and too common. To do anything that doesn't fit into this mould doesn't require a compromise; it requires mums to 'let' dads care for the babies, and for dads to 'let' mums go to work. It just props open the paternity and gender pay gaps.

This raises some difficult questions. The ability not to have to compromise with others and being the ultimate decision-making authority, on your own, is always nice. Being told as a woman that you shouldn't veto your partner's ability to look after the kids, or as a man that you shouldn't veto your partner's career progressions, means you're giving something up. But this isn't about having to do something that you as a couple don't want to, it's about not being limited by the default expectations that, depending on your sex, you don't have a full say over how you're going to organise your lives.

Government cannot, or certainly should not, reach into people's homes and dictate how they are going to live their lives and behave as parents. But it can create a framework to encourage equality and a legal backstop to let parents make fully free decisions.

But most normal people do not pore over the intricacies of the law to look for their cues as to how to behave. They just look around them, at the culture they live in. And changing that is a big task, and one that starts with our kids. It starts with a pig.

Part VI

RAISING LITTLE DADS
Freeing the next generation of parenting limitations

25

LEARNING TO BE A 'MINI MUM' AND 'MY LITTLE SOLDIER'

The trouble with this story so far is that it doesn't have a bad guy. Well let's change that, because it's nice to focus all our anger on one person, or one pig. Peppa Pig may have taken the world of kids' TV by storm. She's had countless TV series, a feature film, her name and image on every conceivable knick-knack and there's even a Peppa Pig World theme park (which is quite good: I even took the family to the opening press event and celeb-spotted Natasha Kaplinsky and Sonia from *EastEnders* there).

But angelic little Peppa is not the problem. It's her dad. In the course of writing this book two frequent truths from interviewees have been thrown up. Everybody could relate to being annoyed by the idea that men 'babysit' their own children and any man taking on the stereotypes gets irritated by Daddy Pig. As MP Jess Phillips told us, "My husband HATES the representation of Daddy Pig in *Peppa Pig*. He absolutely hates it. He'll often raise it. He's not an identity politics sort of person my husband but he absolutely hates that."

Mummy Pig is the sensible problem solver who stays at home, and Daddy Pig goes to work (or the odd football match whilst Mummy looks after the piglets). When Daddy Pig is spending some weekend time with his kids, he becomes the family idiot, who can be relied on to lose Peppa's toys, get the family lost, make unnecessary calls to the emergency services, boast skills that he doesn't have, and generally make a fool out of himself.

For the first season Mummy Pig very occasionally also joins in the idea that parents can get things wrong. But somewhere along the line as the show evolves, the writers started to give up the idea that kids can have two equally involved and capable parents.

Kids are treated to how funny it is to pick on the discomfort of the idiot Daddy Pig, whether he's been forgotten buried under some sand at the beach, or suspended from a helicopter whilst suffering from vertigo. Meanwhile, Mummy Pig is keeping Peppa safe, and serenely reminding Peppa that daddies play the role of the family idiot well, but they shouldn't be trusted on their own as they're disaster prone.

Sure, Daddy Pig is an engaged parent, of sorts, at the weekend but he's also a bumbling buffoon. It's not so much that he's irresponsible, just that he's daft. As the show moves on he turns into a character that exists mainly to be laughed at.

If he was designed *purely* to wind up 'meninists' – those nutters who like to claim that men are getting oppressed by the 'matriarchy' – then that would be okay. That's not the case.

He is typical of the way fathers are portrayed on TV, as we explored in Part IV on the Babysitting Handicap. But, as Daddy Pig shows, the idiot dad trope isn't just aimed at making adults laugh, it's also aimed at kids, just at the age they're looking for the rules that define the roles they should play in the world. These parents are sanitised and little kid-friendly versions of Homer and Marge Simpson, and Pete and Lois Griffin from *Family Guy*.

If they appear at all, they are invariably somewhere on what you might call the idiot dad scale. Dad in popular kids' culture is a hopeless figure of fun but, as a man – or a hog – he is allowed to do interesting activities whether that's being rubbish at running or being rubbish at driving a boat. Mummy, on the other hand, is the predictably less adventure-prone voice of reason knowingly taking responsibility for family wellbeing and childcare, and nudging the know-it-all useless daddy back into place. It's a trope, and it persists because viewers identify with it rather than object to it. For now.

If we are truly to move towards making equally shared parenting an expectation-free choice for parents, we need fewer stereotypical impressions that tell us what parents of a particular sex 'should' be doing. And that means starting young. Very young. The first thing most children hear upon entering the world is "It's a boy" or "It's a girl". And from then on they are set on different paths, sometimes wildly divergent, sometimes all but parallel. But the striking thing is that they are separate.

In the book *The Gender Agenda*, we (James and his partner) recorded all the different ways we treat boys and girls and showed how seemingly innocuous moments build into a great weight of gendered expectation. Cues can include toys presented to the children as babies – a fluffy white bear for his daughter, a knitted dinosaur for his son. Babies don't go together well with anything white whether that be toys to drag through mud, clothes to poo and dribble on, or walls to scribble on. And why would anyone knit sharp pointed teeth into a toy; babies are best kept away from anything pointy.

There's the language used such as "boys will be boys" and "there's a good girl". There's also the way people handle the baby. The childminder I chose because she was sparky and delighted our daughter by throwing her around did the same with my son and declared he liked it because he was a boy (another case of confirmation bias reinforcing the rules).

But the people who had the most influence on the kids? Me and my partner. The two big unexpected takeaways from the process of putting together *The Gender Agenda*, which grew from the @

GenderDiary Twitter account, was that boys are disadvantaged by stereotypes too and that even the most feminist and gender-aware parents carry the baggage handed to them by their own upbringing and by the society around us.

But as parents we can change our behaviour. It's moot whether we can ever attain the higher state of gender neutrality aimed for by the likes of pop star Paloma Faith, who refuses to reveal or refer to the sex of her child, but we can be aware. It's that awareness thing again. Harder is taking on those outside influences.

Kids look for a huge range of social cues almost from the moment they're born. When they start to understand that they're separate little people in the world, sex tends to be the first marker that kids place on themselves: they're either a boy or a girl. This isn't particularly surprising, given their entry into the world will be quickly followed by a determination of their gender.

If the parents haven't picked a name in time the baby may be simply known to the medical professionals as either girl or boy followed by a surname. And of course it starts even before the baby is born, as parents swither over what colour to paint the nursery, as if the baby will even notice. And who hasn't heard a parent or a grandparent opine that a son will be able to play football with his father or a mother can look forward to shopping with her daughter? This stuff matters because it places expectations and limits on those babies. Just as parents and grandparents project what hobbies the newborn might enjoy, so they, wittingly or not, carry and cast expectations of what male and female roles will be in the future around work and family life.

The evidence for strong, innate differences in behaviour and preference for boys and girls is weak. If it exists, it only hints at small relative differences. The evidence for the social expectations kids have on them to conform to gender stereotypes, on the other hand, is strong and much more within our control. As Lise Eliot argues in her book *Pink Brain Blue Brain*, if we want our kids to have the most options to choose from in the future, should we reinforce the small limits that they might have, or should we put more effort into making them more rounded individuals[166]?

Children quickly pick up that males and females are different because they are treated differently. It's remarkable how they pick up the tiny cues that adults often unwittingly give out. But having worked out which they are they then look to determine what it means to be a boy or a girl. And they start with toys. Which is why so much research and so much activism focusses on play.

Play preferences – dolls and diggers

Plenty of studies have shown that, although there isn't much of a difference in small babies, as they get bigger (especially when they're old enough to pick up social cues and know their gender), boys have a tendency to play with cars, and girls with dolls[167]. Unlike the tiny scale of differences reported by research into other character traits, this one looks fairly big by the time they're around six[168].

The sex difference writers we mentioned in Part III, about biology, tend to argue that these toy preferences are there to prepare girls for motherhood, and boys for killing (or other impersonal tasks). So when a girl learns to take care of a doll and 'play mummy', she is acquiring the essential fine-motor skills, empathy, and caring techniques required for childrearing babies. When a boy learns how to build blocks and imagine that a tree-branch is really a laser-rifle, he is acquiring the essential spatial skills and imagination for the workplace. Sounds reasonable?

They even couch it in pseudosciencey language and certainly sound quite convincing. As many dads who are trying to battle gender stereotyping being imposed on their kids can attest, it's tough to push against the tide. Despite their gender-neutral efforts, parents can find that their daughter gravitates towards the Disney princess cult or that their son has a habit of picking up sticks and using them as guns.

The writers obsessed with biological sex differences go further. They implicitly argue that a boy building blocks then fails to acquire the skills to care for a baby because he never touched a doll, or that a girl playing with dolls is then disadvantaged in the modern office environment. But let's put to one side the faulty inferences these writers are making for the moment.

At twelve months old around half of children will pick up a doll to play with, regardless of their gender. A year later, as those children are just beginning to make sense of whether they are boy or girl and what that might mean, strangely the choice of toy changes. They haven't had a sex change at age three, there hasn't been some massive dump of special gendering hormones, they've just become aware of what gender they are and the expectations placed upon them as such. In fact, hormone levels in boys and girls are roughly the same from birth all the way to puberty.

Illustrative of the point, my son started becoming *more* not less interested in pushing dolls and cuddly toys around in his toy pushchair around the age of two. He also loves building Duplo and pushing his trains around their track. But when a train falls off the bridge, the little guy picks it up at pats it, putting it in the pushchair so it can get a kiss from Pappa to feel better. My son might just be seeing how men, his dad, behave and copy it, in the way that when he gets hurt I pat and coo over him and kiss him better. Not in the sense that I kiss trains (anyone that says I kiss trains is definitely lying).

Recalling Part III, the more sophisticated, innate difference arguments rely on the idea that the brain is 'organised' by hormones in the womb. The innocent prenatal brain of a boy starts by resembling a 'girl's brain'. Then along come the boy hormones and destroy all those bits in the brain that cause them to be empathetic and nurturing, leaving them instead with the

246

cold and mechanical reasoning power of the boy brain. The future child is therefore biologically repelled by the idea of holding a doll and has an unstoppable urge to pick up a toy sword and whack people.

To prove this, these writers have to demonstrate sex difference *independently* of social factors. Because if we're left with it just being social factors, then our job is clear: to challenge, change and improve social expectations on kids and parents.

Distracted by monkeys

There are people who claim the proof of this innate gender differences in toy choice can be proved by an experiment involving monkeys, and whether male monkeys choose cars or dolls to play with because of course monkeys don't watch *CBeebies* so have no gender stereotypes to contend with.

In one of the most cited studies, some 'boy-toys' which had wheels and some 'girl-toys' – a soft toy or doll – were put out for a group of monkeys to play with. Now, you may be expecting the punchline here to be that the male monkeys played with the boy toys and the females with the dolls. But the experiment didn't even prove that. True, the male monkeys apparently preferred to grab a digger. The females played with all the toys equally. So even this monumentally crap experiment didn't show that girls naturally favour dolls. As for the male side of the experiment, it involved just eleven adult monkeys.

The *New Scientist* write up of the research stated, "This conclusion may upset those psychologists who insist that sex differences – for example the tendency of boys to favour toy soldiers and girls to prefer dolls – depend on social factors, not innate differences."[169] In fact that conclusion may upset anybody who rates decent science (and, in defence of the lead researcher, he did warn against extrapolating too much from the results). A test group of eleven is not enough from which to draw any robust conclusion. Never mind the whole issue of the researchers projecting their beliefs about what constitutes boys and girls toys on to the items chosen.

If this monkey business proved anything it's that there's a problem with the concept of girl toys, given the female monkeys played with both items equally. But we'd contend it proved nothing, given that monkeys are not children.

If the sex difference writers want to claim that the monkey brain is in fact like the human brain (questionable), then they would also agree that monkeys pick up social cues. Monkeys do in fact operate within communities and a lot of their behaviour is indeed learnt.

So we could easily point to the Macaca Sylvanus monkeys, frequently used by researchers for having the most similarities with the human brain. In Morocco, the baby monkeys are looked after by the female monkeys. But we could equally point to the *same species* of Macaca Sylvanus monkeys on Gibraltar, where the male monkeys take care of the young, keeping the boisterous female monkeys away from their precious charges. We find similarly diverse patterns of parenting from other species of monkeys from around the globe[170].

The point here is that looking at monkeys, flies or rats (another popular evidence base for sex difference writers) doesn't tell us a lot about the inner workings of the human brain. But even if we ignore the fact that the human brain is so much more adaptable than other animal brains (allowing us to dominate the planet), the sex difference theorists appear to be being selective about the evidence they're presenting, and ignoring the evidence against them.

Back to people

So what evidence is used to explain the impact of prenatal hormones on humans? The problem is that, once we start controlling for social differences, the only convincing difference we are left with in kids is the toy preference one. The differences between boys and girls in empathy, verbal or cognitive skills are weak, and tend to only become stronger when they're under the watchful gaze of their peers or are hearing the expectations of the adults around them[171].

Despite the popular implications that girls are emotional ninjas and boys are budding psychopaths, most girls are able to act selfishly, and nearly all boys are perfectly capable of understanding how others are feeling, and acting on it.

The evidence on whether hormones have a 'nudging' effect on the developing baby brain is mixed. There is research into girls exposed to high levels of male hormones in the womb that suggest when they come out they are more likely to play with 'boy toys'.

Most studies however have shown that more male hormones (androgens) in girls have had no impact on any of the other 'male-brain' traits. Rebecca Jordan-Young explains that, whilst one experiment (quoted by sex difference writers) shows better spatial awareness in these girls, there are three others that show no difference, and one that shows a lower level of the 'boy' trait in these girls[172]. Far from conclusive then.

So we're left with play preferences. But, while boys are more likely to play rough-and-tumble, hormones don't seem to be the cause of this, with the androgen topped-up girls preferring the calmer pursuits of girls, based on Barron-Cohen's own studies[173] (the Ali G bloke, remember?). In fact when boys were exposed to more of these hormones in the womb, they appeared to be *less* inclined on average to play rough-and-tumble.

The only demonstrated difference caused by hormones appears to be that, when exposed to boy hormones in the womb, girls are simply more willing to play with trains and trucks. Notably, they are not less willing to play with dolls.

So there is no decisive evidence to suggest that a boy's hormones drives him away from dolls. Try asking a four-year-old boy why he doesn't want to play with a doll, and the likely response might be revealing. He will probably explain that he doesn't want to because it's a 'girl toy'. Not because his urges make him find it repellent. In contrast to this at best ambiguous and developing field of research, our understanding of social and cultural impacts on kids play preferences is much more extensive.

In fact, if we take away the gender-imbued nurturing toy, the doll, and replace it with an equally valid object for showing parental caring, like a cuddly toy or even a pet, differences disappear. Research shows that boys show the same affectionate and nurturing behaviour towards their soft toys compared to girls[174]. They're also more keen on average to have and look after something actually living, a pet. Stroking and feeding a pet tarantula is in fact more realistic training for parenthood than waving a doll around.

What kids learn about gender – 'Boys don't like red, it's a girl colour!'

So if you look hard enough you can conclude that there's an inconclusive possibility that sex hormones may provide kids with a little nudge towards certain toy preferences. To claim that therefore toy choice is innate is a huge leap. Not least because there are other larger and more obvious reasons to consider. To blame testosterone for toy choices is to visit the Grand Canyon, ignore the monoliths and crevasses, and focus on a tiny speck of sand, which probably isn't even there. The bigger picture is more informative and rewarding.

The first influence we tend to hear in conversation is about what the parents do. The number of times we've heard (or said) "I tried giving him a doll but he just hated it", or "she's just not interested in building things". The next sentence after these claims by parents that they have tried their hardest to defy gender toy preferences is invariably that, since their attempt failed, the preferences of their offspring *must* be "biological": "he's just being a typical boy".

Parents are right to assume they have a big influence on their kids, but it's often more subtle than they think. Simply giving a boy a doll isn't enough. There are cues in the way it's handed over, the reaction when he does actually play with it, the encouragement you give him and how other friends, peers, and relatives react to his choice. We can't underestimate how kids will react to our hesitation and awkwardness when we hand them toys that we worry they might be judged for holding.

Watching grown-ups

Play-group, nursery, and school are the places where gender conditioning really kicks in.

The wheels on the bus may be a rhyme-time favourite, no matter the gender of the children singing it, and thankfully wheels cannot be gendered, but an innocent nursery rhyme can. After all, invariably "the mums on the bus go chatter, chatter, chatter"; and we've heard one version that includes a verse involving "the dads on the bus go snore, snore, snore" or equally the dads enforce a bit of uncalled for discipline on the bus by telling all the kids to be quiet. Ever wondered why there are five "little men" not aliens in the flying saucer? Or why Mummy is the only parent looking for her ducklings or ringing the doctor when her kids get ill?

It really is remarkable that the cod scientist that extrapolates strong claims from tiny absolute numbers behind hormones gets blanket media coverage, even when similar studies have shown the opposite result, while the person that suggests nursery rhymes that kids hear over and over might have some sort of impact on shaping their views on stereotypical roles is written off as PC gone mad.

Kids can be raised as gender neutral as you like within the walls of your own home. Drop them into a group of peers and they are suddenly subject to a whole new range of incredibly strong forces directing them to behave in one way or another. And it's not just the kids that are responsible. The teachers, being only human and raised in the same culture, are often equally guilty of treating the boys and girls in their classes differently. That's not a crime or even unexpected: parents invariably treat their own boys and girls differently.

The 2017 BBC series *No More Boys and Girls* brilliantly demonstrated just how gendered schooling was. How ingrained it was for the teacher to start each day not by saying simply "Good morning children" but with a cheery "Good morning boys and girls". Now that might seem innocuous but actually just by reminding the kids that they weren't the same but that there was some fundamental difference between them triggered all sorts of emotions and deep-seated ideas.

Girls bought into the idea they were lacking in strength and confidence; boys swaggered. The teacher featured in the programme, the redoubtable Mr Andre, was horrified to find that, not only did he have a bad habit of calling the boys "mate" and the girls "darling", but that he invariably selected boys to answer questions thrown out to the class.

But Graham Andre is a good example of masculinity. Faced with his failings, he's set out to roll out the lessons he learned to all schools through his Primary Rocks project and by engaging with government.

The programme was sciencey rather than scientific, but compelling enough to suggest that more research around what can be achieved by tiny nudges in the classroom would be welcome. By the end of the experiment the boys were better able to express their emotions, the girls more confident. They were more rounded individuals and better equipped to make choices about their future.

Kids are learning social rules and expectations and not challenging them at this pre and early school age, so they generally aren't trying to deny the sex split. They are actively looking for every rule they can find that explains this social split, and everything they can get their hands on to explain why they belong to this newfound tribe.

Kids pick up a lot more from us than we think they do, and not just that swear word we rather hoped they wouldn't repeat in public. They look at what parents are doing. If they notice that only mummies hold babies, and daddies handle spanners and don't care for dollies, then the little sponges are going to pick these things up as rules about what they can and can't do, as my son's affectionate attitude to his toys shows.

Another classic example from *The Gender Agenda* was the six-year-old surprised to see his uncle putting in contact lenses: he'd assumed contact lenses were a girl thing because the only person he'd previously seen using them was a woman, his mum. They see an association and extrapolate it into a rule.

Kids will be kids – learning what to play with

The theory about testosterone organising the boy brain in the womb suggests same-sex twins should have the same toy preferences. There is evidence to show that this is the case to a small degree. However, the far bigger impact on toy preferences in twins is not what the twin's womb-mate likes to play with, but what their older siblings, who they did not share prenatal hormones with, like.

They look to their older siblings significantly more than they look to younger kids for ideas about what they should be doing. In fact, many little kids are so wanting to identify with their big brother or sister, that if they are different sexes they are more likely to pick up their toy preferences from their older siblings than other kids.

A girl with an older brother is likely to partake in more 'masculine' behaviour and a boy that displays more 'feminine' traits is likely to have an older sister[175]. The obvious conclusion is that testosterone can move between siblings by osmosis and we can expect the researchers to get next year's Nobel prize for this breakthrough. Or perhaps little kids just look up to another role-model.

Most kids want to show that they fit into the social expectations, especially of their peers. They look for every rule they can get their hands on.

Research shows that on their own, boys are more likely to play with dollies and tea sets than when just one other kid is present[176]. What's more, if they are repeatedly given the private option to play with boy and girl typical toys alone, the more likely boys are to show curiosity in playing with dolls and boy-toys equally. The moment another kid is present though, the tea set is dropped and the ray-gun grabbed.

So the evidence on this poorly understood area offers us two most convincing possibilities: either the innate sex differences between boy and girl toy preferences are essentially non-existent; or they are relatively minor, only to be augmented through the expectations pushed on kids as they grow up.

So what?

Despite the weakness of the evidence, sex difference writers infer that these toy preferences carry over into childcare preferences. The little girls that like playing with their dollies are also more likely to show interest in caring for babies as they grow up, they claim. The boys and men who squash ants, on the other hand, should probably be kept away from other living things.

Girls engaging in 'normal' behaviour are encouraged and noticed, boys diverging from their anti-caring behaviour are not.

To borrow an example from *The Gender Agenda* again, when my six-year-old relative spent a significant amount of time cooing over my baby son it wasn't commented on, but when that boy's sister finally expressed an interest, their mother paid attention and reinforced that this was normal.

But fast-forward to adulthood, and we're seeing increasing numbers of men say they want to look after their babies, despite their childhood toy preferences (this is a generation raised on Action Man and Lego before Lego had any lady minifigures). So why should we care about toy preferences at all, when even the most rough-and-tumble dolly-breaking tyke can grow up to become a super-dad?

DOES IT REALLY MATTER?

GIVING KIDS MORE CHOICES IN LIFE

We now know that the urge and ability to be a good parent is not determined in childhood. Most girls may well start to acquire the basic cognitive skills of becoming a parent by putting a doll to bed or pouring tea from a tea set. They may even learn it from putting dummies in their baby-sibling's mouth. But the skills they are learning are multi-purpose skills that all kids learn.

Boys are learning the same skills if they are feeding their pet tarantulas and building a tree-house. They are learning important competencies about how to carry their babies safely when they play with building blocks, and they are learning essential parental problem-solving skills when they are deciding where to dig for pirate treasure in the garden.

To put it another way, holding a doll at age five doesn't make you a better parent age twenty or age forty, just as stirring an empty pot on a pretend cooker for hours at age five isn't going to make you a master chef later in life. But what about the 'empathy' of little girls?

The empathy that we're spuriously told girls have more of is not something you can leave to genes, as we saw in Part III, it's something that we learn. It's something we have to teach kids and it's something that even adults continue to develop. By the time kids reach adulthood in fact, there is very little difference in empathy skills.

As we've shown, the big change in instincts and ability to parent doesn't come from what sort of games we played as kids. It comes from that moment when, as adults, a baby is placed in our arms and we're told that it's our responsibility. Crucially, however tough a bloke can be, science tells us that they become softer and more nurturing when they become the carer of their baby and the dad hormones get flowing.

So was the last chapter a pointless distraction? All the efforts of the sex difference writers and their focus on the whats and whys of kids play preferences is all for naught if it becomes irrelevant the moment your baby is put in your adult arms.

Unfortunately, we can't be so hasty. The paternity gap is still there. Dads are increasingly wanting to take up a role as co-parent, but are nudged away from doing it. The reason that what we teach our kids is so essential is that it plays a critical role in starting and steering those expectations. We are giving messages to kids of what they should and shouldn't do in parenting because of their sex, and these are more often than not carried through into adulthood. We are limiting the choices that our kids will feel they can pursue in the future.

Broadening what boys and men feel is socially acceptable for them to do as dads is bound up with something much bigger. It's very much a chicken and egg situation, or perhaps more of a rooster and egg situation. For if men become more involved in family life, that will inevitably seep into the way families are seen by kids. In turn this will spread into changing the way men see themselves. Not just as warriors and breadwinners outside the home and bumblers or adjuncts inside the family setting, but rather as possible equals in the parenting axis and the workplace.

Assuming the egg comes before the chicken, and that of course is a big assumption, then changing the workplace and parenting culture is the chicken. But the egg has to be addressed too. That is the early years, the culture that smiles benignly on 'boys will be boys' misbehaviour but scowls at girls who engage in a bit of rough and tumble. As well as toys, parents, and other kids, there's the impact of TV, adverts, books, even just the world around us[177].

When kids are learning about their identity, they seek out every subtle rule that they can to steer them in the 'right' direction[178]. While young kids may be better at enforcing rules than listening to the ones we set as parents, they are biologically built to pick up social signals about how their peers and adults expect them to behave.

Deviations from this are punished by peers and adults[179]. There is even research to show that when kids are developing their identities, they interpret deviations from the rules they find not as eccentricities (as mature adults would), but as morally right or wrong. This is probably because they are still developing the cognitive tools to see the difference between moral rules and differences in taste. Every parent who recognises the moral affront and outrage of a toddler faced with the wrong colour food/plate/cutlery can see this in action.

When one of the first big things you learn about your identity is your gender, and adults, books, TV, and other kids are commenting on how different from you the other sex is, you're going to look for every rule you can so you can conform to that. As discussed in Part II, adults are looking for and following the social rules they see around them. Kids do this and they do it on overdrive.

So being a boy isn't about having a penis to the three-year-old, it's about playing with trucks and pirates, liking blue, and staying well away from pink dolls. If we want to broaden the choices that our kids think they have as they grow up, we need to start by showing them that they can cross the old stereotypical split of roles pushed on them by their sex.

The adult factor – How we encourage our kids to care

A boy, around six, ran up to Little Bear [eighteen months], and pretended to punch him, all the while looking at his little friend smiling. It's easy to call the six year old a little s*it and scare him off. But he was just trying to perform 'like a boy' to show off to his mate. Instead, a gentle reminder that that's not what we do to babies, and that in fact us boys need to look after babies, changed this little kid's whole demeanour. Something switched inside and I could see a light bulb turn on in his head as I spoke.

Somewhat surprised at his reaction, I then watched as the boy took Little Bear by the hand and started taking him around the playground helping him on the play equipment. All the while looking at me for approval. I couldn't believe the care he started showing towards my son in such a quick turn of events. "Is this what us boys are meant to do?" his glances at me were saying. Yes, that's exactly what boys and men are meant to do. Care for the babies.

Raising Little Dads
D Freed, Dad's Turn blog[180]

Unfortunately after only three minutes of him being kind to Little Bear his mum woke up and ran over to him to tell him off for "bothering the baby", and that he needed to "stay away from the babies". Without a doubt, had the kid been a girl, the parent would have encouraged her to carry on playing with Little Bear.

When my toddler son pats or tries to feed a baby or a doll, I praise him for being a "great little daddy". Not only have I not yet heard another adult say this to a boy who shows any caring behaviour, but every time I say it, the adults around pop their heads up intrigued. They notice that praising a boy for playing dad is strange, whereas praising a girl for playing mummy is expected.

Older boys and girls have both been caring towards my toddler, and both have also been less than nice. But when girls are caring, their mums step up and, rightly, praise them. When boys do the same, there are too many incidences when an anxious parent steps in and tells their son not to touch the baby or even not to be 'mean' in response to their boy's caring behaviour. The assumption is always that boys will not understand how to look after smaller kids, nor should they be encouraged to do so.

It will come as little surprise that evidence shows adults can have a big impact here[181]. Studies show that the stronger parents hold gender stereotypes, the stronger they encourage them in kids. The kids of parents with more traditionally sex-split roles and attitudes about the differences between what men and woman can do and can't do are more likely to carry those rules (limits) into nursery and the playground[182]. The less important gender is to how Mum and Dad run the home, the less likely kids are to think it's important – and the less likely they are to limit themselves with those expectations.

Our kids are learning limits every day they grow up. Just as much as it's our parental duty to be clear on some of the good limits that keep them safe and happy, it's also our responsibility to take away or neutralise those limits that might stop them from being happy in the future.

If we feel uncomfortable with telling a five- or ten-year-old kid who wants to become a doctor that they are wrong, and that instead they need to become a lawyer or an accountant, then why not extend that same aversion to railroading our kids into the roles they take on in their future families? Why not give the message to our daughters that they can be good doctors, engineers, and managers, and to our sons that they can be good parents, and responsible dads?

If letting your boys play with dolls is too radical and strikes you with the terror that you might get your son bullied, then it could be worth building on other caring instincts with personalising their cuddly toys and explaining that they need to be looked after. If you were weighing up whether or not to buy the boy a dog, lizard or even rat, then put this in the pro-column. It doesn't hurt to talk to your kid about his potential as a nurturing 'dad' that looks after his toys or pets, and let him feel he's got some responsibility over it. Of course, this will all be small change compared to role-modelling being an active and responsible dad directly to them.

Role-modelling – 'I wanna be just like my daddy'

When I went part-time to look after my toddler I hoped this would provide some balance for my son, but every time we went to a soft play area nearly all the other parents were mums, and the people running the kids activities and play groups were all women. Clearly it's not the women that are lacking here, it's the men. The first and consistent message kids see in the wider world once they start to understand gender is that it's almost exclusively women that care for kids. And care is the vital word here.

98% of carers for pre-school are women, and a quarter of primary schools have no men working in the classrooms at all[183]. That's a serious lack of male caring role-models for our boys. And don't think that our girls aren't affected as well. Studies in Swedish nurseries have shown that the nearly exclusively female staff have a bias to quickly perform caring roles for boys, such as just handing them the water cup they grunt at. In contrast, they expect girls to ask for the objects using words, and even to get it themselves[184].

At my son's nursery, there's a particularly cute little girl who 'looks after' my son during the day. When it comes to home time, she'll run to find his hat and shoes and get the attention of a nursery worker. The study of the Swedish nurseries indicates that this is widespread, with the girls aged two and above identifying with the female carers, and toddling around the room 'helping' them look after the boys. This is the foundation for the pressures of the 'super-mum' from Part V. More men as role-models in these situations would demonstrate to our girls and boys that it is also a man's job to care and nurture: that boys should also be running around 'helping' when they can.

If children invariably only seen women doing the minding and caring, they will draw the same conclusions as everyone else has down the decades – it's a job for women. Men are out doing work, important work, more important work. And so the vicious circle is drawn that boys not only regard childcare as something that's not for them but is low status work. It's below them, and those that do it are below them.

But the messages aren't only from the adults around them, and it's difficult to enact this sort of radical social change on our own. We need to look at the other places they get the messages from.

Kids and Toys – 'You can't touch dolls, they're for girls'

Toys have become a totem for the ways in which children are limited into their stereotypical gender roles. As we've shown, toy preferences may not limit what adults can do in the future, but what the gendered preferences can do is limit what kids think they *should* do in the future. Most boys shy away from dolls by the age of three. But worse than that, they don't just take a different path; they are raised to actively shun dolls, to disdain and dismiss anything associated with them as being 'girlish'.

And of course it's not just dolls. It's anything domestic – play kitchens, dressing up clothes, even craft kits come in pink boxes. My seven-year-old son was given a craft box containing all the usual stuff like glitter, pompoms, pipe cleaners, and stickers, but dressed up as a pirate treasure chest of craft. Pirates are cool so suddenly it's okay for boys to play with craft kits. Making insects out of lolly sticks is a largely peaceful and imaginative activity. Apparently boys will only think about starting such a project if there's the prospect of making someone walk the plank at the end of it (and never mind that two of the most badass pirates were female: Anne Bonny, and Mary Read).

The impact of all this is that boys are taught from an early age to want to be pirates, policemen or builders. Girls are taught that they must be demure and caring – neither are attributes that are regularly attached to pirates. Both boys and girls are taught that playing with dolls (invariably attached to something pink in case the kids need more signals) is something that only girls can do. Girls are taught to be mums, and boys are taught that parenting is a 'girl thing' and so not for them.

It is self-evident that this is going to have an impact when, after at least twenty years of this sort of conditioning, men have to start thinking about what their role might be in a family context. As we know, they are no less capable of performing caring roles. But they are discouraged from them thanks to the gendered baggage from their childhood.

Will they choose the caring role looking after the kids, with all its pink and fluffy connotations, or the more active role outside the home? Even if they want to do the former, overcoming a lifetime of brainwashing is tough, as we've seen in previous chapters. Men who are committed feminists have trouble fighting these childhood expectations.

Kids are looking around for everything that can clearly mark them out as being from their sex – especially boys, as all the cultural signs around them are pointing to their sex being the most important part of their identity[185]. This is the genesis of the aversion in most adult men to being classed as feminine.

The mighty *Let Toys Be Toys* pressure group have done a remarkable job in raising the issue and challenging it successfully, at least as far as doing away with pink and blue aisles in toy shops goes. Of course there are still signals. Hamleys were praised for tearing down the signs that said boys toys and girls toys in their flagship Regent Street store. Walk in there today and you'll still find one floor full of dolls, domestic toys, and pink boxes and another with primary colours, construction toys, and wheels. This is bound to have an impact when it comes to later life.

It's flagging to boys that, since they need to avoid pink like the plague, they need to avoid toys that role-play caring. Those sort of things are pink, and so for girls. This reinforces the expectations that they get when most parents they see that are looking after babies are mums. And it's not just toys.

Kids' TV these days

Every parent worth their salt has given thanks for *CBeebies* during their child's formative years. But what are the kids watching? Boys appear as adventurers, not caregivers. See the likes of Peter Rabbit, Timmy the sheep, and Tree Fu Tom. A typical day's viewing on *CBeebies* – the most watched kids channel – features a slew of shows led by active male characters – Baby Jake, Raa the Noisy Lion, Bing, Postman Pat, Mr Bloom, Grandpa in my Pocket, Peter Rabbit, Andy's Dinosaur Adventure, Octonauts, Justin's House, Timmy Time. In these shows, the boys are getting up to all sorts of antics, but are very rarely shown in a caring light.

The thing is, there are caring roles in these TV shows. It just so happens, these tend to be filled by the girls. Think of Peter Rabbit's mother or Kanga in *Winnie the Pooh*. In fact, Kanga is the only female regular in *Winnie the Pooh*, and her only real role is to dote on her boy, Roo. Research has shown that even when there are female-led shows like *Everything's Rosie*, and the all-conquering *Peppa the Pig*, those characters are significantly less active than their male counterparts.

They also take on a caring role that their boy-counterparts in other shows are never given. Peppa takes care of her little brother George and teaches her baby cousin his first word, following Mummy Pig's nurturing lead. How many toddlers do the male care-bears look after in the same way? It's in their job description to care, but all the boy-bears seem to be focused on is building things and defeating the diabolical whims of Mr Beastly.

Tree Fu Tom goes off battling baddies with a combination of nous and action. There aren't even any baddies in *Everything's Rosie* for the eponymous star of that show to contend with. The only action Peppa ever undertakes is jumping in muddy puddles.

Research shows that kids, once they understand their sex, start identifying with these characters[186]. They pick up the messages that if they're boys they go on adventures and don't bother with the nurturing stuff. If they're girls they do pretty and gentle things.

A particularly depressing report by the *Common Sense Media Foundation* in the US found that media reinforces gender stereotypes – that boys' attributes including lots of fighting are valued more highly than those associated with girls, including being sexy and allowing their body to be used by others. And kids lap it up.

The roles kids see played by each sex on TV and in books has a big impact on how they develop their sense of identity. When boys and girls start developing their understanding of what being one sex or the other means, between three and five years old, they are heavily influenced by prevailing cultural stereotypes. The list of studies backing this influence up is long. The idea that being a girl means having long hair (Disney princesses don't do haircuts) or being a boy means being strong are picked up from cultural signals around kids.

The good news is that studies have also shown that if kids are given a fairer portrayal of gender, they are more likely to think men and women can do any jobs, with men caring, and women swashbuckling[187]. But we're not there yet.

One key report found that male characters get way more screen time than females which obviously tells its own story. And while female characters are beautiful and intelligent, male characters are often funnier and more resilient. Crucially for our purposes, male characters are shown in traditional roles like firefighter and president, women are more likely to be shown looking after the children and the home.

When men are shown in a domestic setting they are more likely to be "humorously inept"[188]. And while programmes pitched at older children ease up on the one-dimensional female characters, with men and women equally likely to be portrayed as "brave", the stereotypes when it comes to each gender's role in society does not change – men shown in professional or manual work or with aspirations to that end, women glued to the kitchen counter.

This matters because boys that watch a lot of telly are found to be more likely to believe males are better than females. And these programmes drive their vision of masculinity – they associate being a man with aggression, power, and dominance, emotional restraint and, vitally, status-seeking. If being a man means seeking status, but childcare is not a role with high status, those boys will shun a position they are raised to believe is alien to their gender.

But there's an upside to this. The evidence also shows that media can be a powerful force for altering expectations about the roles our kids feel they can take on later in life. TV and film are catching up, the bosses have sussed that there is a market out there marked 'female'. So we have *Totally Spies, MC2*, the blockbusting Wonder Woman film. And props to the folks behind *Star Wars* who realised that the brand was big enough to sell anything so they boldly went where space movies rarely go and cast a female lead. Not just in the latest trilogy which features shedloads of strong and independent women, but in *Rogue One* too, suggesting they are totally committed to the cause.

But the final frontier will have been breached when we have a slew of kids' programmes and films featuring boys and men in caring roles, when it's normal for Spider-Man not just to rescue the baby from the burning building but to change its nappy. This might sound like a big ask: cast more men in kids shows who are carers. Or go even further and make childcare the main role of some male regulars.

But it's not at odds with what many of us are expecting and hoping for in our own families, as the paternity gap shows. The only impact it could have is show boys and girls that they have more options for when they grow up. Boys can be little adventurers *and* take on lead caring roles because it's seen as normal and in line with what we expect.

Books

The same goes for books. Parents know that reading to and with their children is one of the most rewarding and valuable ways to spend their time. Essentially, the earlier you start reading to a baby – no matter the book – the better it'll be at language later in life. But there's no harm in being discerning in choosing reading matter.

Literature predominantly follows the same pattern as all other media in featuring females as secondary characters, inevitably caring for or relying on men to decide their fate. Males lead the action. Again there are books out there featuring strong female characters, and that canon is growing. But books about boys who care are few and far between[189]. A study of 200 prominent kids' books showed that "fathers are largely under-represented, and, when they do appear, they are withdrawn and ineffectual parents". Whereas men are predominantly shown sporting their career skills, women are nearly always shown as mothers and are narrowly defined by their role as carers.

A further if smaller study done in 2011 of sixty books showed that mums were significantly more likely to appear at all in picture books than dads, and were much more likely to be mentioned. Dads were less likely not only to be seen but also spoken about. When one parent was present, it was predominantly Mum. When dads did appear, they were significantly less likely to be shown touching or holding their children compared to mums, and were less likely to show emotions such as consoling, being worried or being affectionate.

This is hardly surprising to parents who frequent the children's section of their local libraries in a desperate search to change the monotony of the favourite bedtime read. Whenever most of the books have a parent in, it's the mum and her alone, as if the illustrator ran out of ink when they were sketching the family portrait.

The study did however hint at some progress in recent years. Despite appearing much less often, when dads did appear they were similarly likely to be performing 'non-contact' childcare activities compared to mums (yes, it sounds like a low risk form of rugby).

I found two books in the local library that feature a dad as the main carer of his kids, and which are not subtle in implying that he's just doing Mum a favour. And that's after searching through several dozen I found that talk to Mum performing the role of real parent. I then gave up and decided to read the mummy books to my toddler instead, just replacing the word mummy with daddy. Soon nursery rhymes followed suit. There will be some point when my kid asks why daddies always like to wear dresses and lipstick, but I'm perfectly ready for those questions.

I was told last week that you can't sing a nursery rhyme about monkeys being helped by their daddy when they fall of the bed, because in nature mummy monkeys are the ones that look after their kids. Aside from the fact that, as we know, daddy monkeys can also look after the babies, monkeys in nature also don't jump on beds. Nor do they ring the doctor and get told "no more monkeys jumping on the bed".

If we're willing to make animals behave like people in all these respects because it's a kids' nursery rhyme, then why do we draw the line of acceptable anthropomorphising when it challenges a social rule? Don't let it. Let more dads appear as the carers in kids' books and songs.

Publishers though, along with nearly all other media producers, are capitalists. And they respond to the market. That's why there's been a slew of cartoons, superheroine movies, and all the associated spin-off merchandise aimed squarely at girls in an attempt to address the massive gender imbalance there. Create a market for media featuring dads in caring roles as normal and it'll be reflected. (Unless you're reading this and you run a multinational film studio, in which case come talk to us and we'll pitch you some ideas.)

The answer here is simple, and it involves encouraging kids' books' authors and publishers to challenge themselves and think about making the main carers in their books a little more balanced. It's about accepting the impact books have on kids and about producing books that start to show families the way that more people are wanting to see them run, with dads taking their turn.

Adolescent boys

We've seen that gender stereotypes of one sort and another are still repeated and promoted everywhere we, and our children, go. Whether that's only as far as the living room to watch TV or outside the house in adverts and the sorts of jobs kids see men and women doing. Kids especially pick up the patterns of how others are behaving and what's expected of them. If our boys see men and boys staying away from childcare, girls being cast in mainly caring roles, and then get reminded that things that girls play with should be avoided, then they'll start laying their own limits. There will be a limitation inside our boys to nudge them away from diving headfirst into responsible parenting.

If there's no magic trick for making those stereotypes and differences disappear overnight we can at least make children aware that they exist. Sex and Relationships or Citizenship education at school is a good place to start. It needs to have a higher profile and be taken more seriously than it is today. Preparing kids for adulthood doesn't just involve equipping them with a maths A-level. It also involves making them more aware and able to challenge the limits they're faced with. It involves them being able to be critical and analytical about the things they read and watch.

Teaching kids to recognise gender stereotypes and letting them think about the limits those stereotypes impose could really start to shake things up. For example, a man who wants to be involved in family life, who wants to work part-time after he becomes a father, will be more empowered if he knows that when his request to reduce his hours is rejected it's because of prejudice not because there's something wrong or unusual in his asking. Make kids aware that there are stereotypes and that, if they want, they can challenge them, and a seed is sown.

If many years down the line a couple are making a choice about how they divide up the childcare, being aware that they are fulfilling stereotyped roles would be progress. Even if in the end they decide that the woman is going to take on most of the childcare and the father is going to stick with his five-day-a-week job, the very fact that they know about the limits society puts on the genders is something. It's a huge leap from doing something just because you're used to it, because it's expected, because it's how it's always been, to making an informed decision.

For the same reason it's worth investing in teaching kids about relationship skills and how kids should respect their partners as they grow older. Some might argue that it's not for anyone to decide what constitutes a healthy relationship and what doesn't. All relationships are different. But already society has a say if it's setting the limits on what we can freely choose as parents, and on pushing both boys and girls down blinkered and limited paths.

Teaching boys to be more emotionally intelligent, to be more open and empathetic and to turn their back on toxic masculinity, will lead to better, more equal relationships, and that means happier men, women, and children. Toxic masculinity stops boys and men from developing the tools they need to manage their own emotions and to support others.

The broad parameters of what constitutes a healthy relationship – consent, respect, equality – should be critically thought about by kids and hopefully later adults too. And this will have an impact when it comes to not just forming those relationships but the way they play out. Discussions about how to divvy up the domestic roles, including childcare, should start from a different base to where they do now. As is so often the case with discussions and decisions, information is key.

And we can tackle toxic masculinity in the same way. Show boys that they don't need to behave in any particular fashion and they will enjoy improved mental health and better relationships with their partners, friends, and children.

A 2017 Lynx deodorant advertising campaign focused on the idea that young men turn to Google for reassurance, asking "is it okay to…?" completing the question with all sorts from be thin, wear pink, be depressed. Essentially the question was "is it okay to be like a woman?" Now, Lynx is almost exclusively worn and bought by gauche youngsters making their first forays into the world of sweaty teenagerdom. But this is the brand that used to advertise itself by suggesting that wearing it would lead to hordes of half-naked women chasing you across the beach. Something's changed. Something's changing.

Unfortunately "Is it okay to stay at home and look after my children?" was not included in the ad. Mainly because the boys wearing Lynx are not of an age to start thinking about settling down or about a smell to actually pull. But it belongs on the same list. Each question was a chip at the edifice of toxic masculinity. The whole basis of toxic masculinity is that it prescribes what is and isn't okay for a man.

The fact that boys have to turn to Google to question it sums up the problem. They can't turn to friends because it is not okay to appear weak, to push the boundaries of male behaviour. The internet allows men to do that in the privacy of their own home. It's a fascinating inversion of the toxic masculinity view of men – that what they do on the internet is look at pictures of naked ladies. In fact boys and men are looking for knowledge, reassurance and the feeling that they are not alone. Just like any other person of any gender of Lynx-wearing age.

Good sex and relationship education at school, and more positive messages that challenge the toxic image of masculinity are what teenagers need to start breaking down the limitations gender imposes on them. Boys and young men can then start to feel more free in what they decide to do with their lives.

Caring, nurturing, empathy, and talking about how you feel shouldn't be the preserve of only one sex. Boys, from toddlers to teenagers, need to hear the message loud and clear that caring for kids can be their thing, full time and fully responsible, and that they would be more, not less, of a man by doing it. They can then carry these more open expectations about their role in the world into adulthood to choose more freely for themselves.

CONCLUSION – MAKING IT HAPPEN

WHAT NEEDS TO CHANGE

We've seen that if men get more involved in parenting it is not just a win-win scenario, it's a win-win-win-win scenario. Men, women, children, and the broader economy all benefit if equal parenting is supported and everyone can make genuinely free choices about how they order their family lives.

Men get better health and relationships, the two being closely linked, and a more fulfilling version of fatherhood. Women too could see mental health benefits and a wider vista of options after motherhood with regard to what work they take on within and outside of the home. Children benefit from having two involved parents, bringing a string of advantages from better educational attainment, to healthier friendships, to a more well-rounded personality and outlook. Society takes a step closer to something resembling equality, and a happier, more flexible workforce is a more productive workforce with a positive impact on the nation's bank balance.

On that basis it is something everyone ought to be agitating for.

But we've looked at the reasons men are dissuaded or downright barred from getting fully involved in parenting: the barriers – cultural, financial, and psychological – that make it understandable to describe men as victims of outdated social rules. Women of course have been victims of the same strictures that can keep dads at arm's-length from the kids.

However it is not enough to simply ask for equal parenting or just generally expect men to do more (or to expect women to expect men to do more, thereby adding to their burden). We need a set of simple asks. Achievable goals that everyone can get behind. And we need a strategy for how to achieve equal parenting and an end to the idea that men can babysit their own children.

This effort involves government, companies, the media, and importantly civil society, but at its core, parents need to take ownership. Some of the things we've discussed will need broader action to bring down the barriers for families. But the real change starts at home.

Dads and mums should have honest conversations about how to split childcare and what they want out of life, giving all the alternatives, including shared parenting or letting Dad take the lead, a fair chance to make a quality choice on this momentous decision. Those parents who really believe that they want to parent equally will need to look for the breaches in the ideas that keep the paternity gap open, and dive in. It's the only way to make this change really happen.

Let's start at the beginning.

GETTING THE RIGHT PATERNITY RIGHTS AFTER BIRTH

Introducing parental leave in 2010 and making it more flexible in 2015 was undoubtedly a good thing, with the power to transform the expectations and reality of childcare in that vital first year. However it has not fulfilled its potential. Take-up is still disappointingly low, those that take it are an exception and even out of those who use it, most use relatively little. That needs to change. We need to improve the quality of the choice for a couple's decision of how to split the first year. In fact the way the state values a man's involvement with his family needs to change.

The first step towards that is to make paternity rights automatic the moment a man starts a job. Currently women are rightly entitled to maternity leave from the very first day in work. Maternity pay is dependent on doing six months' service. However for men there are no rights unless the father has clocked up six months in work first. There's a clear message being sent here that, come what may, a baby needs its mother while a baby only needs its father if he qualifies.

There should not be any qualification to being with your baby and if we want equal parenting – and as set out above it is unequivocally a good thing and a sensible aim for any progressive society – then mothers and fathers must as far as possible be treated the same when it comes to rights and responsibilities.

We need to get this right and equalise early maternity and paternity rights because the beginning really matters. It's the time that parents start bonding with their babies, and forming their sense of responsibility. As we've seen, it's when the habits of childcare start settling in. The more dads are able to be fully involved at the beginning, the easier it gets to share parenting equally as the kids grow.

Therefore our first ask with regard to birth, rights, and the world of work is that paternity rights kick in on day one, or even sooner. Health services need to take a look at whether they do enough to include men in the journey to parenthood. It shouldn't be their job to screen out deadbeat dads but the health benefits provided by a supportive and engaged father are worth maximising. Measures could include simply going further to include dads at antenatal appointments to looking at providing the option of allowing dads to stay over the first night rather than being kicked out and the (more) exhausted mum told to cope on her own.

Then there's paternity leave. The first chunk of maternity leave is the most generous. Women are entitled to six weeks paid at 90% of full pay. Many employers improve or extend that. And, to be fair, an increasing number of employers are upgrading paternity leave from the statutory two weeks paid at £140.98 per week (at time of writing) available as a minimum to those that qualify. However that backstop needs to be beefed up.

We've witnessed rather than experienced childbirth but it certainly seems a huge physical event and mothers definitely need time to recuperate. Yet they are expected to recuperate and look after a tiny, helpless baby as well. That doesn't make any sense. If their partner is able to be around for longer then surely that would aid the recuperation process.

Partners taking on the upheaval of a child's arrival are likely to cope better. With a first child a couple will find their lives turned upside down: it's a cliché but it's true. There are few life events as momentous and discombobulating as parenthood and inevitably it takes time for most people to adjust. Neither gender has an advantage on coping and consequently both should get an equal opportunity to take the necessary time and space to get used to their new circumstances and to support their partner in making that change.

Of course there are some people, some couples, who find it all terribly easy and who serenely take this momentous change in their stride. They are annoying to the rest of us. Policy should never be constructed to suit annoying people.

With second and subsequent children the upheaval may not be as stark but there are different needs. Simple logistical stuff – the older ones may well need to be looked after while the mother breastfeeds for example – or emotional and psychological needs – the older ones may just need a bit of attention given the inevitable cooing over the new arrival. Again those situations are better handled by two than by one.

Apart from the practical considerations there are mental health concerns too: dump too much on a mother in those early days and she will have to work harder to maintain mental health.

Then there is the mysterious issue of bonding with the baby. As with so much about parenting, it works for both parents – decent midwives know that skin to skin contact within the first seconds of birth help bonding and breastfeeding.

That's the only reason why there's a picture of me on Facebook in y-fronts. I was snuggling skin to skin with my daughter just after she'd been born. And for anyone who's seen the pictures, the pants were brown before the birth started not as a result of watching the horror unfold.

Science has shown that dads also need to bond with their babies in similar ways and with similar hormones to mums, and it's those close and involved relationships in the first year that allow them to do that.

Women are granted that first six weeks to allow them to bond with their offspring and that is sensible and understandable. What is weird is that men are expected to either achieve the same level of bonding on fast forward and get there in just two weeks or are sent back to work after a fortnight because bonding is not for them, work is for them. That's a silly, outdated outlook.

There's also another practical issue. Being a parent may be natural, but the mechanics of parenting are not. For example there's nothing natural about disposable nappies, and learning not only how to apply a nappy and the importance of doing it right or, more pertinently, the horrific poo-based consequences of doing it wrong, takes a little time and practice. As do the mysterious ways of soothing babies.

I well remember a friend yet to have children asking in wonderment how we knew that doing the so-called space walk

– holding the baby diagonally across us while taking big, slow, bouncy strides up and down the room – was the best way to settle a baby. The answer: days and nights of bitter experience trying everything else.

At the moment women are forced to learn and learn quickly in those first six weeks. Men are shut out from picking up the tricks of the parenting trade. Consequently if dads try to take over at the weekend or evenings then inevitably the mum has to take time explaining what works and what doesn't. Sometimes she'll conclude quite reasonably that it's just easier to do it herself.

The same issue applies to shared parental leave; with women encouraged to take that first six weeks off, the implication is that the early days are for women and, even should a man take over after that, six weeks or six months down the line the mum may well find herself having to teach her partner the details of how to look after their own child. That sends a message that he's doing something new, difficult, and unnatural – no-one teaches the mother what to do.

So to get the start right, from the day the baby is born, each parent should receive the same paid maternity and paternity leave, at 90% of full pay, as mums do today. Having six weeks together at the beginning is not an outrageous ask and could be essential in helping many families settle into a shared and happier parenting routine. It would send out a clear message that the involvement of both parents is equally valued in those early weeks. And it would be a win-win. Men get to not just bond with their newborns, but learn to parent.

BETTER PARENTAL LEAVE AND USE-IT-OR-LOSE-IT

The first month is important, but establishing the bonds and habits and getting the real benefits from having kids comes from sharing parenting across the whole of the first year.

Currently mums are able to donate part of their twelve months of maternity leave and nine months' maternity pay to their partners. As we've seen that sounds nice in theory, but in practice pesky issues like the gender pay gap and decades, if not centuries, of cultural build-up make it invariably easier and more cost effective for the woman to do the bulk of that time, if not all.

The obvious solution is to split leave down the middle, with each parent entitled to six months each. That would force men to think about their role more, to walk in women's shoes when it comes to the career sacrifice they've historically been expected to make, and hopefully eventually drive out the imbalance between a man and a woman's career prospects. Employers deciding whether to employ or promote would be faced with some stark equality – either gender equally likely to take six months out to bring up a baby.

However, while the six months each of shared parental leave is appealing on the grounds of equality, in the real world things are more complicated. For a start there's a question around the government forcing the issue. Few parents would welcome the choice when their baby is just six months old (likely less given mothers usually start their maternity leave before the actual birth) between dad taking over and potentially taking a huge financial hit, or putting the child into paid childcare and potentially taking a huge financial hit. An element of choice must remain.

Plus giving a woman six months' maternity leave is actually reducing her current rights to nine months' paid maternity leave. That can't be right. As vocal equality activist Jess Phillips MP puts it, "You're expecting a woman to lose something, a hard won right."

The destination we'd like to get to is the one proposed by Jess – nine months of paid parental leave each. She explained: "I think I deserve nine months off when I've given birth and then you can have the next nine months. That's what I want." She adds that it would have a practical and financial spin off: "You'd have paid childcare for eighteen months." That's if the parents decided to take the leave consecutively.

That would still require some sacrifice of current rights but the benefits outweigh the downsides. David Lammy MP, chair of the All Party Parliamentary Group on Fatherhood, a collection of MPs from all parties who look at issues affecting paternity and fathers, questions the idea of maternity leave belonging to the mother. He told us "Some on the feminist position are gatekeeping those hard won rights and freedoms.

> "It's interesting that when I called for three months of non-transferable leave for men there was a debate within and among women, among feminists who take a different view about some of the gatekeeping."

That debate needs to be had in the open. It would be problematic for policy makers to simply demand or dictate that some maternity leave is handed over. But equally there is an inherent flaw in the idea that a dad does not really have a right to shared parental leave, as his partner can simply block him from taking it.

It doesn't only reinforce the idea that women can block their partners from opting for childcare, it also reinforces the assumption that men have the opposite veto to stop their partners from returning to work after baby arrives. Just like deciding how to parent, it needs to be a shared and equal decision to allow both parents a genuine choice in childcare responsibilities. Both parents should start from the same position when they come to deciding how to split parenting and earning responsibilities. It should not be biased against an equal split.

This brings us to the issue of household finances. When most parents are making decisions about how to divide leave, one thing tends to rule out a lot of good and more equal options – cash.

The gender pay gap is real, as evidenced in the first part of 2017 when the Equality Act came home to roost and companies had to fess up the difference in pay between their male and female employees. This wasn't necessarily equal pay for work of equal value, the issue that's bedevilled the BBC. This was the evidence that female employees get much less pay then male employees. When certain companies squealed that this was because women were on the shop floor while men were in the boardroom, they only demonstrated how blind they were to the problem. And it feeds into the shared parental leave calculation.

A couple looking at the balance sheet are likely to find that the family takes a bigger financial hit if the dad's income drops to the standard parental pay compared to the mum's. This matters because continued economic sluggishness means most new parents are of a generation less well off than their parents and are having to struggle with paying the costs of housing, heating, rising food prices, and all the rest before they even start to factor in the not inconsiderable cost of kids.

So any revamp of shared parental leave must be properly funded. That's not straightforward. But, as ex parental leave minister Jo Swinson pointed out to us, there's an irony in men looking at the rate of statutory parental pay and deciding it's not for them. "People go 'but there's hardly any pay' and you go 'you know this is what statutory maternity pay is and you haven't been moaning about maternity pay but now that it affects men you're suddenly moaning about it.' The thing is I'm glad that they're moaning about it but it is just as if this is uniquely affecting men when actually SMP is fairly rubbish and has been for some time."

This is a different but related issue, for it perfectly shows why it's good to get men interested and involved in parenting. Once they start taking an interest, conditions might improve for everyone, particularly while men still hold so many of the levers of power. An increased rate of parental leave pay will make it easier and more attractive to men to take parental leave.

Relying on the goodwill of companies is not enough. Not only does it mean that being a responsible and involved dad in the first year becomes limited to those lucky enough to work in the right companies, it is also inherently unfair on the companies that do pay. The ones that don't are free-riding on the ones that do.

There are no shortage of good and successful examples of how parental leave policies could work. It is affordable. As we know, we can look to the sustainable approaches taken in the Nordic countries and Germany. Notably, while generous, these policies have been financially sustainable. They have promoted benefits for families, and for the wider economy. This is like the Government investing in growth-enabling infrastructure projects, growing both the social and material wealth of the country.

There is also, without a doubt, a need for use-it-or-lose-it parental leave for each parent. There is practically no reporting of shared parental leave that does not recommend the need for a big chunk of shared parental leave to be reserved for dad. And that's because, in every country where it's been employed, uptake of parental leave by dads has shot up as the stigmas attached to fathers taking responsibility at home start to look ridiculous.

So our ask when it comes to better shared parental leave for couples is to work towards each parent being entitled to nine months' paid leave with their baby, for at least half of that to be properly funded, and for some but not all of the leave to be transferable to the other partner.

That would be a big leap to take place at once but it's a reasonable and achievable aim. We'll support any and every small step along the way because equality has the potential to be transformative. It also adds to maternity rights, without handing much over.

But, as we've seen, it's only half of the journey to allowing equal parenting. There are many other cultural barriers that prop open the paternity gap. When leave ends it's back to work. Things need to change there too.

THE FLEXIBLE WORKING REVOLUTION

The right to request flexible working already exists and has been expanded massively in the relatively short period since New Labour first took it up. That's because it's a good thing. We're building on success here but we have to go further. The right to flexible working is not enough. We need to normalise it. Because it works. Those that do it rarely regret it.

Too often flexible working is taken as shorthand for less working. Sometimes that's what it means – but never does it mean less work for the same money. Unfortunately all too often it actually means doing the same work for less money in fewer hours. That's because it's not taken seriously enough.

There is plenty of evidence that shows those that break out of the nine-to-five make happier, more productive employees. A key plank of the growing campaign for a four-day week is that, counter intuitively, when people work fewer days they work smarter and more productively. For businesses and subsequently job creation, the ultimate goal is higher productivity and more economic value. Flexible working delivers that.

But flexible working only makes people happier and harder working if it is accepted fully. There can be no scowls from a boss or, more devastatingly, from a co-worker when a dad ends their shift halfway through the day because they are working two and a half days a week, or when a mum switches off her computer at 2.30 to go and collect the kids because she started the day at 7am. Jokes about 'working from home' meaning watching *Loose Women* have got to stop.

And they will as flexible working becomes normalised. Extending the right to request flexible working to everyone was little understood but actually quite a good coalition policy as it removed any resentment from non-parents that only those that had reproduced could access this better way of working. Now anyone can do it: few do, but more are considering it. Everyone – men and women, whether parents or not – ought to.

Jo Swinson MP, author of the law on Shared Parental Leave and the 2018 book *Equal Power*, sketched out a vision of the workplace of the future which appeals: "What we're talking about is a revolution in the workplace in terms of not only how parents are but how people's life and work in the round is balanced.

> "The workplace that we need to have is one where flexibility is assumed to be the norm. Where 'presenteeism' or 'face-time' is banished. Where people are judged on their outputs rather than on the number of hours they put in. Where it's understood that there will be periods in peoples' lives whether for parenting reasons or for caring reasons or for volunteering reasons or for personal development reasons where if we're going to have a fifty year career from twenty to seventy or whatever there will be times when we are working more and times when we are working less."

Given the amount of time spent at work we'd like to see more attention given to this issue by government, think tanks, and HR organisations. We'd like to see a good practice hub set up, whether that be under the auspices of ACAS, business associations, trade unions or government where employers and employees can turn for advice and support to change corporate culture. It shouldn't just be reactive, it ought to be properly funded to reach out and positively advertise the benefits of a more flexible approach in workplaces.

Forcing big firms to publish their gender pay gaps has been enlightening for employees and embarrassing for many companies. It's been a success and we expect it'll be rolled out to smaller firms in the near future.

We think that success can be built on further. Firms should be forced to reveal their parental policies – that's shared parental leave, parental pay, flexible working, onsite childcare, and whatever other benefits they want to throw into the mix to make life easier for their employees and more attractive to their potential employees.

But good words are only the first step. Real culture change needs to happen and we need to stigmatise the stigmas against flexible working. Potential employees are increasingly taking parental policies into consideration when deciding where to work. The best firms will not only get the best people, they'll get the best returns as the most progressive workplaces are invariably also the most productive.

Companies should not only reveal their policies, but also the outcomes: showing how many people work flexibly, work reduced hours, and what those reduced hours look like. Crucially, an employer's score needs to show whether only women take up flexible working opportunities, or whether men are also allowed to opt for them. This will be the litmus test on whether flexible working policies have really changed a company's culture.

Working Families, an organisation promoting different ways of working that celebrates its fortieth anniversary in 2019, currently has an excellent voluntary benchmarking scheme to help companies compare themselves. But this only applies to companies that are already committing to changing their workplace cultures. Extending this to all medium and large companies and making a company's performance against this accessible to potential employees would be a huge step in the right direction, incentivising companies to promote a better work-life balance for everyone.

Working Families CEO Sarah Jackson has argued that "the lack of flexibility in how we organise work brings very real costs in lost skills and experience and a reduced talent pool for employers".

Her organisation has been pushing for employers to adopt a flexible-by-default approach to job design and recruitment.

> "All jobs should be advertised on a flexible basis unless there is a specific, good business reason not to. The government has the power to introduce this in the public sector whereas it would take legislation to get all private sector organisations to take it up. So we believe that in local and central government it should be adopted as soon as possible. Ministers should act and recruit business leaders as 'flexible working' champions, and should encourage private sector employers to adopt the Working Families' Happy to Talk Flexible Working strapline."

This follows the path of our Nordic neighbours as we saw, with Sweden giving parents the right to reduce their hours by a quarter until their kids are eight. Similar rules in the UK could help change attitudes and make flexible working the norm. Also, but as technological change sheds more and more jobs whilst pushing up productivity, the Scandinavians, by embracing flexible working, may be in a better position to protect their workforce in the future .

But ultimately, putting the policies in place and enforcing them can only go so far. We need a culture change and that needs leaders. If you haven't considered flexible working – part-time, condensed hours, different hours, home-working, job share; it's a term that covers something for everyone really – then ask for it. If you're successful, the time you'll get with your kids will more than pay off.

CULTURE – ENDING DADDY PIG AND KEVIN

Media

On a very hot day in summer 2017 I squeezed into a meeting room in the bowels of parliament to hear the Advertising Standards Agency trumpet their new rules outlawing gender stereotypes from adverts. There was a meninist there who pointed out the irony that all those serving the drinks were women, and stereotypes exist for a reason. Except he was lying. There were male and female servers. Stereotypes exist because folk repeat them without thinking, often ignoring the evidence around them in real life.

That's what adverts relied on for decades: an outdated model of family life but one which everyone understood as a shorthand for safe and secure normality.

The ASA, apparently out of nowhere, decided that it shouldn't happen anymore. And more power to their elbow. We'll have to wait and see the impact it has, whether complaints are upheld and such like, but it's given the advertising industry something to think about. And thinking is key to tackling stereotypes.

If the ASA can do it, then so can others. We've mentioned the problems with what messages characters like Homer Simpson and Daddy Pig put across: cultural lodestones to some degree and very unhelpful. We're ready and waiting for the inevitable ridicule for targeting fictional characters but the evidence shows that culture impacts a kid's worldview, an influence that carries on into adulthood.

If children see women doing the majority of domestic work in the home and on the TV they think that's the normal way of the world. If they see an equal distribution of housework among their parents and among the families on the gogglebox they think that is the normal way of the world.

Adult TV also has its role to play. Starting with *Motherland*, characters like the idiot stay-at-home dad Kevin are only a problem if there are no dads in his position that men want to relate to. A few more stay-at-home dads who aren't prats would go a long way to changing things. Giving people role models through TV is tried and tested.

TV can make a huge difference. One program where there is a stay-at-home dad who comes across as funny, competent and likable is the US show *Modern Family*. But it's not Cameron's stay-at-home dad status that has rocked the expectations of men on TV, it's the fact that he's a gay dad, and his husband is out working the long hours to support his family. Plenty of people have spoken about the change in attitudes towards gay parents that *Modern Family* caused. It's a pity then that in the two families in the show where a mum is there, the dads fall back into the out-at-work, dumb and hopeless dad stereotypes.

We should take lessons from the show and be ready for the change in social attitudes that will come from a dad taking on a lead role in a show even when a mum's around and heading off to work. If shows that challenge traditional ideas about parenthood are well written and acted to grab the interests of men and women, it'll help shake of some of the limits we face to equality.

Should Homer Simpson be banned from the airwaves? Probably not. Should he be peddling the vision of a buffoonish and inept fatherhood at 6pm? No. *The Simpsons* started out as a segment on Tracey Ullman's comedy programme for adults. Stick it on much nearer the watershed when those watching will be better equipped to understand and critique the worldview they are being presented with.

Should *Peppa Pig* only be screened post-watershed? No. But, just as ASA rolled out guidelines to tackle gender stereotypes aimed at making sure the bits in between the programmes are more modern in their outlook, so Ofcom can take on the programmes themselves. We'd like to see gender stereotypes challenged, particularly in viewing aimed at children. Some rules from the regulator would supercharge that process and give programme makers something to think about.

But it doesn't just need to be top-down and rule driven. There is huge scope for encouraging better challenges to existing limits through the media. Civil society has a role to play here.

And this isn't just limited to TV. As we've seen, kids' books and even nursery rhymes can also play a big role. Not just in shaping what kids see about parenting, but what new dads see about parenting. With nursery rhymes and books heavily leaning on mum as the responsible parent and often forgetting about dad, there equally needs to be a redress. The easiest way to do that is rewarding more kids' books that aren't about dad being a dad, but just show dad as a caring and nurturing parent more.

Producers, publishers and writers have a role to play, to be ready to resist the temptation to just fit into the stereotypes when they're making new material. The paternity gap shows that audiences of current parents and the next generation of parents are looking for, itching for, a stronger role for dads to be shown and to be made more acceptable. This is an untapped market and an interesting take on TV and other media.

'Death to Daddy Pig' is quite a rallying cry but we don't really want Daddy Pig bumped off (even though you'd get a helluva lot of sausages off him) but we do want balance, challenge, and alternatives. Children's TV by its very nature does not have to adhere too closely to the laws of real life. If the folk making it can dream of schools in space, talking racing cars, and floods of jelly, surely they can cope with the idea of Daddy Rabbit looking after the babies when Mummy Rabbit (not to be confused with her childless but successful twin Miss Rabbit) heads to one of her many jobs.

Kids' telly already often presents a world as we want it to be, even if it's not there in reality yet; a world where the good guys (and yes they usually are guys) always win and folk act according to their consciences. So it's not a huge leap to ask it to reflect family life as it often is and always should be: equal. Because to create an equal world and break down the stereotypes that still exclude men from family life we have to start early.

One message that came out loud and clear from talking to *Working Families* and the Fatherhood Institute is that changing the word 'mother' to 'parent' is not the fix-all solution we all wish it was. Opening up the world of parental support, advice, and advertising to dads will need more effort.

Support services

As a stepping stone, but an important one, parenting advice and local parenting networks should not only extend to include dads, but focus on dads. They should make it clear dads are also their customers, and that they are dads in their own rights, not back-ups to mums.

We should also challenge the culture in support services for parents. The Fatherhood Institute's training of parental support services has shown that there is a serious gap in understanding dads. But the reach of their efforts is going to be limited. There is no reason why government cannot expect its services that regularly interact with parents and kids to undergo similar training: training that challenges their assumptions about what parents are doing, and seeks to more actively involve dads in what has traditionally been a mum's domain.

This includes local government, but it also requires bigger efforts from the NHS. Experiences of dads being asked by nurses where their baby's mum is when they come in for an appointment should not be acceptable for services today. But, by their nature, most NHS staff are considerate people. Just a little bit of awareness raising amongst health care professionals will do a lot to nip this problem in the bud.

Reaching parents

But by far the most important group of people amongst whom we need to raise awareness of the benefits of sharing parenting are parents and parents-to-be. There are countless couples who do not consider sharing parenting more equally because they simply don't understand why they should, or even what it means.

The overwhelmingly positive messages from dads participating in the *Making Room For Dads* project[190] looking at dads on shared parental leave was tempered by the low uptake of the policy. Dr Ben Kerrane, heading the project with Dr Emma Banister, explained that "the research is pretty clear, many people just don't know about the real benefits that bigger paternal involvement can bring to the family". He noted that in Norway, when parental leave was introduced, people "could see it everywhere, from labour wards, TV, to the sides of busses".

The *Making Room For Dads* project is doing what it can to fix this. With the help of *Working Families*, the project is promoting the positive experience those taking shared parental leave have had. But projects like this will only have a small reach because of their funding. We need more of that.

The Government has at the time of writing committed to investing a little cash in its own publicity project. Hopefully it'll add to the mix. Unfortunately when you're looking for the Government's new Share the Joy campaign online, you're more likely to find the embarrassing fact that the Minister promoting it was about have a kid, but that he claimed he wasn't eligible. Case in point, and not a great way to change minds about parental leave.

David Lammy MP argues that, since for many families sharing parenting could bring huge health and wellbeing benefits, it deserves more dedicated promotional support to start to change the culture. "The amount the Department of Health has put into campaigns on breastfeeding… Imagine if just a quarter of that money was spent on promoting the shared aspects of parenting. Campaigns around seatbelts and drink driving have changed attitudes. The same could be achieved on shared parenting." And as a career-enhancing tip for Minister Andrew Griffiths, fix it and try out your parental leave. Parents deserve to see role-modelling responsible dads to know their choices.

BREAKING LIMITS ON THE NEXT GENERATION

Kids soak up influences like a sponge. The stereotype of a therapy session starts with a Freud-like chap saying, "Tell me about your childhood" precisely because they are formative years, in the sense that people and personalities and outlooks and views are formed at the start of your life. That's not to say people can't change their views, but it's good to start young with instilling good habits. Feminism is a good habit.

Boys learning from the off that they are no better or worse than their female counterparts is self-evidently a good thing. And if they take that view to its logical conclusion in the home – that domestic tasks, including childcare, can be shared equally – we've surely showed by now that everyone, not just within the family but in society too, more widely will benefit.

Redefining what boys think it means to 'be a man' as someone who is paternal, caring about kids, and wanting to take on childcare can't be bad. Manly men can be nurses or stay-at-home dads, and they're no less of a man for doing so. Getting school kids to challenge their pre-school revulsion of doing 'girly' things, and questioning whether any of those things really are feminine or masculine at all, is worth every second.

Parents have the biggest influence; they are the people that children spend most of their time with. But when they start school for five days a week teachers take up a huge role in a kid's life. Do the maths – a child that gets up at 7am and goes to bed at 7pm spends most of their waking hours with their teacher and classmates for the entire working week. That's why even the most gender-neutral toddlers often go awry in terms of their attitudes when they get into the classroom. Being exposed to up to thirty new classmates all with different upbringings, backgrounds, and worldviews is marvellous but discombobulating. Teachers can take a role in guiding kids through that and mentoring them in how to understand their place in the world.

Sex and relationships education (SRE) is a fiercely fought battleground but we seem to have got to a place where it is to be compulsory in all schools. Children don't just learn the three 'r's at school. Just by sharing a space with other people they learn how to socialise. The idea that they don't need help to do that is absurd. For a teacher they respect to instil in them the importance of healthy personal relationships can be very influential.

It's not creepy or nanny state to want children to emerge from school as fully rounded human beings with a limitless horizon in front of them. That vista ought to include parenthood, no matter their gender, and it ought to offer the hope of a healthy and fulfilling relationship. Government can boost shared parental leave legislation, workplaces can encourage flexible working, but if we continue to raise boys to think that fatherhood is a part-time pursuit and that relationships rest on disrespect for the opposite sex, then the options and opportunities that fatherhood can bring will be missed.

Teaching children about healthy relationships, whether that be with their playmates or their mates for life, can help them to question when things aren't right, and that questioning attitude could be brought to bear in another part of the curriculum.

Science education should be bolstered to include lessons on spotting and calling out bad science in the media so that those shoddy pink brain/blue brain experiments don't get the coverage that they really don't deserve. If folk can spot such stories that don't stand up to scrutiny they will quickly turn the page of their newspaper or keep scrolling down through their news feed. To make things better, you have to be aware of what's not right in the first place. Awareness is key to all of the above. And it's key to getting it fixed.

The above list of demands – automatic paternity rights, better paternity leave, beefed up shared parental leave, a workplace revolution in flexible working, an end to unhealthy cultural stereotypes, and an increase in teaching and awareness – constitute a manifesto for a better fatherhood.

But we need a plan to make it happen.

MANNING UP AND MAKING IT HAPPEN

Achieving the aims set out in this book is a process made up of three fairly simple steps – talk about it, agitate for it, just do it.

Achieving change is about remodelling the world as we want it to be. However, the process has to recognise the world as it is and will only succeed if we meet men, and women, where they are now rather than relying on others to either seek out alternatives or to magically be hit by some sort of epiphany.

Let's be clear. This book is not about telling others what to do (well, it is a little bit). What we are drawing on is the experiences of parents, our own journey to believing in equality and what we've learned from applying egalitarian ideas to our own time as fathers, and how we think everyone can benefit. Lived experience and practice tends to be the biggest driver to taking up new and better ways of looking at the world.

One of the key things I learned from the process of setting up the @GenderDiary Twitter project that spawned *The Gender*

Agenda book was that I was part of the problem. It's a humbling experience to set out gunning for those guilty of spreading stereotypes that limit kids' lives only to find the barrel pointing back at yourself. But it's the first step to making things better and being better at persuading.

If you're a parent, or are about to become one, then the one thing you can hopefully take away from this book is the will to challenge your expectations and those of your partner. Think hard about the benefits that doing childcare differently from what everyone's expecting you to do could bring to you, your partner, and your kids.

Try not to fall down at the first hurdles – it's complicated to understand parental leave or that there might be a financial hit. For some couples it really isn't possible financially, but try to challenge that before accepting it. Many couples put savings aside for holidays, and we pay interest and go through mountains of paperwork to get out a mortgage. Few would argue that having a child is less of a life-changing decision than either of these.

Give shared parenting an honest and open hearing and be ready to shake things up. If you think you can, then we'd welcome you joining the fight for equality. To make change happen we need to act, communicate, and agitate for a fairer parenting deal.

Act

We're not advocating blowing up post boxes or throwing things at prominent politicians; it's much more low level and achievable than that. The biggest key is modelling the alternative.

As Cordelia Fine explains in her excellent tome *Delusions of Gender*, small or big actions change the culture. "Our actions and attitudes change the very cultural patterns that interact with the minds of others to coproduce their actions and attitudes that, in turn, become part of the cultural milieu... When a woman persists with a high-level maths course or runs as a presidential candidate, or a father leaves work early to pick up the children from school they are altering, little by little, the implicit patterns of the minds around them."[191]

Model the alternative. Don't just wish it, talk about, yearn for change – be the change. That starts with the mental load – look hard at how much you do around the house in terms not just of mechanical stuff like putting the washing on and making the dinner, but how much the responsibility for thinking ahead and keeping the household running lies with you, if you're a man. If you're a woman, demand more from your partner. It doesn't have to be equal, it does have to be fair. But equality brings further benefits.

Children who see an equitable distribution of domestic tasks grow up thinking that is the norm, and they model the same behaviour when their turn comes. The 2017 State of the World's Fathers report found "in nearly every country where data exists, men who reported that their fathers had participated in conventionally 'feminine' domestic work were more likely to carry out this work themselves as adults."[192]

That domestic load includes childcare. You can choose your reason for getting more involved – just because it's fair, because you'll live longer, because it benefits everyone in the household including yourself in terms of mental health, prosperity, and all round wellbeing – but be sure to do it. Be around at the start of your child's life and we're confident you'll like it (maybe not at the time when you haven't slept for a week and that, but you'll look back and recognise the rewards: trust us on this one).

When dads-to-be see more dads taking responsibility for their kids, more parental leave, and more flexible working arrangements, the stigmas start to weaken. They get the impression that maybe this is something they should be looking at and maybe something they can try. It becomes okay. It becomes the new normal.

Take shared parental leave. Talking to your friends about whether they've considered doing SPL is a whole lot easier when you've done it: you can give an honest account and you can answer the questions they might have.

Be brave. As a dad, if you really want the benefits to come flooding in; if you really want the kids to come to you as much as their mum; if you want to maximise the satisfaction you get from childcare, then think about taking as much time as you can on your own with the kid.

Think about months not weeks of shared parental leave, and a substantial part of it not crossing over with your partner. It's the surest and quickest way to go from the back-up 'mum's helper' to the fully involved and responsible dad. Be ready to go through the same learning curve as your partner and you'll reap the rewards.

But your action doesn't need to be limited to, or give up at, parental leave. Turn up to playgroups, soft plays, swimming lessons, and rhyme-times (if you can stomach singing *Wheels on the Bus* and don't feel too confused by what a 'bobbin' is). And think about how you can make them more agreeable to dads. It's that point about the world as it is again – men, unless they are Welsh, are not brought up to sing. So suggest a parent and baby group eases up on the rhyme-time element and includes more games or physical activities perhaps, if you think these things are putting off the guys.

Change is coming. SPL will be normalised, it's just a question of how long it takes to get there; we're confident of that. Quite confident. If we really have to appeal to baser desires – if you get in early enough you'll be considered a hero, with all the bonuses that brings.

We've both felt the upside of being an early adopter to responsible fatherhood. James has been cited in at least two books by other people as a positive example of good parenting. One author even dubbed him a 'hero' for working part-time, conveniently ignoring the seven previous years when he was still playing by the stereotypical rules. You should see the comments on Dave's *Dad's Turn* blog.

There's nothing heroic in discharging your basic responsibilities as a parent, doing what women have been given little choice in doing for years. But if some in society want to say you're a hero, lap it up. It might even appeal to that competitive or envious streak that accompanies traditional masculinity. If another man sees you getting plaudits for childcare, he might decide that he wants a bit of that action too and be more likely to do the same. Whatever it takes.

Question what it means to 'man up'. Being a real man is no longer being the meathead who can get drunk and head-butt the bartender at his local pub for "looking at me funny". If we're successful, being a real man in the next decade will mean getting stuck in to childcare and being ready to take on serious responsibility for looking after your kids. To do that you need broad shoulders (figuratively, although literally does help too).

Model and sell the idea that a man in the middle of the working week holding a baby in one hand and bottle in the other while ushering an older kid into the park is what it means to be manly – even if he does have a baby-vomit stain on his t-shirt (more so then). It's becoming the new cool, just as the 'power-women' of career successful mums has become a role model for women, the dad that really gets stuck in will become the role model for men.

And the same goes for flexible working. Ask for it. Harness that male sense of entitlement for more noble aims than just demanding grubby money. Cash won't make your children smarter and happier: your time will.

Whether you get a flexible working deal or not, don't be afraid to work your hours and speak out. If you need to leave early to collect the kids, don't pretend it's a doctor's appointment or a meeting somewhere else. If other people in your organisation see a man leave at 5pm on the dot because he has caring responsibilities they will be more likely to follow suit.

And if you're an employer then consider your approach to flexible working. The evidence suggests a more enlightened culture will lead to a more successful workplace, whether you measure success in happiness, productivity or simple profit. Even better, if you're the boss then adopt flexible working yourself. If you leave on time and admit it when you have to go early for parents' night at school, or because your child is sick, then your employees will find it a whole lot easier to do the same.

Don't give in to *Facetime* pressures or fatherhood stigmas – push back. And over time your staff will reward you with more loyalty and more effective work. Modelling the alternative is the easiest and most potent step you can take to make equal parenting a reality and to bring our manifesto for a better fatherhood to life. When you model it, be ready to talk about it and spread the word, because it's awesome.

Communicate

Preaching rarely converts anyone. Talking does. Talking about fatherhood is the easiest and perhaps most important thing men can do to change opinions and change the world.

Too often men talking about fatherhood reduces the conversation to how the arrival of offspring has ruined their sex lives (let's not shy away from the fact that your partner just pushed a baby out through her vagina: your penis wouldn't work quite the same way if you had to piss a melon). Putting to one side the evidence showing that sharing parenting more equally boosts your sex life compared to leaving the baby with an exhausted and overburdened mum, it's not a very helpful view of the biggest and most fundamental change in a man's life.

Men are not trained to talk, and certainly not about emotions. The old adage about babies that "boys mobilise and girls socialise" is true. Because we make it so. Handed a baby in a pink Babygro, adults will coo and talk to it; handed the same baby in blue, and the same adult will engage in much rougher and more active play[193].

But men need to talk. A range of mental health campaigns are trying to encourage men to talk to their mates when they're feeling bad. That's to be welcomed. But we can double the benefit if men are encouraged to talk to each other about being a dad. Because, as we've seen, men who do more dad stuff enjoy better relationships and better mental health.

Recent changes in the media landscape have highlighted the fact that people trust and believe information shared by friends over other news sources. It's why political parties are desperate to get shares on Facebook. That phenomenon can be harnessed in the service of the manifesto for a better fatherhood.

Let men talk to other men about the wonderful experience of being a dad. The heart-bursting love you feel when you watch your child sleeping (something we've got a feeling doesn't change, no matter how old they, and you, get!), the pride in their achievements, whether that be their first steps, a good school report, or just a kind act towards another child that surpasses the pride you might feel for any of your own achievements.

Yes, your sex life will have deteriorated for a bit but, heaven knows, that drawback is cancelled out by the deeper bond you feel with your partner because you made a **whole other person** together.

But many men (including ourselves) are not necessarily comfortable with talking about the emotion of it all. As discussed above, men are not raised to maximise their emotional intelligence, so let's meet them where they are rather than where we want them to be.

Jo Swinson put it like this: "Often the conversation between men about a baby coming along is banter and it goes along the lines of 'sleepless nights, dirty nappies' which is fine as far as it goes. Talk about the joy. Talk about how amazing it is. Make that part of the conversation honestly and openly so fatherhood can be celebrated. If you can get out of that slightly piss-take banter mode sometimes you can have a genuine connection about what is one of the most momentous things that'll ever happen to you in your life."

So when a mate says he's going to be a father you don't have to overwhelm him with a gushing spiel about what a wonderful alteration is coming his away. But if it's appropriate don't be afraid to do so. Be practical if you want, it could even make a bigger impact. Ask him if he's going to take shared parental leave. If he's not aware of it or thought about it then talk him through it, point him towards the websites that have the details, lend him this book (or, better still, buy him his own copy). Gently point out that it's worth giving some serious thought to because it's great to spend time with his child, but also that most couples initially think it's unaffordable yet when those same couples consider the logistics and economics in detail many find that it is eminently doable.

We've set out why it's good for men and women to do shared parental leave and share parental responsibility. There is no shortage of these arguments out there, they just need to be spoken about more.

The same goes for flexible working. Remind your friend of his rights, suggest he has as much right and as much responsibility as his partner to consider changing his working pattern.

Women are much better at talking (of course, not all women, but as explained women are trained from early on to communicate more) and we'd urge women to take up the talking baton too.

Talk to your partner about whether they might think about taking shared parental leave, changing their working pattern, and discuss whether the benefits outweigh the idea that you're giving up 'your' maternity leave.

Talk to female friends. As new dad Ben told us, "One of the things I found really surprising was going along to the baby and toddler groups and quite often I was the only dad there. The amount of times I'd hear from other mums saying 'my husband wishes he could do what you're doing but X, Y, Z'. Whether it was 'his career is really important' or 'he's really busy with work' the X, Y, Z was never a particularly good excuse. I'd ask if they worked before they had a baby and they'd say yes and there was this kind of, are you making excuses for him or repeating what he said to you.

"The idea that you can't take three months out, which is the minimum really, to look after your child is ridiculous, unless you are the Prime Minister." We don't need to push as hard as Ben, but it's worth remembering that now we know even the Prime Minister can take time out to look after their child, after New Zealand premier Jacinda Ardern announced she was pregnant early in 2018.

Women have a huge part to play in this, in talking to their partners and expecting more from them. Men occupy an odd position in the sense that their responsibility for a child starts once they've made it, yet while the baby remains in and part of the woman's body she has ultimate oversight. But that must not be used as an excuse, the idea that women are crowding men out by seeking to retain autonomy over their own person. Biology is how it is; we are not slaves to it, as Part III of this book made clear.

Agitate

Men need to talk, not just to each other, but to power. And for this one the responsibility really is on their shoulders. And this bit requires little or no retraining. For boys are taught from a very early age that they are entitled. So, to be clear, men's rights to fully active fatherhood are being held back (ironically by a set of rules that have kept them on top for so long). Men, dads in particular, need to fight for those rights.

While women are encouraged to lean in, men need little encouragement to speak up. It's why more boys than girls put their hands up to answer questions in the classroom and why men tend to sit round the table at meetings while women are confined to the margins. It's why research has found that women are far more likely to ask a question at an event if the first person picked to speak is also female and why men are twice as confident about asking for a pay rise as women[194].

This last statistic speaks to the oft repeated trope that part of the blame for the gender pay gap is somehow on women for not asking for extra recognition. We should look at why women don't feel as comfortable speaking up (because those that do are written off as gobby or shrill, for example), not blame those that don't.

But if men have no problem demanding more pay then they should channel that confidence in another direction and start making more complex but rewarding requests. And researchers ought to ask a different question. Instead of looking at the difference between men and women when it comes to pay negotiations, why not ask how each gender feels about requesting flexible working or family leave?

But it goes further than taking requests to the boss. Pressure must be brought to bear on government. If men want to spend more time with their children, and the evidence suggests most do, then they are going to have to fight for it.

As MP Jess Phillips told us, she somehow expected the male witnesses that spoke to the Women and Equalities Committee to have the agency to act on their situation, whereas she understands she has to be a voice for women. She explained: "I believe that if men really wanted to have the same equal parenting rights as women they'd have it. They're not agitating to get it. But then they haven't had to agitate, they're not such good agitators. When people say it happens to men too I say, 'Well crack on and do something about it then! I can't be the one that has to agitate on your behalf all the bloody time!'"

She's right that it's unreasonable to expect women to campaign for men to get more rights when there are still so many feminist battles to be fought. But, just as men have supported feminists down the years from the men's arm of the suffrage campaign onwards, so we hope we will have convinced women to back up our calls for action.

For it's not just men that gain. To quote Jess Phillips again, "It's the bloody panacea I think, giving men equal parenting rights. I want men to have equal parenting rights because I think it'd be good for women as well." If men demand more paternity leave and beefed-up shared parental leave – both properly funded – they will get a hearing. If men demand real changes to make workplace culture more family friendly for both sexes, it will start to happen.

At the risk of being accused of 'mansplaining' or of telling women what to do, we get that there will be women who feel resentment at the unfairness of the need for them to let go of a privileged status for mums to shake up the privileged status for men in politics and business. But we need to put those concerns aside and back moves to make it easier for men to play a full part in family life as soon as possible. The result will be fairness and improved equality, which is good for everyone.

There are organisations out there already campaigning on this stuff such as The Fatherhood Institute and Working Families. Get in touch. But be sure to do due diligence – there are other organisations out there who like to portray themselves as arguing for a more equal world when in reality there is a deep seam of misogyny beneath their respectable veneer.

The Campaign Against Living Miserably is doing good, if narrowly focused, work on male mental health. Why not get involved and persuade them to make the benefits of engaged fatherhood a part of their mission?

And policy makers do respond to their constituents. Members of parliament, the Scottish parliament, and assembly members in Wales and Northern Ireland mainly want to make the world a better place. And lots of them want to get their mugs in the headlines as often as possible, whether in the hope it'll lead to better recognition among voters or that they'll catch the eye of someone who can give them a job as a minister or whatever.

If a bright politician spots a lot of emails on a topic, he or she will take it up. Whether that's asking for day one paternity rights, more money for shared parental leave or for Ofcom to take a close look at the activities of Daddy Pig, if enough people make the ask it will be heard. It'll start slowly with a debate away from the cameras perhaps, but if other MPs are getting the same messages they'll go along, the numbers will swell and the issue will gain momentum.

So get in touch with your MP. They want to hear from you. Really. David Lammy, chair of the All Party Parliamentary Group (APPG) on Fatherhood told us: "Bother your MP. Do more to break open this political conspiracy that exists to keep things as they are. We're stuck politically while families are making changes. Send emails, go to surgeries, send letters, send petitions, sign up to fatherhood organisations. Get in the face of your local MP." He asked for it, so bother him. Since the APPG is a cross-party organisation it could prove particularly fruitful. The more attention the parents and voters give it, the higher up the political agenda it will travel for all political parties.

The suffragette creed was "deeds not words". It's a good motto for any dad or mum that feels they could benefit from more equal parenting. Ghandi never said "Be the change you want to see", but, as ever, he did say something like it that is perhaps even more apt here. He said, "As a man changes his own nature, so does the attitude of the world change towards him." We think he was talking about people rather than just men, but the point stands. If you change and there's enough 'yous' then attitudes alter and broader change will come.

DAD'S TURN

You have an action plan in your hands now. We've set out in detail why we need equal parenting, why men getting more involved in family life benefits everyone – themselves, women, children, and society as a whole, socially, economically, and physically. The argument is strong.

And we've explained why that's not happening right now. There are social, cultural, and historical barriers that must be overcome.

But we've explained the policy initiatives that can drive difference, the cultural changes that can embed alternative attitudes to those that hold sway right now for no other reason than "just because". The fundamental message is simple and effective and applies particularly to men but also to women as allies and potential beneficiaries of the changes we envisage – talk, agitate, act.

The barriers men face to taking their full place in the family are the same as those the pioneers of feminism faced and overcame. The battle for women's rights is not won but, as the title of Dave's blog makes clear, it's Dad's turn.

You can regard taking your turn as an onerous duty, something that must be done just because everyone must have a shot. Or you can regard it as an opportunity, the same way a child excitedly yearns for their turn on the swings.

Frankly, we don't care which way you view it as long as you accept the argument and act on it. Do shared parental leave, do talk to male and female friends about the realities of parenthood and the benefits and joys it can bring, do email your MP to ask them to support extending paternity leave, do question canards about pink brains and blue brains, do your hours at work and no more unless absolutely necessary, do challenge anyone who says you're babysitting when you are looking after your own children. (But also, if you can, do actually babysit. Looking after other people's kids shows that men as well as women take on caring roles.)

Ultimately we want a fair and equal society in which everyone can make their own choices about the role they play: in reality they'll likely choose those that maximise happiness for themselves and those they love. That means more men playing a full and equal role in the family, and when they do that it will free up women to do the same outside the home.

Many women have fought and campaigned for that fair and equal society for decades, yet still the balance between the sexes is not set straight. We need to alter the law and the culture to give men equal opportunities in the domestic sphere. It's up to men to complete the equality puzzle by putting themselves into the picture and changing what it means to "be a man". Yes, they've had the power to make change all along, but now the circumstances are such that they, we, must use that power.

We're not asking women to step aside. At the risk of drawing a war analogy, it's more like we are the reinforcements joining the battle against old and limiting stigmas (some might even have swapped sides). Men can make the difference, achieve victory for equality, and everyone will share the spoils.

It is Dad's Turn.

ACKNOWLEDGEMENTS

This book has been largely a labour of love for both of us, but it's been a labour nonetheless. We've many people to thank for their help in making it happen.

First and foremost we must express our gratitude to our respective partners, Ros and Charlotte, for their unstinting support, encouragement, and the constant stream of improvements, ideas, and interventions that have made this a better book. However when it comes to them, and everyone we'd like to thank, the bottom line is that all omissions, errors, misinterpretations or slurs directed at fictional characters off the telly are entirely the authors'.

We'd also like to thank our publisher, Alice Solomons, whose instant enthusiasm for the idea was as refreshing as it was overwhelming. It is surely no coincidence that, after a string of male big beasts of the publishing world seemed incapable of understanding our premise, a woman publisher got it immediately. Her continued enthusiasm coupled with grace and practical support has been greatly appreciated.

Friends and professional contacts gave helpful and constructive feedback and for that we are grateful to John Millar, Rosie James, Clare Beavis, Cat Wildman, and Nicole Ponsford. The help from the Fatherhood Institute and Working Families has also been essential. Alex Hardy deserves a special mention for her support along the way, and for encouraging us to get these ideas into a book before we even knew that's what we wanted to do. Thanks to Kelly, Justin, Cher, Chloe, and Lear for your ideas and for putting up with the blog and book related rants while herding the toddlers around London.

A lot of people gave up their time to be interviewed for this book. Our thanks go to all the parents who spoke candidly and generously about their experiences. Your insights lie at the heart of this story. These committed parents gave up their time willingly which we really appreciate. (In particular Chris Mason who took time off the BBC Breakfast sofa to speak at length of his enthusiasm for Shared Parental Leave. When he inevitably joins the line-up for a future edition of *Strictly Come Dancing* he'll get our vote.) But we're also grateful to the parents who were interrogated in buses, trains, cafes, playgrounds, and airports around the country and abroad to give us their insights into modern parenting.

MPs are inevitably busy people and yet Jo Swinson, Jess Phillips, and David Lammy found time to share their expertise with us and it was all invaluable when thinking about how policy has been formed, is formed, and ought to be formed in the future.

Experts may be unfashionable among some but we spoke to a range of people with brilliant ideas and a wealth of knowledge that massively helped to inform our outlook. Thanks to Ben Kerrane, Jeremy Davis, Jonathan Swan, John Adams, Bridget Hargreave, Jasmine Kelland, and Matthew Webster.

If we have forgotten anyone from the above list we offer sincere apologies but rest assured your contribution was as appreciated as your omission is unforgivable.

This book began with an email to James' @GenderDiary Twitter project from Dave's Dad's Turn blog. It is a tangible demonstration that the internet brings people together. Ideas can be kicked around, talked about, expanded, and acted upon. We hope our readers might get in touch with us and others mentioned in the book who believe it's Dad's Turn and together we can make it a reality.

REFERENCES AND NOTES

INTRODUCTION

1   http://punchng.com/serena-williams-multimillionaire-husband-babysits-as-wife-returns-to-court/
2   Cory, G. & Stirling, A. (2015) *Who's Breadwinning in Europe* https://www.ippr.org/files/publications/pdf/whos-breadwinning-in-europe-oct2015.pdf
3   https://plantingmoneyseeds.com/when-women-earn-more-can-this-destroy-your-marriage/
4   O'Brien M. & Wall K., (2017), *Fathers on Leave Alone: Comparative Perspectives on Work-Life Balance and Gender Equality*

PART I

5   Quoted in Asher, R., (2011), *Shattered: modern motherhood and the illusion of equality*
6   Burgess, A. & Davies, J., (2017), *Cash or carry? Fathers combining work and care in the UK.* Fatherhood Institute http://www.fatherhoodinstitute.org/wp-content/uploads/2017/12/Cash-and-carry-Full-Report-PDF.pdf
7   Levtov R., van der Gaag N., Greene M., Kaufman M., & Barker G., (2015), *State of the World's Fathers* https://sowf.men-care.org/
8   Burgess, A. & Davies, J., (2017), *Cash or carry? Fathers combining work and care in the UK.* Fatherhood Institute http://www.fatherhoodinstitute.org/wp-content/uploads/2017/12/Cash-and-carry-Full-Report-PDF.pdf

9   O'Brien M. & Twamley K. (2017), Fathers Taking Leave Alone in the UK – A Gift Exchange Between Mother and Father? In: O'Brien M. & Wall K., (2017), *Fathers on Leave Alone: Comparative Perspectives on Work-Life Balance and Gender Equality* https://doi.org/10.1007/978-3-319-42970-0_10

10   http://dadvworld.com/treasure-every-moment/

11   Burgess A. & Davies J., (2017), *Cash or carry? Fathers combining work and care in the UK.* Fatherhood Institute http://www.fatherhoodinstitute.org/wp-content/uploads/2017/12/Cash-and-carry-Full-Report-PDF.pdf

12   Emma, *You should have asked*, Blog, https://english.emmaclit.com/2017/05/20/you-shouldve-asked/

13   Levtov R., van der Gaag N., Greene M., Kaufman M., & Barker G, (2015), *State of the World's Fathers* https://sowf.men-care.org/

14   Burgess A. & Davies J., (2017), *Cash or carry? Fathers combining work and care in the UK.* Fatherhood Institute http://www.fatherhoodinstitute.org/wp-content/uploads/2017/12/Cash-and-carry-Full-Report-PDF.pdf

15   https://www.amazon.co.uk/Fine-Not-Perspectives-Experiences-Depression/dp/1853432202

16   https://www.telegraph.co.uk/women/10192274/Warning-maternity-leave-can-damage-your-career.html

17   Burgess A. & Davies J., (2017), *Cash or carry? Fathers combining work and care in the UK.* Fatherhood Institute http://www.fatherhoodinstitute.org/wp-content/uploads/2017/12/Cash-and-carry-Full-Report-PDF.pdf

18   https://www.theguardian.com/society/2018/jan/06/uk-firms-including-easyjet-and-virgin-money-reveal-huge-gender-pay-gaps

19   ONS, https://www.ons.gov.uk/employmentandlabourmarket/peopleinwork/earningsandworkinghours/articles/understandingthegenderpaygapintheuk/2018-01-17

20   e.g. http://www.huffingtonpost.ca/lydia-lovric/working-mothers-childcare_b_7835022.html ; http://www.dailymail.co.uk/femail/article-1042454/Are-super-mums-selfish-Here-mothers-fiercely-opposing-views-mothers-place-home.html

21   https://www.theguardian.com/lifeandstyle/2010/aug/01/babies-dont-suffer-working-mothers

22 Burgess A. & Davies J., (2017), *Cash or carry? Fathers combining work and care in the UK.* Fatherhood Institute http://www. fatherhoodinstitute.org/wp-content/uploads/2017/12/Cash-and-carry-Full-Report-PDF.pdf

23 *ibid*

24 Levtov R, van der Gaag N, Greene M, Kaufman M, and Barker G, (2015), *State of the World's Fathers* https://sowf.men-care.org/

25 Lamb M. (1981), *The Role of the Father in Child Development* https://www. researchgate.net/profile/Michael_Lamb/publication/31670039_ The_Role_of_the_Father_in_Child_Development_M_R_Lamb/ links/00b4952399d43485f1000000/The-Role-of-the-Father-in-Child-Development-M-R-Lamb.pdf

26 Fatherhood Institute, (2013), *Fathers' Impact on the Children's Learning and Development* http://www.fatherhoodinstitute.org/2013/fatherhood-institute-research-summary-fathers-and-their-childrens-education/

27 LSE, (2017), *What would you trade to be happy?* http://www.lse.ac.uk/ News/Latest-news-from-LSE/2017/07-July-2017/What-would-you-trade-to-be-happy

28 Thevenon O. *et al.* (2012), *Effects of Reducing Gender Gaps in Education and Labour Force Participation on Economic Growth in the OECD* http://www.keepeek.com/Digital-Asset-Management/oecd/ social-issues-migration-health/effects-of-reducing-gender-gaps-in-education-and-labour-force-participation-on-economic-growth-in-the-oecd_5k8xb722w928-en#.WldRgqhl_IU#page39

29 https://startupsventurecapital.com/10-most-impressive-facts-about-stockholms-tech-scene-6531de033c27

30 Rodríguez-Domínguez L., García-Sánchez I.M. & Gallego-Álvarez I., (2012), *Explanatory factors of the relationship between gender diversity and corporate performance* https://doi.org/10.1007/s10657-010-9144-4; Campbell K. & Mínguez-Vera A., (2008), *Gender Diversity in the Boardroom and Firm Financial Performance* https://doi.org/10.1007/ s10551-007-9630-y ; Francoeur C., Labelle R. & Sinclair-Desgagné B., (2008), *Gender Diversity in Corporate Governance and Top Management* https://doi.org/10.1007/s10551-007-9482-5

31 http://www.dads-turn.co.uk/

32 http://www.worktolive.info/blog/the-scientific-link-between-work-life-balance-employee-engagement-and-productivity

33 Burgess A. & Davies J., (2017), *Cash or carry? Fathers combining work and care in the UK.* Fatherhood Institute http://www.fatherhoodinstitute.org/wp-content/uploads/2017/12/Cash-and-carry-Full-Report-PDF.pdf

34 Fatherhood Institute, (2009), *Fathers and Parenting Interventions* http://www.fatherhoodinstitute.org/wp-content/uploads/2013/11/Fathers-and-Parenting-Interventions-What-Works.pdf

PART II

35 Humans treat their experiences differently based on what they have already accepted as 'the rules'. When they see evidence confirming their expectations, they take it as evidence for the rule. When they see something contradicting it, they either ignore it or give it special attention as an exception. When this confirmation bias is working, people are resisting changes to how they see the world function; for instance, see Wason P., (2008), *On the failure to eliminate hypotheses in a conceptual task* https://www.tandfonline.com/doi/abs/10.1080/17470216008416717

36 OECD, (2016), *Parental Leave, where are the fathers?* https://www.oecd.org/policy-briefs/parental-leave-where-are-the-fathers.pdf

37 The Economist, (2014), *Why Swedish Men Take So Much Paternity Leave* http://www.economist.com/blogs/economist-explains/2014/07/economist-explains-15 ; https://www.svt.se/nyheter/inrikes/sa-manga-foraldradagar-tog-papporna-2017

38 https://www.svt.se/nyheter/inrikes/sa-manga-foraldradagar-tog-papporna-2017

39 Fatherhood Institute, (2011), *Fathers, Mothers, Work and Family* http://www.fatherhoodinstitute.org/2011/fi-research-summary-fathers-mothers-work-and-family/

40 Equal Opportunities Commission, (2015), *Time Use and Childcare* http://www.fatherhoodinstitute.org/uploads/publications/29.pdf

41 Fatherhood Institute, (2011), *Fathers, Mothers, Work and Family* http://www.fatherhoodinstitute.org/2011/fi-research-summary-fathers-mothers-work-and-family/

42 Equal Opportunities Commission, (2015), *Time Use and Childcare* http://www.fatherhoodinstitute.org/uploads/publications/29.pdf

43 ONS, https://www.ons.gov.uk/peoplepopulationandcommunity/
    births deaths and marriages/families/bulletins/
    familiesandhouseholds/2015-01-28

44 Burgess A. & Davies J., (2017), *Cash or carry? Fathers combining work and
    care in the UK.* Fatherhood Institute http://www.fatherhoodinstitute.
    org/wp-content/uploads/2017/12/Cash-and-carry-Full-Report-PDF.
    pdf; ONS, https://www.ons.gov.uk/employmentandlabourmarket/
    peopleinwork/employmentandemployeetypes/articles/familiesa
    ndthelabourmarketengland/2017#fathers-who-are-economically-
    inactive-are-less-likely-than-mothers-to-cite-looking-after-the-
    family-or-home-as-a-reason-for-inactivity

45 Department for Business, Innovation and Skills, (2015), *Shared
    Parental Leave: public attitudes* https://assets.publishing.service.
    gov.uk/government/uploads/system/uploads/attachment_data/
    file/394623/bis-15-32-shared-parenting-leave-public-attitudes.pdf

46 Equality and Human Rights Commission, (2015), *Work and Care: a study of
    modern parents* https://www.equalityhumanrights.com/en/publication-
    download/research-report-15-work-and-care-study-modern-parents

47 NatCen Social Research, *Attitudes to Gender Roles: change over time*
    http://www.bsa.natcen.ac.uk/latest-report/british-social-attitudes-30/
    gender-roles/attitudes-to-gender-roles-change-over-time.aspx

48 Working Families, (2017), Modern Families Index Report https://
    www.workingfamilies.org.uk/publications/mfindex2018/

49 Department for Business, Innovation and Skills, (2015), *Shared
    Parental Leave: public attitudes* https://assets.publishing.service.
    gov.uk/government/uploads/system/uploads/attachment_data/
    file/394623/bis-15-32-shared-parenting-leave-public-attitudes.pdf

50 https://www.tuc.org.uk/news/two-five-new-fathers-
    won%E2%80%99t-qualify-shared-parental-leave-says-tuc

51 http://www.thisismoney.co.uk/money/news/article-3448120/Cost-
    raising-child-spirals-230-000.html

52 Cory G. & Stirling A., (2015), *Who's Breadwinning in Europe?* https://
    www.ippr.org/files/publications/pdf/whos-breadwinning-in-
    europe-oct2015.pdf

53 ONS, https://www.ons.gov.uk/employmentandlabourmarket/
    peopleinwork/earningsandworkinghours/articles/understand
    ingthegenderpaygapintheuk/2018-01-17#headline-measure

54 https://www.theguardian.com/money/2016/aug/23/gender-pay-gap-average-18-per-cent-less-uk-women

55 https://www.tuc.org.uk/news/two-five-new-fathers-won%E2%80%99t-qualify-shared-parental-leave-says-tuc

56 O'Brien M. & Twamley K., (2017), Fathers Taking Leave Alone in the UK – A Gift Exchange Between Mother and Father? In: O'Brien M. & Wall K., (2017), *Fathers on Leave Alone: Comparative Perspectives on Work-Life Balance and Gender Equality* https://doi.org/10.1007/978-3-319-42970-0_10

57 Working Families, *Shared Parental Leave: sharing the leave with a partner or splitting up the leave* https://www.workingfamilies.org.uk/articles/shared-parental-leave-sharing-leave-with-a-partner-or-splitting-up-leave/

58 ONS, https://www.ons.gov.uk/employmentandlabourmarket/peopleinwork/earningsandworkinghours

59 Data from: European Parliament, (2015), *Maternity, Paternity and Parental Leave,* http://www.europarl.europa.eu/RegData/etudes/STUD/2015/509999/IPOL_STU(2015)509999_EN.pdf

60 My Family Care, *Shared Parental Leave: where are we now?* https://www.myfamilycare.co.uk/resources/white-papers/shared-parental-leave-where-are-we-now/

61 My Family Care, *Maternity and Paternity Benchmarking* https://www.myfamilycare.co.uk/news/update/maternity-and-paternity-provision-benchmark.html

62 https://www.harbottle.com/shared-parental-leave/

63 OECD, *Babies and Bosses,* http://www.oecd.org/els/family/34906050.xls

64 OECD, *Effects of reducing the gender pay gaps in education and labour force participation* http://www.oecd-ilibrary.org/social-issues-migration-health/effects-of-reducing-gender-gaps-in-education-and-labour-force-participation-on-economic-growth-in-the-oecd_5k8xb722w928-en

65 European Parliament, (2015), *Maternity, Paternity and Parental Leave,* http://www.europarl.europa.eu/RegData/etudes/STUD/2015/509999/IPOL_STU(2015)509999_EN.pdf

66 http://www.dads-turn.co.uk/raising-little-bear-blog/mrs-dad

67 Pleck, (1981), *Gender role strain paradigm;* Levant, (2011), *Research in psychology of men and masculinity*

68   Wason, P., (2008), *On the failure to eliminate hypotheses in a conceptual task* https://www.tandfonline.com/doi/abs/10.1080/17470216008416717

69   Serbin *et al*, (1979), *Effects of peer presence on sex-typing of children's play behaviour* https://doi.org/10.1016/0022-0965(79)90050-X

PART III

70   http://amumtrackmind.com/career/shared-parental-leave-can-not/

71   Department for Business, Innovation and Skills, (2015), *Shared Parental Leave: public attitudes* https://assets.publishing.service. gov.uk/government/uploads/system/uploads/attachment_data/ file/394623/bis-15-32-shared-parenting-leave-public-attitudes.pdf

72   O'Connor C. & Joffe H., (2014), *Gender on the Brain: A Case Study of Science Communication in the New Media Environment* https://doi. org/10.1371/journal.pone.0110830

73   Richard Udry quoted in Rebecca Jordan-Young (2011), *Brain Storm*

74   http://www.dailymail.co.uk/femail/article-2382139/I-proud-stay-home-dad-Now-I-fear-harmed-daughter.html

75   Brescoll V. & LaFrance M., (2004), *The Correlates and Consequences of Newspaper Reports of Research on Sex Differences* https://doi. org/10.1111/j.0956-7976.2004.00712.x

76   Fatherhood Institute (2014), *Dads and Hormones* http://www. fatherhoodinstitute.org/2014/fi-research-summary-dads-and-hormones/

77   *Ibid.*

78   Warren-Leubecker A. & Bohannon J., (1984), *Intonation Patterns in Child-Directed Speech* http://www.jstor.org/stable/1130007?seq=1#page_ scan_tab_contents

79   Kelly D. *et al* (2007), *The Other-Race Effect Develops During Infancy* https://www.ncbi.nlm.nih.gov/pmc/articles/PMC2566514/

80   Eliot, L., (2009), *Pink Brain Blue Brain*

81   De Vries G., (2009), *Sex Differences in the Brain: the Relation between Structure and Function* https://www.ncbi.nlm.nih.gov/pmc/articles/ PMC3932614/

82   Fine C., (2011) *Delusions of Gender*;
     Haier *et al*, (2005) *Neuroanatomy of general intelligence* https://www. sciencedirect.com/science/article/pii/S1053811904006822; Poldrack,

(2006), *Can cognitive processes be inferred from neuroimaging data?* https://doi.org/10.1016/j.tics.2005.12.004

83   Saturn S., (2014), *Flexibility of the father's brain* http://www.pnas.org/content/111/27/9671.full; Fine C., (2011), *Delusions of Gender*

84   Rivers C., & Barnett R., (2013), *The Truth about Boys and Girls*

85   Brizendine L., (2006), *The Female Brain*

86   Eliot, L., (2009), *Pink Brain Blue Brain*

87   *Ibid.*

88   Nash A., & Grossi G., (2007), *Picking Barbie's Brain: inherent sex differences in scientific ability?*

89   Fine C., (2011), *Delusions of Gender*

90   *Ibid.*

91   *Ibid.*

92   See Fatherhood Institute (2014), *Dad Hormones* http://www.fatherhoodinstitute.org/2014/fi-research-summary-dads-and-hormones/ ; and Lamb *et al.* (2010) *A biosocial perspective on paternal behaviour and involvement* in Beckman J. *et al. Parenting Across Life Span*

93   https://www.newscientist.com/article/mg19626352-400-mega-mouthy-which-is-the-talkative-sex/

94   Fatherhood Institute, (2009), *Fathers and Parenting Interventions* http://www.fatherhoodinstitute.org/wp-content/uploads/2013/11/Fathers-and-Parenting-Interventions-What-Works.pdf

95   Fatherhood Institute (2014), *Dads and Hormones* http://www.fatherhoodinstitute.org/2014/fi-research-summary-dads-and-hormones/

96   http://sciencenordic.com/girls-have-better-motor-skills-boys-do

97   Kokstejn J., *et al.* (2017), *Are sex difference in fundamental motor skills uniform throughout the entire preschool period?* https://www.ncbi.nlm.nih.gov/pmc/articles/PMC5407840/; http://sciencenordic.com/girls-have-better-motor-skills-boys-do

98   Marklund L. & Snickare L., (2007), *Det finns en särskild plats i helvetet för kvinnor som inte hjälper varandra*

99   http://www.dads-turn.co.uk/

100 Fine C., (2011), *Delusions of Gender*

101 Pleck, (1981), *Gender role strain paradigm*; Levant, (2011), *Research in psychology of men and masculinity* https://www.ncbi.nlm.nih.gov/pubmed/22082409

102 Brescoll V., & LaFrance M., *The Correlates and Consequences of Newspaper Reports of Research on Sex Differences* http://journals.sagepub.com/doi/abs/10.1111/j.0956-7976.2004.00712.x

103 ONS, https://www.ons.gov.uk/employmentandlabourmarket/peopleinwork/employmentandemployeetypes/datasets/employmentbyindustryemp13

104 Jordan-Young, R., (2011), *Brain Storm*

105 *ibid.*

106 Brizendine L., (2006), *The Female Brain*

107 For a summary of research see: Fatherhood Institute (2014), *Dads and Hormones* http://www.fatherhoodinstitute.org/2014/fi-research-summary-dads-and-hormones/

108 Among others: Atzil S., *et al* (2012), *Synchrony and specificity in the maternal and the paternal brain: relations to oxytocin and vasopressin* https://scholars.huji.ac.il/sites/default/files/atzillab/files/atzil_et_al._2012.pdf ; Gray P. & Anderson K. (2010) *Fatherhood: Evolution and Human Paternal Behavior*

109 Saturn S., (2014), *Flexibility of the father's brain* http://www.pnas.org/content/111/27/9671.full

110 Fatherhood Institute (2014), *Dads and Hormones* http://www.fatherhoodinstitute.org/2014/fi-research-summary-dads-and-hormones/

111 http://www.dads-turn.co.uk/

112 https://www.sciencedaily.com/releases/2014/11/141106131853.htm

PART IV

113 http://www.dads-turn.co.uk/

114 Steele C. & Aronson J., (1995), *The Effects of Stereotype Threat on the Standardized Test Performance of College Students*;
Fine C., (2011), *Delusions of Gender*

115 Burgess A. & Davies J., (2017), *Cash or carry? Fathers combining work and care in the UK.* Fatherhood Institute http://www.fatherhoodinstitute.org/wp-content/uploads/2017/12/Cash-and-carry-Full-Report-PDF.pdf

116 TUC, (2016), Pay and Parenthood, https://www.tuc.org.uk/sites/default/files/Pay_and_Parenthood_Touchstone_Extra_2016_LR.pdf ; http://www.bbc.com/news/business-36126584

117 http://www.independent.co.uk/news/business/news/fathers-part-time-work-negative-bias-men-apply-employers-gender-stereotypes-society-changes-a7591661.html

118 Kelland J., (2016), *'Fatherhood forfeits' and 'motherhood penalties': An exploration of UK management selection decision-making on parent applicants* https://www.cipd.co.uk/Images/fatherhood-forfeits-and-motherhood-penalties_2016-an-exploration-of-uk-management-selection-decision-making-on-parent-applicants_tcm18-20005.pdf

119 Burnett *et al.*, (2013), *Happy Homes and Productive Workplaces* http://knowledgebank.oneplusone.org.uk/wp-content/uploads/2012/03/Happy-homes-productive-workplaces.pdf; Gatrell & Cooper, (2008), *Work-life balance: working for whom?* http://www.mamsie.org/wp-content/librarypapers/Gatrell.+C.J.+and+Cooper,+C.+(2008).+Work-life+balance.+Working+for+whom. European+Journal+of+International+Management.+2(1).+71-86.pdf

120 Berdahl J. & Moon S., (2013), *Workplace Mistreatment of Middle class Workers based on Sex, Parenthood and caregiving* https://spssi.onlinelibrary.wiley.com/doi/abs/10.1111/josi.12018; Fuegen K. *et al.*, (2004), *Mothers and fathers in the workplace: How gender and parental status influence judgments of job-related competence*

121 Working Families & Bright Horizons, (2018), *Modern Families Index* https://www.workingfamilies.org.uk/wp-content/uploads/2018/01/UK_MFI_2018_Long_Report_A4_UK.pdf – 5% of dads and 11% of mums reduce their hours, but men were far more likely to be forced to reduce their hours because of their employers, meaning that the real gap between mums and dads *opting* to reduce hours for childcare reasons is likely to be wider than this.

122 Equality and Human Rights Commission, (2015), *Work and Care: a study of modern parents* https://www.equalityhumanrights.com/en/publication-download/research-report-15-work-and-care-study-modern-parents

123 Kelland J., (2016), *'Fatherhood forfeits' and 'motherhood penalties': An exploration of UK management selection decision-making on parent applicants* https://www.cipd.co.uk/Images/fatherhood-forfeits-and-motherhood-penalties_2016-an-exploration-of-uk-management-selection-decision-making-on-parent-applicants_tcm18-20005.pdf

124 Kelland J., (2016), *'Fatherhood forfeits' and 'motherhood penalties': An exploration of UK management selection decision-making on parent*

applicants https://www.cipd.co.uk/Images/fatherhood-forfeits-and-motherhood-penalties_2016-an-exploration-of-uk-management-selection-decision-making-on-parent-applicants_tcm18-20005.pdf

125 https://www.theguardian.com/careers/fathers-choose-not-to-take-paternity-leave

126 https://www.thehrdirector.com/features/flexible-working/stigma-of-the-part-time-dad/

127 Working Families & Bright Horizons, (2018), *Modern Families Index* https://www.workingfamilies.org.uk/wp-content/uploads/2018/01/UK_MFI_2018_Long_Report_A4_UK.pdf

128 Dex S. & Ward K., (2010), *Parental Care and Employment in Early Childhood* http://www.fatherhoodinstitute.org/uploads/publications/257.pdf ; Fatherhood Institute (2011) *Fathers, Mothers, Work and Family* http://www.fatherhoodinstitute.org/2011/fi-research-summary-fathers-mothers-work-and-family/

129 http://www.telegraph.co.uk/women/womens-life/10601408/Fathers-twice-as-likely-as-mums-to-have-flexible-working-requests-turned-down.html

130 Working Families & Bright Horizons, (2018), Modern Families Index https://www.workingfamilies.org.uk/wp-content/uploads/2018/01/UK_MFI_2018_Long_Report_A4_UK.pdf

131 https://www.citizensadvice.org.uk/work/discrimination-at-work/common-situations/discrimination-at-work-flexible-working/

132 Working Families & Bright Horizons, (2018), *Modern Families Index* https://www.workingfamilies.org.uk/wp-content/uploads/2018/01/UK_MFI_2018_Long_Report_A4_UK.pdf

133 https://www.theguardian.com/careers/fathers-choose-not-to-take-paternity-leave

134 Pencavel J., (2014), *Productivity of Working Hours* http://ftp.iza.org/dp8129.pdf

135 https://www.workingfamilies.org.uk/news/happy-to-talk-flexible-working-the-new-recruitment-strapline/

136 http://www.radiotimes.com/news/2011-11-24/the-simpsons-named-us-tv-show-with-greatest-influence-on-britain

137 https://psychcentral.com/news/2016/02/08/first-time-dads-vulnerable-to-media-messages/98808.html

138 Pleck, (1981), *Gender role strain paradigm*; Levant, (2011), *Research in*

psychology of men and masculinity; Wason P., (2008), *On the failure to eliminate hypotheses in a conceptual task* https://www.tandfonline.com/doi/abs/10.1080/17470216008416717

139 Originally by David and Kelly Sopp, https://wrybaby.com/ ; reviewed by http://knowyourmeme.com/photos/407502-baby-instructions-101

140 Cartoon by Kelly and David Sopp, published in Safe Baby Handling Tips, Running Press (2015)

141 https://www.mumsnet.com/Talk/parenting/1567-dads-why-are-they-so-hopeless-sometimes

142 https://www.forbes.com/sites/jefffromm/2016/09/21/when-marketing-to-millennial-parents-authenticity-is-required/#12e9fcc54d85

143 https://www.thinkwithgoogle.com/consumer-insights/marketing-millennial-parents-youtube-insights/

144 Bandura (1977), *Social learning theory* http://www.asecib.ase.ro/mps/Bandura_SocialLearningTheory.pdf

145 Gregory A. & Milner S., (2007), *Fatherhood regimes and father involvement in France and the UK* https://core.ac.uk/download/pdf/1584307.pdf

146 https://www.mum2mum.com/about-us/

147 Marshall D. *et al.*, (2014), *From overt provider to invisible presence: discursive shifts in advertising portrayals of the father in Good Housekeeping, 1950-2010* https://www.researchgate.net/publication/271943265_From_overt_provider_to_invisible_presence_discursive_shifts_in_advertising_portrayals_of_the_father_in_Good_Housekeeping_1950-2010

148 http://saatchi.co.uk/uploads/140984300765298/original.pdf

149 Working Families (2017), *Top Employers Benchmark* https://www.workingfamilies.org.uk/employers/benchmark/

150 No shortage of research. Examples: http://onlinelibrary.wiley.com/doi/10.1111/j.1467-6494.2009.00577.x/full; http://onlinelibrary.wiley.com/doi/10.1002/j.2164-4918.1981.tb00282.x/full

151 Chu J., (2014), *When boys become boys: development, relationships and masculinity*

152 https://www.theguardian.com/lifeandstyle/2016/may/14/shared-parental-leave-mothers-fathers-childcare-paternity-maternity

PART V

153 https://www.confidentlykylie.com/2017/01/29/supermum-does-exist-so-stop-trying-to-be-her/

154 https://www.babycentre.co.uk/a25017591/uk-mums-feel-huge-pressure-to-achieve-perfection

155 https://www.babble.com/parenting/going-out-in-public-when-youre-a-parent/

156 Cartoon by Babble (courtesy of Disney) and published on their website (2015)

157 ONS, https://www.ons.gov.uk/employmentandlabourmarket/peopleinwork/earningsandworkinghours/articles/understandingthegenderpaygapintheuk/2018-01-17

158 https://www.54k.org.uk/

159 Kelland J., (2016), *'Fatherhood forfeits' and 'motherhood penalties': An exploration of UK management selection decision-making on parent applicants* https://www.cipd.co.uk/Images/fatherhood-forfeits-and-motherhood-penalties_2016-an-exploration-of-uk-management-selection-decision-making-on-parent-applicants_tcm18-20005.pdf

160 TUC, (2016), *Pay and Parenthood* https://www.tuc.org.uk/sites/default/files/Pay_and_Parenthood_Touchstone_Extra_2016_LR.pdf

161 https://www.amazon.co.uk/Fine-Not-Perspectives-Experiences-Depression/dp/1853432202

162 https://www.psychologytoday.com/blog/kith-and-kin/201312/the-maternal-myth

163 http://www.dads-turn.co.uk/

164 *Ibid.*

165 https://www.express.co.uk/life-style/life/675117/dad-tried-being-mum-for-a-day

PART VI

166 Eliot, L., (2009), *Pink Brain Blue Brain*

167 See here for a fun video on one such study – http://www.madeformums.com/school-and-family/is-it-time-to-rethink-the-toys-were-giving-our-boys-and-girls/41468.html

168 Eliot, L., (2009), *Pink Brain Blue Brain*

169 https://www.newscientist.com/article/dn13596-male-monkeys-prefer-boys-toys/; contrast with critique in other studies, including Fine C., *Delusions of Gender*

170 Burton F., (1972), *Integration of biology and behaviour in the socialization of Macaca sylvan* http://utsc.utoronto.ca/~burton/burt-web/poir-social.pdf; Itani, J., (1959), *Paternal care in the wild Japanese monkey, Macaca fuscata fuscata* https://link.springer.com/article/10.1007%2FBF01666111

171 Eliot, L., (2009), *Pink Brain Blue Brain*

172 Jordan-Young, R., (2011), *Brain Storm: flaws in the science of sex difference*

173 *Ibid.*

174 Eliot, L., (2009), *Pink Brain Blue Brain*

175 Rust, J. *et al.*, (2000), *The role of brothers and sisters in the gender development of preschool children* https://www.ncbi.nlm.nih.gov/pubmed/11063630; Iervolino *et al.*, (2005), *Genetic and environmental influences on sex-typed behaviour during preschool* https://onlinelibrary.wiley.com/doi/full/10.1111/j.1467-8624.2005.00880.x

176 Serbin *et al.*, (1979), *Effects of peer presence on sex-typing of children's play behaviour* https://www.sciencedirect.com/science/article/pii/002209657990050X

177 Kane, E., (2012), *The gender trap: parents and the pitfalls of raising boys and girls*

178 Lobel, T. & Menashri, J., (1993), *Relations of conceptions of gender-role transgressions and gender constancy to gender-typed toy preferences* http://dx.doi.org/10.1037/0012-1649.29.1.150

179 *Ibid*

180 http://www.dads-turn.co.uk/

181 Jacobs, J. & Eccles, J., (1992), *The impact of mothers' gender-role stereotypic beliefs on mothers' and children's ability perceptions* http://dx.doi.org/10.1037/0022-3514.63.6.932

182 Blakemore, J., (1998), *The Influence of Gender and Parental Attitudes on Preschool Children's Interest in Babies* https://doi.org/10.1023/A:1018764528694

183 https://www.nurseryworld.co.uk/nursery-world/opinion/1155693/time-for-action-on-men-in-childcare

184 Marklund L. & Snickare L., (2007), *Det finns en särskild plats i helvetet för kvinnor som inte hjälper varandra*

185 Chu, J., (2014), *When boys become boys: development, relationships and masculinity*

186 Gotz M. & Lemish D., (2012), *Sexy Girls, Heroes and Funny Losers: Gender Representations in Children's TV around the Word*

187 e.g. Karniol R. & Gal-Disegni M., (2009), *The Impact of Gender-Fair versus Gender-Stereotyped Basal Readers on 1st-Grade Children's Gender Stereotypes* https://www.tandfonline.com/doi/abs/10.1080/02568540909594670

188 Common Sense Media (2016), *Watching Gender: How Stereotypes in Movies and on TV Impact Kids' Development* https://www.commonsensemedia.org/research/watching-gender

189 Adams M. *et al.,* (2011), *Invisible or involved fathers? A content analysis of representations of parenting in young children's picturebooks* https://www.academia.edu/838078/Invisible_or_involved_fathers_A_content_analysis_of_representations_of_parenting_in_young_children_s_picturebooks ; Anderson, D. & Hamilton, M. (2005) *Gender Role Stereotyping of Parents in Children's Picture Books: The Invisible Father* https://doi.org/10.1007/s11199-005-1290-8

CONCLUSION

190 http://www.research.mbs.ac.uk/makingroomfordad/

191 Fine C., (2011), *Delusions of Gender*

192 https://sowf.men-care.org/wp-content/uploads/sites/4/2017/06/PRO17004_REPORT-Post-print-June9-WEB-3.pdf p36

193 This video isn't science but sums it up nicely – https://www.youtube.com/watch?v=fwiY2JQRz5U

194 http://www.mintel.com/press-centre/social-and-lifestyle/uk-women-half-as-confident-as-men-asking-for-payrises